ADAM PIGGOTT

PUSHING RUBBER DOWNHILL

1

Copyright © Adam Piggott, 2015

The moral right of the author has been asserted

All rights reserved.

Cover and text design by Ivan Cannon ©

I have tried to recreate events, locales and conversations from my memories of them. In order to maintain their anonymity in some instances I have changed the names of individuals and places, I may have changed some identifying characteristics and details such as physical properties, occupations and places of residence.

For my darling wife, Bianca

Special thanks to the crew at the El Diablo forum

1

Perth, Western Australia, 1995

Sex is power. That's all there is to it, particularly if you're a twenty-three year old male. As in you have no power and it runs roughshod over you. You spend most of your time thinking about how to get it, any way you can, and preferably with the most beautiful girl possible. So when you actually do stumble across a stunningly beautiful woman a few years your senior who thinks you're God's gift to women, well, you're in serious trouble.

I should know. When I met Jodi and we hooked up, I was elevated to another plane on the social scale. I was that guy who went out with her. The two of us arrived at parties and people stared at her with open mouths. Then they looked at me and tried to work out what the fuck was going on. Hell, I didn't know what the fuck was going on. All I knew was that I was in love with the most beautiful woman in the world.

But a few weeks into our intense relationship she dropped a bombshell on me: she was moving to Sydney to become a model, and nothing could change her mind. She had purchased her plane ticket and given notice at her job before the two of us had even met. I tried to reason with her. I tried to make her see that something as special as what we had was so rare that it couldn't be tossed aside. At least it was rare for me. Thinking back, maybe it hadn't been that rare for her at all.

And then she blew my mind with the suggestion that I move to Sydney as well. This was a pretty big deal, and something which I had never considered before. My entire life was in Perth, an oversized town perched in complete isolation on the left side of Australia. I had a job in a chic bar. I rented a groovy inner-city apartment. But the most important thing in my life was my band. We had worked hard to get to a point where we stood a chance of actually making it. And now this girl just blithely suggested that I chuck all of this and head on across to the other side of the continent.

Like I said, sex is power. It took me about a day to make the decision to go. I told my band-mates on the night of what turned out to be both our most successful and final gig. They promptly quit in disgust. I couldn't believe it. I thought that they could keep going with someone else, but apparently I was the glue that bound everything together. But I didn't want to be glue. I wanted to be with Jodi.

And so I sat on my over-loaded bike at the top of the low scraggy hills above Perth. Jodi had already left over a month ago, after the most obscene make-out session ever seen at a boarding gate. I'd divided the rest of the time between phone sex with her and packing up my entire life. And today was the day of my departure.

I should have felt excited to be finally on my way. But the truth was that I was nervous and scared. Not just because I was about to ride my motorbike all the way across Australia. I had no idea what my reception in Sydney would be like. Jodi had hung up on me on our last phone conversation after I made the dreadful mistake of drunk-dialling her to confess my undying love.

And she hadn't answered the phone since. But I was still going because hey, love conquers all, right? The thing is, when you're young and clueless, you really need to find these things out for yourself. And the only way to do that is to make terrible decisions like I was about to do. So I kick-started the bike's big old engine and, after waiting for a break in the traffic, pulled out and headed east.

There's probably an optimal way to ride a twenty year old motorbike alone across Australia, but I didn't do it that way. First of all, you don't ride a bike that's almost as old as you are. In the desert, if you break down, you can die waiting for someone to turn up. Tourists check out like this all the time. So do Australians, though you think we'd know better. They'll be driving their vehicle down a lonely desert road and something will go wrong. Then they'll sit there for an hour or so wondering what to do, until finally they make the deadly mistake that is common to all of these unfortunate deaths.

They'll leave their vehicle and walk off looking for help.

Fifteen kilometers is usually about as far as they get, depending on the time of year. And then they find a little tree, and they sit down, and they die.

So if you're riding across Australia, you need to have some sort of back-up plan. I didn't have one of those. And you need to carry a lot of water. Assuming you don't want to die. Call-in points at pre-arranged intervals to someone back home is also a very good idea, but neither myself or any of my friends or family thought about this one. A first-aid kit is also highly desirable in case you get bitten by a scorpion that was sleeping in your boot or a snake crawls into your tent and snuggles up for warmth.

I did none of these things. I had a vague idea to travel 800 kilometers a day, I had a map, and my dad had given me a contact for one of his childhood buddies who now lived in Adelaide. I figured I would be okay because I was staying on the main highway.

Well, after I loaded my tent, sleeping bag, inflatable mat, cooking stove, and bags of clothes, I didn't really have that much room for things like water. I took a few liters, but that was it. Some tools would be good, in case my bike broke down, but I was mechanically illiterate, so what was the point?

On the evening of the second day, when I was well into the desert section of the trip, I began to worry about camping on the main road. I was concerned about being run over by swerving road-trains driven by speed-addicted drivers, their eyes popping from lack of sleep. I also wanted to avoid the chance of an unwelcome visit from any of the potential lunatics who roamed this sparse land, bored out of their minds and hoping to stumble across a lone traveler whom they could debase with unspeakable acts of savagery. In other words, I wanted to keep my white honkey ass in pristine condition.

So I decided to camp off the main road. I spotted a track and I followed it slowly for a few hundred meters as it wound its way through the desert scrub and became a small sheltered clearing. I figured this was nice. It was out of sight from the highway and there was a flat area to pitch my tent. There was no sign of snake tracks. All good news.

Then I waited for the sound of a passing vehicle. This spot was only good if they couldn't see me, and that meant a campfire, which would stand out like, well, like a fire at night in the middle of the fucking desert. After a time I caught a faint dull sound from a far distance. It gained intensity as it approached and then it was a loud roar as it hurtled away on the flat desert road, its body reflecting in the evening light. I watched it for a while, and then I stepped back down into the little hollow and began to set up my camp.

I didn't need an alarm clock as the following morning the tent became a furnace as soon as the sun hit. After making a coffee and packing up my little camp I sat on my bike and pressed the starter button. And the bike started beautifully.

Let's stop here for just a moment. What if it hadn't started? What on earth would I have done then? I'm half a mile from the highway. Do you think I'm going to be able to push my bike on a sandy track all the way to the main road? It's not happening. I would have to walk back to the road and hail a passing car. And it's probably over five hundred kilometers to the nearest mechanic. How much do you think that would cost me? They would lick their lips and take me for everything I had. That's if the bike was still there when we got back to it.

But the bike started the first time, and I motored slowly back to the hard asphalt strip, and then I rode off into the new day in a state of blissful ignorance to how lucky I was.

It took me five days to reach Adelaide. By the time I arrived I desperately needed a wash and a decent bowel movement. More than that, I needed my head read. Five days alone in the desert, alone on roads that stretched for 146 kilometers at a time without curve or undulation, alone at night in front of a fire that struggled in the evening wind, alone when I woke in the morning, not knowing where I was or even why, alone with my thoughts and with my doubts and insecurities.

I'd realized early on that I'd put myself in this paradox. The closer I got to Jodi, the further we were actually apart. But there was still a small chance it would work out, so I kept going. Hope and sex are a gloriously self-deceiving combination. And nothing seems to make much sense when you're in the middle of doing it.

So I arrived in Adelaide and I negotiated the streets and found the address of my father's friend. The couple and their three young children came out to greet me. The kids looked at me as if I were an astronaut. I shooed them away from the hot exhaust pipes as I didn't think giving them third degree burns would make me very popular. My hosts gave me a wash and a beer, and for that I was truly grateful.

After dinner I answered questions about the trip. It was good to take my mind off my immediate problems.

"Did you meet any pirates?" one of the little boys asked.

"Thousands," I told him. "But luckily my bike was too fast for them."

The kids oohed and ahhed.

I stayed for a couple of days and explored the city, but I was eager to be on my way and aware that every guest is intriguing for only a very short time.

The morning of my departure, the kids helped me bring out my gear. I explained to them how to load a bike and then they each posed for photos sitting on the seat and straining forwards over the gas tank to reach the handlebars. Then I shook hands with my hosts, thanked them for their kindness, and climbed on my bike. With a final wave to the kids I gave it a dramatic kick-start.

Nothing happened. I looked at the controls and saw that none of the lights were on. The bike refused to respond to my increasingly desperate attempts to start it. My hostess had a look of distress on her face and I didn't think it was concern for me. The kids ran around, excited that I could stay longer.

My bike had decided to die in the middle of a large city while I was a guest at someone's home, which in the possible circumstances was very fortunate indeed. As usual, I didn't realize at the time how lucky I was.

I asked if I could use their phone and they rushed me into the house. I didn't know who I was going to call until I picked up the receiver and dialed my father's number. The old fallback for tough bikers everywhere: when you get in the shit, call dad.

Between the two of us we worked out that my uncle knew a bike mechanic in Adelaide. Uncle Billy was a bit of a live wire, and accepting his help was fraught with unknown risks, but I didn't appear to have any other options. I called his Perth number and explained the situation. He called me back half an hour later.

"Adam? It's Bill. I've fixed it up."

"Oh, that's great Uncle Bill. How'd you manage to do that?"

"There's a guy there, he owes me a favor. You can't trust him on your own. Like, if you went to see him he'd probably do you over. But 'cause you're associated with me, it'll be righty. He's got a bike shop over that way. You call him up and he'll be able to get you sorted. But remember..."

"Remember...?"

"He's not to be trusted." The words hung like danger in the phone line between us. "You got that?"

I rang the mechanic with no little trepidation. Uncle Billy had briefed him but I still needed to explain the specific details. I followed his instructions and the bike coughed and spluttered. I coaxed the throttle with careful desperation. It caught, almost died, caught again, and then it finally roared into life. I saw my hostess catch herself as she clapped her hands.

I took the bike to the mechanic. The shop was in a battered structure of corrugated iron on the other side of the city. A cheap radio struggled to be heard above the sounds of a young apprentice bashing a hammer on an unidentifiable piece of metal. I parked my bike and located the small office. The man behind the desk had greasy hair that matched the stains on his overalls. I caught sight of faded tattoos on his hands and knuckles. I had visions of him asking me if I wanted to go out with him to rob a bank.

He spent half an hour looking over the bike while I kept a respectful distance.

"It's fine," he eventually said.

"Really?" I hadn't seen him doing very much to it.

"Yep." He looked at me. "It's fine."

"Great," I managed to say. "How much do I owe you?"

I saw a shadow of pain settle over his eyes. "Nothing. You tell Bill that I did me part, okay?"

I had lost some time but I was on my way. From this point I was confident that the trip would be much easier than the nightmarish country I had already travelled across. There were even parts of countryside that looked vaguely green, as opposed to the death-rattle brown which had been the hallmark of the journey to date.

I pulled into a clean looking truck stop for lunch, where I spotted an old bike loaded up similar to my own. I gave it a quick look over. What interested me was that it was old. A new bike, even loaded to the gunnels, meant the rider was older than me, wealthier than me, and wouldn't even want to talk to me. But this old piece of scrap metal signified that the owner was a fellow member in the travelling-without-a-penny-and-a-clue brigade.

I pushed open the door with a little ding-a-ling from the bell and walked inside. There was a young guy standing at the counter dressed in riding leathers. He had long straight hair that almost reached down to his waist. I reckoned that he was my guy.

The lady behind the counter wrote my order with a laugh. "You two are a pair," she said as she walked back to the kitchen.

The other biker grinned at me. He had a friendly face and was about my own age. We stood in silence for a little longer, and then I decided to take a chance.

"Is that your Yamaha outside?" I asked him.

"Yes, yes. Are you a rider too?" He had a French accent and a broad smile.

"Yeah. I've come from Perth. I'm heading to Sydney, planning on taking the Great Ocean Road."

"I flew into Darwin a few weeks ago. I got the bike there and I too am going to Sydney."

I thought for a moment. "Perhaps we could ride together."

"It would be good to have some company," he said. "I think this idea is good."

So now I had a travelling companion, and I had found one in the best way possible. It's usually not a good idea to begin a long journey with someone you know, the reason being that you'll probably be at each other's throats in a matter of days. You're thinking that it's probably a rare case for best friends not to travel well together.

Well, you're wrong. It's a rare case if things don't turn into a giant cluster-fuck. When you travel with someone you have to agree on *everything*. Where to go, where to stop, what to do, where to stay, what to eat, what time to start, what time to finish. The list goes on and on. Pick the wrong travelling partner and not only do you risk ruining the trip, you risk ruining a friendship. And you won't be able to fix your mistake during the trip. How do you say to your best friend that you don't want to travel with them anymore because they're making your life miserable?

But someone you find on the way, like I had just done? This is the perfect situation, because it's easy to ditch them if they turn out to be a flake. You want to go there? Oh, what a pity, because I have to go to this other place. Gee, it's been great, thanks for all the memories.

Of course you must be judicious; you can't just pick up any old potential freak that stumbles across your path. But this guy seemed cool, I got a good vibe from him, and most importantly we shared the same travel budget – spend as little as possible.

Towards the end of the day we stopped at a town for supplies, and after a bit of searching we found a good camp on the edge of some fields shaded by large river gums. The road curved away behind the trees and we were out of sight of a small farm house sitting in the distance. I went into the trees and found some dead branches while the Frenchman picked out some large stones from a weedy area. We cracked open some beers, and I sat down by the fire and smoked a cigarette. Then we prepared some hot food and opened a bottle of red wine. Afterwards, the Frenchman rolled a joint.

"I'm impressed," I said. "You must have found that pretty quick."

"Is not so hard to find dope in a backpacker hostel in Darwin." He thought for a moment, and then he frowned. "I do not even know your name."

I stuck out my hand in an awkward manner. "Adam."

"Eve." He shook my hand.

I looked at him. "Is that a joke?"

"No, it is my name." He seemed surprised.

"Adam and Eve? Come on, you can do better than that." His poor attempt at humor made me suspect that I could be travelling with a moron.

He laughed. "Not Eve. Ha, ha, I understand the joke. No, but I am French-Canadian. My name is Yve." He spelled it for me. "It is a common name where I am from."

"Well this is a little hard to believe," I said. "Adam and Yve travelling around Australia together. Who would have thought it?"

"The world is always strange. Or we are the strange ones and it is the world who is normal."

We laughed, and he refilled the glasses, and we smoked some more weed as the night grew dark at our little camp beneath the stand of river gums.

"So why are you riding all the way across Australia?" he asked me. "Is it a holiday adventure?"

I considered my options before replying. "I'm moving to Sydney. My girlfriend's there. She moved across to become a model."

"There are no models in Perth?"

"Apparently Sydney is where you need to go if you want to make it big."

He drank from his glass. "Have you been there before?"

"Once when I was a kid, to see my grandmother. She lives a few hours up the coast. But I suppose that doesn't count."

"Do you have plans for your work?"

"I have no idea what to expect." I poked a stick in the fire. "To tell the truth, I'm not even sure about my girlfriend. We had a bad phone conversation before I left. I was drunk, so I suppose it was stupid to call her and express my undying love at that time."

My companion winced as I went into more detail, and I told him how I hadn't spoken to her since then. "We spoke all the time when she first left. Quite graphic phone sex if you want to know."

Yve held up his hand. "I believe you."

I smiled. "Yeah, fair enough. The really bad thing is that now, riding across Australia, the closer I get to her in a physical sense, the more I feel we're getting further apart. I ride all day, and then I sit at night and try not to think about it. About that moment when I get to Sydney and either way I'll know for sure."

We sat in silence and sipped at our wine. I lit a cigarette and savored the harsh smoke in my lungs.

"All you can do is ride," Yve suddenly said. "You must enjoy the ride. Then you are in Sydney and then you must look at your problem. But here we have the wine, and the smoke, and the company. And tomorrow we can ride again to new places. It is good to ride. You must have concentration. No thinking of problems. Otherwise you cannot see."

"Yeah, I suppose you're right."

After a time he said, "How long have you been with this girl?"

I sighed. "About two months."

Yve whistled. "We should have got two bottles of the red."

The next morning my bike was dead. It wouldn't start, I didn't know what to do, and I was monumentally annoyed. I figured I had to do something, so lacking any better ideas, I walked off towards the distant farmhouse with a vague idea of asking for help, but halfway there my courage failed me and I turned back towards our little camp behind the stand of trees.

Yve had my bike up and running. He nodded his head at me while he fiddled around with his own bike.

"What did you do?" I felt stupid asking the question, but sometimes curiosity gets the best of you.

"It was not so hard. I put the battery from my bike in yours. Now I put it back in mine. You don't need the battery once it is going."

I stood there, wondering what to say. "No shit. I should have been able to work that out."

"One of us was enough."

"Lucky I bumped into you yesterday or I would have been stuck out here on my own."

He gave me a Gaelic shrug and then we finished loading our bikes and headed back to the main road. We were close to Mount Gambier, a large town located just before the next state border. The plan was to get a real mechanic to find out what was wrong with my bike.

We found a small motorbike garage. There were two mechanics working out the front in the early morning sun. They stopped work as we arrived and came over to look at our bikes.

"Honda 750," the taller one said to me. "Is that the '76 version?"

"Yeah," I said. "It's a tough old beast."

"Where have you come from?" the other mechanic asked.

I pointed to my companion "He came down from Darwin and I came across from Perth."

They both looked at me. "You came from Perth on that?"

I assured them that I had, and then I explained the problem. They told me to leave it with them for an hour, so we walked down the main street until we found a nice place for breakfast where we leafed through the morning papers and watched the locals walk by.

An hour later, my bike was ready. The mechanics explained that the alternator had burnt out, ruining my battery on the long run across the desert. I thanked them and asked how much I had to pay.

The older mechanic shook his head. "There's no charge, mate." I must have had a confused expression. "Bikers look after bikers. You get a lot of respect for this trip on that bike. Just a little bit we can do for you."

I was blown away by this unexpected generosity, but I was careful not to make a fuss as I didn't want to embarrass them. We all shook hands and then Yve and I rode out.

Over the next two days, Yve proved to be a boon travelling companion. He rode his bike well, he was quick to come to an agreement, he was a good conversationalist, he held his drink admirably, he said he liked my cooking, and he didn't crawl into my tent in the middle of the night and murder me. But I had a dilemma that needed to be resolved.

On our third night together we stopped on the Omeo Highway in the Alpine National Park, after a nightmare few hours spent negotiating rutted gravel roads that was made even more frightening by the frequent invasion of large groups of suicidal rabbits that sprang from the forest and darted between the wheels of our bikes. We found a campsite sitting in a lush meadow. A small river thundered over smooth bounders and the mountains formed a protective bowl around the clearing. We placed some beer in the cold running water, set up camp, and prepared a meal. The light began to fade and the clear water reflected the purple sky.

"You could kayak that," I said to Yve, and he nodded and handed me a beer. We drank sitting at a rough picnic table, but my thoughts strayed back to the mountain stream, and I imagined the line I would take if I had a kayak handy.

"Tomorrow we arrive in Sydney," Yve said.

I took a sip of my beer and peered at the rapids growing fainter in the evening light.

"What time do you think we can arrive there?" he said.

"I'm thinking of taking a detour for a day or so," I said. "I have an aunt who lives up in Mudgee. She'd probably be upset if I didn't stop in to say hello, and it's a sure bet that my mother has already called her to say I'm coming." I stared out across the meadow. "It would be great if you could come, but I don't know if it'd be cool, me turning up with some other biker. And I haven't seen them in a long time. I've only ever met them twice myself."

"It's no problem," he said. "It's probably best that I arrive in Sydney soon. I have to find a job, make some money."

"I don't want you to think that I'm ditching you. I just really don't know how they'd react."

"Don't worry about it. It's been a great trip," Yve said. "The ride today was crazy with all those little rabbits."

"And we still have a good day's riding together tomorrow. We can track through Tumut and up towards Gundagai. It's a historical town."

"Let's have a look," he said.

I got out the map and we plotted the route of our last day together, and all the while I was aware that these last few days with Yve for company had been a great distraction from the unwelcome reality that I was about to face in Sydney.

We made the town of Bathurst by midday. From there Yve's route was a direct run to Sydney, while mine was a confusing weave of backroads. I gave Yve Jodi's address, and we made plans to meet up in the next few weeks.

"Thank you for taking the chance to ask me to ride with you," he said.

I smiled and shook my head. "Thanks for everything."

"I will see you in Sydney. Then I can learn how things turned out."

I held my hand in the air as he rode away and I wondered if I had made the right decision.

After numerous stops to consult my map, I reached the farmhouse at Cherry Tree Hill farm before dark. My aunt and cousins welcomed me with open arms. I enjoyed the luxury of a shower, and then we sat in deep lounge chairs and I told them of my trip. My aunt was incredulous at my decision not to bring Yve, and I felt deep regret at making the wrong decision.

With my arrival in Sydney due the following day, I knew I could no longer avoid calling Jodi. I asked my aunt if I could use her phone. I had a cold feeling in the pit of my stomach as I dialed the number.

Jodi answered and my breath grew short at the sound of her voice. I tried to keep myself calm as I gave her the news that I was due to arrive the next day. Her reaction was non-committal and her voice was cold. I asked her what time she would be home. She replied that she didn't know. In my head I began to scream into the phone, demanding and pleading with her to tell me what was going on, but my voice stayed casual as I said I would see her tomorrow, and then I replaced the phone on the empty line.

The weather was foul and the long run into Sydney unpleasant. It took me hours to find her address in the convoluted streets and steep hills of Paddington. Finally I lucked upon it and I pulled up outside a stylish terrace house. I had completed the physical journey, all the way across Australia. And now I was going to know the result of my emotional odyssey, one way or another.

Nobody was home.

It was mid-afternoon, about the time I had told her to expect me. At this point you would have thought that I might have gotten the message, but there was still a sliver of hope. I had to know for sure.

My clothes were still damp and a chill wind was blowing. I walked back to my bike and sat on the wet seat. I didn't have the energy to feel angry. Some people came out of the house next door and cautiously asked if they could help. I told them I had just arrived from Perth, and one of them walked inside and emerged a few minutes later with a large mug of hot tea. I wrapped my hands around the cup and spoke with them about my trip as I kept an eye out for anyone walking down the street.

"I think this is your group now," one of them said.

I turned to look, and one member of the group broke and ran on seeing me, and she launched herself into my arms, and I gave her a big hug.

"Hello Suzie," I said. It was Jodi's best friend.

"I'm so glad you made it safely. I got here a few days ago. I tried to look for you from the plane."

I smiled at her joke but my attention was fixed on the rest of the group as Jodi detached herself and walked over and touched me lightly on the arm.

"Hi," she mumbled, and then she turned and walked to the door and Suzie looked at me and bit her lip and I knew without a shadow of a doubt that I was well and truly fucked.

2

Three days later, I got up late and packed my bags after everyone had left for work. Jodi had a bunch of housemates, and although it had taken me a little while, I had eventually understood that every single one of them had been privy to Jodi bad-mouthing me behind my back before my arrival.

On the first night the looks had been of total pity at my unfortunateness. By the third night the looks had changed to exasperation that I wasn't getting the fucking message. And they had a point. Jodi and I had managed the astonishing feat of sharing a bed for three nights without any real form of communication. Her way of telling me that it was all over was by not telling me anything at all. And after three days I got the message. That last little flicker of pathetic hope died.

I had given this one my all, but for me, when a relationship finishes, and particularly if I had no choice in the final outcome, my survival mechanism is to go cold turkey. I don't want to see the person, I don't want to hear anyone talk about the person, and I don't want to know anything about how their life is going. I just want to get on with my own. Because if someone ends a relationship, you can't talk them out of it. Oh, you might think that you can, and you might talk them into coming back, but it's over, and the only thing keeping it together is their own patch of self-doubt that you managed to weasel your way back into.

That's not me.

So I lay in bed and listened to the morning household sounds until every one of them had left and I was alone with my own pathetic situation. I got up and began to pack my bags. I wasn't leaving because I was desperate to get out into a new city and make a new life for myself. I was leaving because I knew that if the household returned that evening to find me still there they would probably throw me into the street.

I didn't leave a note or any indication where I was going, since I didn't know that myself. With my bike loaded I walked back to the front door and pulled it shut until I heard the lock settle in place, and then I gave it a little push just to make sure. The bike started at the first kick and I motored down the street until I came to the main road. I looked right and left, searching for a break in the traffic, and when it came it was towards the right, so that was the way I went.

I spotted a little café with a few small shaded tables on the sidewalk from where I could watch my bags. I ordered a coffee, and then I spread out my map of the city and tried to figure out the next step. I thought about a guy I knew who had tried to make the same move to Sydney. There'd been a big farewell party where he got lots of gifts and plenty of advice. He barely lasted a week and came back with his tail between his legs.

The scary thing for me was that I was at real risk of being in the same boat, and I couldn't face the idea of going back home and having to recreate my life once again from scratch. The only way I saw of avoiding this predicament was staying in Sydney. Easier said than done. My cash reserves were feeble. I had enough either to get back home or to last a few weeks in this new and unknown city.

Maybe the reason for me coming to Sydney was totally lame, but now that I was here I had to make the most of it. First I needed a place to stay. The only thing that came to mind was the numerous backpacker lodgings in Kings Cross, the city's red-light district. When the waitress came with my coffee, I asked her to show me Kings Cross on the map.

"The Cross isn't a suburb," she said. "It's just this bit of Darlinghurst road." She touched the map with her finger. "You're almost sitting in it now. It's just down this road and a bit to the right."

"Can you find places to stay there?"

She looked at me with tired eyes. "If you're desperate."

I rode through the Cross. People were sweeping away the previous night's rubbish from the doors of the bars and the strip-clubs and the gambling houses. Even in the early morning the street was a hive of seediness and desperation in the midst of an otherwise normal city. After a couple of runs of the main street some of the working girls were convinced that I was cruising for action, so I made a quick decision and parked my bike outside a run-down building several floors high. There was a big sign claiming its status as the cleanest accommodation in the Cross. I didn't think they would have to live up to much.

There were a few lost souls moving erratically along the pavement, as well as several figures slouched in doorways and cellar-front windows. I grabbed all of my stuff from the bike and hauled everything inside the door in one go. The lobby was sparse and functional. A man looked at me from behind the counter.

"How many nights?" he barked.

"I'm not sure," I said. "Maybe a week?"

"I can give ya a discount onna week. We got common rooms for eight bucks a night, or ya can take a private room, but that'll set ya back thirty big ones."

"Can I have a look at a common room?"

"Leave ya bags behind here," he said. "I won't steal 'em." He leaned back and yelled a name a few times into an open door until a morose looking individual emerged, scratching his untidy hair. "Show him a common room. Take him to eight."

I followed him up a flight of steep and narrow stairs that suggested the building was a lethal firetrap. We walked down a long corridor illuminated by small naked bulbs set at irregular intervals. He opened a door and pointed into a long room. Belongings were strewn around the floor. Several figures lay unmoving on sagging beds. Someone mumbled at him to close the door. The room smelled of unwashed bodies and socks that would disintegrate before they ever saw the inside of a washing machine.

"Let's have a look at a private room," I said.

He turned without a word and trudged back down the stairs to the floor below, where he unlocked another door. I peered inside. The walls were brown. The ragged carpet was brown. The thin bedspread and tattered curtains were a different brown color. An ancient television squatted on small legs in the corner. One leg had broken off and someone had stuck an empty yogurt container in its place.

I paid for a week. I dumped my gear in a corner and tried out the bed. It sagged alarmingly beneath me and I tried not to imagine the unspeakable acts it must have witnessed. I risked a glance into the bathroom where I saw surfaces marked with large stains that matched the color of the rest of the room. There was an empty toilet roll on the dispenser and a sliver of used soap stuck to the side of the sink.

I went back to the lobby and asked the man if he knew a safe place where I could store my bike.

"There's an undercover car park on the other side of the Cross." He gave me brief directions on how to get there.

I got on my bike and went to start it when a big man with a beard walked straight up to me. I tensed with the threat of a confrontation.

"Watch out, mate," he said, and he pointed at the rear of my bike. I looked back and saw one of my luggage straps still attached to the rear pannier and dangling dangerously close to my back wheel.

"Thanks a lot," I said, and he nodded his head and walked across the road.

Later I sat on the bed and ate some takeaway food and drank a few cans of beer while the television flickered on the single channel that the broken knob allowed me to watch. There was an occasional yell and bump from somewhere in the building. I got up a couple of times to check if my door was still locked. As night fell, Kings Cross kicked into gear, and I fell asleep to the sounds of vehicles stopping and starting and sounding their horns, voices yelling abuse, and doormen calling out the merits of the girls dancing in their clubs.

There was a lot of lying on my hotel bed and wishing I was somewhere else, somebody else, anybody else, just not this miserable loser who had thrown away his life to chase some chick across Australia. I hated who I was. I didn't see in myself anything of value, and my circumstances reflected this belief. It was a real low point.

But thirty bucks a day was going to chew through my cash in no time at all, and that wasn't counting the cost of eating and drowning my sorrows. It was this more than anything that propelled me out of that dismal room and into the streets to search for a permanent place to live.

There were a couple of old Victorian-era terrace houses on the next street with "room available" signs displayed in greasy windows. A man in a dressing robe answered the door at the first one. He showed me upstairs while he lit one cigarette with the burning stub of another. He had a hacking cough and he played idly with his scraggy grey chest hair. The room was in the attic and I had to stoop to inspect the small single bed and battered wardrobe. Someone had seen fit to nail shut the window.

"Four other fellas live here," said the man behind me. "Don't want no trouble. Fifty bucks a week."

I told him I'd get back to him.

Outside I squinted up into the bright sky and pondered my options. I didn't know the city, but I knew that I didn't want to live in some faceless suburb miles from the city center. I was here, so I may as well be in the thick of it. But perhaps Kings Cross was a little too thick even for my tastes. Exploring a little I discovered that just beyond the boundaries of the seedy awfulness were some of the most desirable suburbs in Sydney. Potts Point, Elizabeth Bay and Rushcutters Bay were packed with glamorous apartment buildings and stately homes, many of which had sweeping views of the harbor.

I purchased the major newspapers and found a neat little bar where I went through the classified ads with great care. I made some calls from a public phone, most of which went nowhere as the rooms in questions had already been let. But in the end I managed to score an interview for a room in an apartment in Potts Point.

The next day I walked a couple of blocks to the address I had scribbled on the newspaper. The building was an imposing set of apartments in an art deco style. The dark lobby had deep purple carpet and crafted wood paneling. The lift had a sliding door and cage, and it cranked and wobbled up to the seventh floor. I thought this was very cool and mysterious, and already I could picture myself living there in smart sophistication. The apartment was large and gracious and was furnished in a retro-seventies style. A bright orange vinyl retro hairdresser's chair squatted in a corner, complete with large clear plastic dome.

Francis owned and lived in the apartment. He was in his late twenties, small and thin, and looked like he was rarely exposed to sunlight. He had eclectic red-blonde hair and a Van Gogh goatee. His girlfriend, Anna, was about my own age. She had beautiful pale skin and striking dark hair and I felt an immediate rapport with her. They were very interested in the story of how I came to be in Sydney, and the three of us chatted for quite some time. The second bedroom was available for the tidy sum of $150 per week. Everything about the place was perfect, and I expressed this while trying to contain my obvious desperation. Francis asked me questions about my general cleanliness, honesty, trustworthiness and reliability, and I did my very best to lie convincingly. He told me that he had a number of people to interview and we arranged to speak again in a couple of days.

I loved that apartment. It was hip, it was cool, and it was in a great area. I could see myself living there, having discussions with Francis and Anna about interesting and important things, and suddenly I wanted it with total desperation. All thoughts of love-sick rejection fell by the wayside as I devoted far too much mental energy obsessing over how the room could be mine.

Which was frustrating, as there was nothing else I could do. Now it was all up to Francis. I should have continued to scour the classifieds, I should have gone to the major universities and checked the noticeboards for flyers advertising rooms. I should have done a bunch of things.

What I did was walk into the main part of the city. I crossed Hyde Park and entered a luxurious department store. It made a welcome change from my drab room. I wandered around the expensive displays until I found myself in the homeware section. I realized I would need a lot of stuff as I had no bed, no sheets, no towels or blankets.

I looked over the store's offerings. In the end I chose the most expensive towel in the store, the fabric thick, plush, and luxurious, while the dark purple color expertly matched the lobby of the apartment I had just seen. This wasn't just a towel; it was an investment in my soon-to-be-obtained-room, and it was my way of demonstrating that Francis would choose me as his new flat-mate. It would either be a lesson in willing a dream into reality or abject self-delusion.

Back in my hotel room I placed the towel on a small chair where I could see it from the bed and I did my best to think positive thoughts. When this all got too much I headed out and found a bar where I could watch the hordes of beautiful women that paraded along the streets. At some point it dawned on me that there was a reasonable chance of seeing Jodi walk by. The thought terrified me beyond belief, and what with the added mental pressure from the room, I was soon an incoherent mess. I stumbled home as the sky became dark, a package of takeaway food under my arm.

I rang Francis at the appointed time, prepared for bad news. But he still hadn't made a decision, and he told me to call back the next day. I placed the receiver back on its cradle, but really I wanted to smash it to pieces. I figured I was still in the running for the room as he hadn't told me to go away forever. But that also meant that other people had a chance, and I had no way to identify them and roll their bodies into the harbor, feet set securely in hardened concrete.

Another day to kill, another chance of bumping into Jodi. I knew that there were many things I should have been doing to improve my situation, but until I got word on that room one way or another I was frozen into inaction. I don't know what I did that day, but I'm quite sure it was nothing.

I rang again the next day and Francis told me that I had the room. It's a pretty awesome moment when you've resigned yourself to failure only to be told that you've succeeded. I stepped out of the phone booth with a feeling of total relief. It took me less than a minute to ride my bike to my new home, but the small distance hid the tremendous difference between the two worlds. I unpacked my bags and folded my clothes neatly in the closet, and then I hung the purple towel behind the bedroom door. I set out on an immediate mission to find a bed, and within an hour I had a cheap new futon and some bed linen in my room. I made another trip for groceries, and that evening I prepared dinner for the three of us, and as we sat and ate and talked, I felt the happiest I had been for what seemed a very long time.

3

Now that I had a roof over my head I needed to find a way to pay for it. Through an old colleague back home I had a contact for a small bar which was just around the corner from my new apartment. It opened early, closed late, and the owner was happy to give me a good number of hours. But leaving a bar job in Perth for a bar job in Sydney seemed to me like I was going backward. At least I'd had a band in Perth. Now I just had a job in a bar.

So I searched the newspapers for potential jobs and sent off applications that went unanswered. I wasn't qualified for anything and I had no idea how to make myself qualified. I could have bitten the bullet and gone to university, but I didn't know what I wanted to study either. And as inexperienced as I was in the ways of life, I knew enough to realize that it was unwise to go into a large amount of debt for a degree chosen by throwing a dart at a chart.

To top it off, I began to suspect that my employer was a flake. She was strident, difficult, and didn't know her job. It was one thing to be a bitch, but quite another to be useless into the bargain.

In the beginning I offered a few suggestions to improve the bar's efficiency, but she took this as an attempt by myself to rebel against her because she was a woman. So I tried to stay out of trouble while following her dumb-as-shit procedures. I was conscious of the importance of keeping alive my only source of income, but I also knew that the whole operation was living on borrowed time. One day I took a delivery from one of the suppliers, but when I went to sign the form he apologized and said that he preferred cash. We looked at each other in mutual understanding.

I got on friendly terms with one of the regular customers, a woman in her fifties. She had untidy frizzy hair and an astonishing inability to match clothing from her wardrobe. She came in each morning, ordered a coffee and a small pastry, and sat at a prime table on the edge of the sidewalk, where a large plane tree offered a cooling shade. Then she spent hours writing in an oversized notebook while resisting any attempts from the owner to pry her away from her table. She always left a tiny portion of her pastry uneaten, as well as a smidgen of cold coffee in the bottom of the cup. When a member of serving staff dared to inch forward and remove the items she shrieked that she wasn't yet finished and the staff member scurried away.

I watched this daily performance with amusement. One day the owner came up to me and said that I had to get her to move.

"There are other people waiting for a table," she said.

I looked around. "So what? She comes in every day when we're empty. You need people like that to get the day moving."

"I don't care. If she doesn't order something else I want her off that table."

"Fine." I walked over to the customer in question. "The manager told me to tell you that unless you order something else she wants you off the table."

The woman regarded me from beneath the bird's nest of hair that covered her face. "Why doesn't she come to tell me that herself?"

I shrugged. "Too scared, I suppose."

"Well, I'm still enjoying my pastry."

"So it seems." I looked at her notebook. "What do you write in there every day?"

She set down her notebook. "I'm a writer. So I write things. I also run writing courses, so I have to prepare glorious lessons for my admiring students." She waved her arms around as she said this, a dozen cheap bangles bashing against one another.

"I like writing too," I said, which was true.

"Really?" She leaned forward with a large smile. "Tell me all about it."

We spoke for a few minutes about writing, and what I wanted to achieve, and then before I knew it I had agreed to come to her next series of evening lessons starting the very next night. I walked back to the bar where the owner was waiting. Her foot tapped an erratic nervous rhythm on the floor.

"Well? What did she say? Why is she still sitting there? Did she order something?"

"She's a writer," I said. "And I need the next four nights off work to go to her course." The owner just looked at me, a vacant stare of pure evil. "Oh, and she wants a glass of tap water. But don't worry yourself, I'll get that for her."

The course was held in an old terrace house down in Elizabeth Bay, just around the corner from my apartment. I was the youngest person there by a good twenty years. Unfortunately, by the second night I had scant regard for just about every person in the room, the teacher included. That evening, the teacher made a broad and opinionated statement on what counted for humor in writing, and then attempted to dismiss my objections. The discussion degenerated into an argument in which most of the other students meekly followed the teacher. A middle aged woman named Barbara keenly watched proceedings without offering her own opinion. Afterwards she invited me to go for a drink in a little bar across the road.

"You were right on the money in there," she said. "I've never met such a disagreeable and untalented bunch."

"I'm relieved to hear that. I thought I was going insane."

"Why are you on the course anyway? You don't seem the type to take kindly to the usual personalities who go along to these things."

"I'm not sure. I could barely afford the bloody thing. I don't know many people here. I've just moved over from Perth. I was hoping to maybe meet some like-minded people."

She laughed. "That's my excuse as well. I've also just come over from Perth."

"Really? Why did you come over here?"

"The kids had grown up and moved out, and I no longer had any reason to keep pretending that their father and I had a real relationship. What about you?"

"Young man follows girl across Australia. Girl dumps young man." I decided to change the subject. "What are you doing here for work?"

"I'm the office manager for a well-known self-improvement and motivational speaker."

I was startled when she mentioned his name and I told her that I had read his book and attended one of his courses back in Perth.

"Are you working?" she asked.

"In a bar, although I think my days there are numbered."

"Well, we're gearing up for a new round of courses and I need some help manning the phones. It would only be for a couple of weeks, but the pay is good and you would get to meet and work with Bennett. You could come down to the office in Balmain tomorrow morning if you're interested."

"What the hell," I said. "It's the best offer I've had since I've been here."

Barbara introduced me to Bennett, a large, energetic, gregarious man who had the disconcerting habit of smiling keenly at you with all his teeth—as if his brain kept reminding him that people like it when you smile. The office was small and chaotic, and Barbara showed me to a desk with a telephone and some printed lists containing names and contact details.

"These are the people who have done a free introductory evening course with us. What you have to do is ring them and see if they want to do the full two day course."

She left me to it, but I saw a couple of problems. First, the course was not inexpensive. Second, apart from some prank calls as a kid I'd never called strangers in their home. The phone seemed like a giant obstacle. I looked around and saw the other half a dozen employees speaking calmly into their mouthpieces. I snatched up the phone and quickly dialed the first number. It rang for a few seconds and then a gruff male voice answered.

"Yeah?"

"Is Kathy there, please?" I said.

"Who the fuck is this?"

"My name is Adam, and I'm calling regarding the Mind Improvement course that she expressed an interest in attending."

"Are you seeing her, is that it? Are you the one who's trying to fuck my wife?" In the background I heard a woman's voice protesting. The man said, "Shut up! I know you're seeing someone!" He turned his attention back to me. "Now you listen here you little bastard. I've got ways of finding out who you are, and when I do ..."

I quietly replaced the receiver onto the cradle. I glanced around and caught Barbara's eye. She gave me an encouraging grin and I returned a belated thumbs-up.

Bennett's exotic wife came up to me. "You have to inspire them to come," she said. "It is an inspiration to do the course."

"Inspire them," I repeated.

"You must have an opening line. My line is like this: 'I am calling to inspire you to come to the course.' Say this to them. You will be amazed."

"You want me to say that?"

"It will work," she insisted. "Do it like that." She walked away.

I watched her sultry bottom swing wildly from side to side, and then I shook my head and dialed the next number. Another man answered and I groaned inwardly.

"Hi, my name is Adam. I'm calling in regards to the Mind Improvement course—" I took a deep breath "—and I'm calling to inspire you to come along."

There was a brief silence. "Inspire me?"

"Yes," I said. "Inspire you."

"Did you think up that lame line all by yourself?"

At the end of the day I had only sold three courses. It turned out that this was two more than anyone else had managed to achieve. Everyone was very pleased and we went out for a drink in a bar overlooking Sydney harbor.

Over the two weeks I managed to sell a total of thirteen courses, a clear record at the office. Bennett was suitably impressed and we had a chat in his office regarding a full time position. The thought of being permanently stuck to the phone filled me with dread, but I took it with both eyes open for opportunities to escape the phones. There were a couple of unstable young women working in key positions, and I had a hunch that at least one of them would soon crack. At the end of my first week as a full time employee, the desktop publishing girl quit with a suitably hysterical outburst, pausing on her way out only to gather her personal belongings and the half-eaten packet of biscuits she'd been jealously guarding at the coffee machine.

Bennett was in a state of acute anxiety. There was a great deal of work to do for the upcoming series of courses, but he'd just lost a key employee. I walked past the newly vacated prime office space and knocked on Bennett's open door.

"I don't suppose you know anything about desktop publishing," he said, looking up at me from behind his desk with a sense of weariness.

I didn't hesitate. "Sure. Computers are like second nature to me."

His face lit up and he bounded around his desk and led me into the empty office. I sat down as he stood beside me. The chair was still warm.

"Can you use one of these?" he said, pointing to the large PowerMac computer.

I decided to balance the outright lies with some half-truths. "I haven't seen this model before." I was thinking fast. "Is there a manual for the program she was using?"

He dragged one out from under the desk. A quick flick through it confirmed I didn't understand a single word. "I'll take it home over the weekend and get stuck into it," I said

Bennett patted me on the shoulder. "Be ready on Monday."

Barbara gave me a slow round of silent applause from behind her desk.

I spent the weekend studying the manual with fiendish intensity. Francis played vintage acid jazz records to keep me in the mood, while Anna provided me with a steady stream of coffee and cake. On Monday I set to work, the manual a constant presence by my side. Bennett breezed in and out as he checked my progress, but somehow I managed to make it look like I knew what I was doing. My big test came when I sent my first brochure off to the commercial printers. Shortly afterwards a large package arrived. Inside were the printed results, exactly how Bennett had requested them.

I took them in to show him. "Good job," he said. "But we're going to need something slightly different for the course the following Wednesday. See this section here?"

As we spoke about what he needed, it suddenly dawned on me that I was going to be all right. I had achieved my goal of being able to stay in Sydney, and I had done it on my own terms.

4

I was twenty three years old and I had managed to land myself a job which I wouldn't have even got an interview for if I had applied in a normal fashion. The pain of rejection and humiliation from my failed relationship began to fade as I went about my daily routine. Working a nine-to-five job was a novelty for me. It felt good to have my evenings and weekends free for the first time in my adult life. The problem was what to do with them. I didn't socialise much with my work colleagues and, apart from Francis and Anna, I wasn't really meeting anyone. For the most part I was sticking to myself, which was the opposite of how I had lived in Perth. There I had surrounded myself with an enormous circle of friends and associates. I reasoned that the more friends you had, the better a person you were. But all that was simply a distraction, a way of avoiding the painful process of having a good long look at myself.

Now I had no distractions, and I had ample amounts of free time. So where did that leave me? I was so lacking in self confidence that if a stranger sat next to me on a bus I would spend the entire journey torturing myself on the right way to initiate a conversation. And if I did manage to speak to the person sitting next to me and they didn't respond in kind, I would take this as a mortal blow of rejection. I couldn't handle the small ups and downs of normal everyday interactions. I might have ridden a motorbike all the way across Australia and begun a new life in a strange city, but deep down I was lost and afraid and unable to initiate real change. Changing locations doesn't matter if you don't change what's inside.

But I instinctively understood that in order to like myself I had to become a well-rounded person. I wanted to be someone who was interesting, and who had something to say. So I figured I better have some interests. I found a little guitar shop on Oxford Street and started taking guitar lessons for the first time in many years. It was a way of becoming better at something. My fashion sense was rubbish as nobody had ever taken the time to teach me how to dress. So I started to frequent good fashion stores. I observed what the staff was wearing, I purchased magazines and studied the clothes, and piece by piece I built a small wardrobe of quality items.

I also walked a lot. Sydney was great for walking, at least in the inner-city area. Autumn came and with it the rain and cold. I bought a smart umbrella and spent hours walking along the narrow laneways and streets that wound their paths around the harbor area. I discovered a few secondhand bookstores down on George Street. One of them was located in a cavernous cellar with the books piled high to the ceilings and spilling over and onto the floor, and I spent hours in there searching for first editions of my favorite writers. Sometimes I went to parties, perhaps invited with a bunch of people from work. I stood on the outside of the room with a drink in my hand as some sort of protection, as if I had a reason to be there. I looked at all the relaxed people, talking and laughing in the middle of the room and I wondered what I had to do to be like them.

Bennett's courses ran on the weekends, typically in some mid-rank chain hotel where he could get some depressing convention room located deep in the bowels of the building, away from all natural light and noise. This was important as he was running meditation courses, so between bouts of crazed and animated lecturing, the entire room collapsed into itself for a twenty minute rendition of silence. Row upon row of middle-class desperados who were faced with the impending reality of tipping over the edge into full-blown mid-life crisis, would sit on straight-back chairs and silently will themselves into repeating the latest mantra meant to stop the crazed voices in their heads.

After the allotted time was up, Bennett spoke reassuringly with a low voice into the microphone, rousing the room from its collective slumber.

"Annnnnd…coming back…back to where we are…coming slooooowly back…very good, very good."

Then I'd hit the lights and they'd blink and look around in a nervous manner, perhaps not wholly convinced that we weren't secretly filming them for an episode of *Australia's Funniest Home Videos*.

I liked the meditation courses, and I began to practice the techniques myself. I found them valuable for centering myself, and I felt more awake and able to think clearer as a result. I also thought that Bennett ran his courses well. He skirted the fine line of giving the crowd what they wanted while maintaining a respectful distance.

But I soon realised that the majority of the attendees used these types of New Age courses as a quick fix for their various personality problems. Weighed down by their bad behaviour and numerous poor life choices, they'd attend a two day course and leave with purposeful strides and confident smiles. But a few months later when the effects had worn off and their good intentions had fallen by the wayside, they'd be back at a course from us or someone else and the cycle would begin anew. It was a good way to convince yourself that you were doing something while really doing nothing at all.

The ones who really got up my nose were those who volunteered their services to help out on Bennett's future courses, as he wasn't one to turn down a free, enthusiastic, and hero-worshipping workforce. They resented my presence because I was a part of Bennett's inner circle, but worst of all because he paid me to be there. In their eyes I should have been doing the great man's work for free.

After having attended two courses, one as a paying client, the other as a volunteer, they inevitably became instant experts on all things New Age and philosophical. They hounded all of their friends to attend, dropped quotes devoid of any real meaning at inappropriate moments, and stood beaming on the sidelines as their great hero lectured from the dais.

Convinced of their deep understanding of the subject matter, they each fell into total disillusionment when their own life failed to change in line with their supposed enlightenment. But no matter, as there was always another puffed-up cretin perfectly willing to step forward and take the vacated place.

During one particular course weekend I was standing at the back of the room while Bennett spoke about finding one's own guru. A man in the audience raised his hand and Bennett indicated that he could speak.

"Would you be my guru?" the man asked. All eyes in the room shifted immediately to the stage.

Bennett's smile was warm as he shook his head and expressed regret that this would not be possible. But he said this in a way that every person in the audience felt that, if they were worthy enough, they stood a chance of becoming his personal pupil.

Cairns was a small city far up the east coast of Australia, the gateway to the Great Barrier Reef. Bennett had identified it as being ripe for the picking, and he whisked me, Barbara, and his young protégé Dylan up with him. The plan was to run five days of free evening seminars in order to generate interest for the full two day course on the weekend. This had been preceded by two weeks of all-out blitzkrieg advertising on the local radio networks.

I had never been to the Far North, or on a business trip, so this was an exciting development. It was raining steadily when we landed, and I was amazed at the deep green color that saturated the landscape. I saw the rainforest reaching down over the high hills until it touched the Coral Sea, and I imagined it continuing for miles offshore in the form of the Great Barrier Reef until it plunged far below to the deep ocean floor.

We walked out of the airport into a thick fog of heat and humidity. Downtown was spread along a long esplanade facing the turquoise sea, at the end of which our hotel sat overlooking the harbor. In my room on the top floor, I stood at the window and gazed over the city, wreathed in clouds and shrouded in warm rain.

There was a knock at my door and Dylan entered. "Nothing to do until tomorrow," he said. "Let's ditch the others and go have a look around."

The steady rain forced us to scurry from one awning to another as we pushed through the tourist crowds. We found a sidewalk table and ordered a beer. The Coral Sea sat languid at our backs and the rain rattled the tin awning as we watched the steady stream of people passing our table.

"There's a really different vibe to this place," I said. "It's nothing like Sydney."

"The beer sure is cheaper," my companion said.

A man approached our table. He had long, unkempt hair and a scraggy beard, but his shirt was clean, and he had a friendly smile. "Mind if I join you?" he said. "You guys bagged the last table."

Dylan and I were used to the social behaviors of inner-city Sydney, where you guarded your own space with an enclosed intensity bordering on neuroticism. We glanced warily at each other, but the man smiled and continued to talk as he pulled out a chair, and within moments he had settled back and ordered a drink.

"Where are you fellas from?"

"Sydney," I said. "How'd you know we're not from here?"

He laughed. "You're too uptight. You almost shat yourselves when I sat down with you."

"We're here to run some self-improvement courses," Dylan said.

"Oh yeah, them mind courses. I heard the ads on the radio. I reckon you'll do well up here."

"Why's that?"

He took a long drink from his glass. "Everyone's half a loony up here. This is the last stop. North of here there's nowhere to go. People who are on the run from their own failures eventually end up in this place."

"Not a bad place to fail in," I said.

"Hide yourself under a tropical sky with a rum and coke and a kilo of cooked prawns. Yeah, it's not bad. And it's open-minded. It's the last frontier. You probably think all these Japanese tourists are here to see the Barrier Reef, and they are, no doubt about that. But they're also here to see us. They come here on their five day holiday; that's all they get in a whole year, five days, and they soak up the whole vibe of laid back nothingness. It's probably what keeps them going."

He suddenly looked past us and signaled to someone in the crowd. In short order, a large group of people were seated around our table. The discussion was animated, friendly, and spontaneous. We purchased several rounds of drinks, and as the sky darkened behind the rain clouds, I got talking to a lithe brunette about my own age. Her hair fell past her shoulders, and her skin was tanned a deep shade of amber. There were a scattering of freckles over her pert nose, and liquid brown eyes that flashed when she laughed.

By now food was a priority. Her apartment was around the corner, and a few of us agreed to the idea of a home cooked meal. After a chaotic group effort at preparing some sort of stir-fry dish, we sat on various mismatching chairs and lounges scattered around the large room and talked and drank into the night.

Later, Dylan and I walked back to the hotel, the silence of the town broken when we ventured past some late night bar filled with young drunken tourists. I thought about the girl; about the fact that in all my time in Sydney I'd never met so many people socially as I had in this one evening. Sydney was a city that supported my self-imposed isolation. Meditating alone on the lounge room floor was all well and good, but now I wanted to get out and meet girls.

Cairns made Bennett. The locals clawed over each other while throwing money at our shocked boss. One week became two, and then it went to three. By the time we checked out of the Hilton, the hotel bill was enough to bankrupt most touring rock stars. Bennett didn't even blink when he paid it. Back in Sydney he launched into frenzied planning to get back to Cairns as soon as possible. He spoke of building a vast meditation retreat in the countryside south of Sydney.

Francis took a three month contract on the Gold Coast writing episodes for a dubious television production, and left me with instructions for how to pay the rent. At night I prepared a single meal while listening to neighbors argue a few feet from where I stood. Alone in the apartment, I began to dream of beautiful girls on tropical beaches, of a laid-back lifestyle bathed in a balmy tropical calm, of lazy heat settling over chilled glasses of gin and tonic filled with crushed ice and wedges of lime. I braved winter storms to sit in cafes, but no strangers asked to share my table, and I didn't meet any more brown eyed girls.

The second trip to Cairns was almost as successful as the first, but in my free time I wandered along the waterfront and marveled once again at the contrast in lifestyle between this small city and the one where I lived. Dylan had a greater sense of diligence on this trip. He shadowed Bennett in an attempt to understand how his presentations were organized, as he was determined to get in on the grand money-making machine. I expressed doubt that he would be able to pull off presenting Bennett's courses; after all it was Bennett they were paying to hear.

"You need to sing your own song, not someone else's," I said.

Dylan thought about this for a long time.

Back in Sydney I received a call from a friend. Mark had left Perth a few months after me and had spent the winter working in the Australian snowfields. I suggested that he come to Sydney to catch up, and a few days later he was at my door. We went out for drinks and I told him about Cairns, about the laid-back lifestyle. Then I told him about the chicks.

Over the next few days we worked out a plan. The logistics required a fair bit of running around, but in essence I was to follow him back to Perth on my motorbike, where we'd tie up some loose ends and then head to Cairns in his car. All the stuff we couldn't carry I left at my grandmother's house just north of Sydney. Mark's brother got my room, and all that went with it.

I gave Bennett a week's notice. He was gracious and gave me a little speech about how I was destined for great things. I appreciated that quite a bit, although I appreciated the unexpected holiday payout even more. Eleven months after I arrived in Sydney I headed out to see if Cairns was the answer to what I was looking for.

5

A good friendship can take a few knocks and bruises. Mark and I had been good friends for a long time. I had met him when I started work as a barman at *The Queens*, a gentrified and hip inner-city suburban pub in Perth. Mark had already been there for a while. He was *the* barman on a staff roster that ran into triple figures, and he held down the prime position on station three during the epic Sunday afternoon sessions when the crowd was ten deep at the bar and screaming for drinks. I sensed in Mark a fellow spirit of the hard-working, take-no-prisoners, and suffer-no-fools variety, and more importantly he recognized the same in me. Officially, a vast collection of managers, assistant managers, and duty managers ran the show. In reality, Mark and I ran it.

So a road trip across Australia and back should have been a snore for us. The part from Sydney to Perth went well, as I was on my bike while Mark was trapped in his car with a couple of English backpacker girls, one of whom he was shagging.

We had a week or so in Perth where I caught up with a lot of friends and family. I purchased an expensive backpack from a family friend who owned an adventure supplies store. He'd taught me kayaking when I was a teenager, and on hearing that I was off to Cairns, he casually mentioned that there was a lot of whitewater rafting up that way.

Finally Mark and I got in his car together with Nicole, one of the classier bargirls we knew from our *Queens* days. She decided to come at the last minute, and the three of us took off for Cairns, a distance of 6500 kilometers.

Mark didn't want to share the driving, which was fair enough as it was his car. But he didn't want to share the decision making either. On anything. Nicole and I didn't even get to pick any music, let alone a say on any of the logistical aspects of the trip. By the time we arrived in Cairns I'd reached the limits of my patience, but I kept my mouth closed. Cairns was the goal, and as we rolled through the outer suburbs I was convinced the trip had been worth it.

I gave Mark directions to the Esplanade, and as we passed the colonial houses facing the sea I pointed out the various backpacker hostels that I considered good possibilities for us to stay. More than anything, I wanted a celebratory drink, perhaps at the very sidewalk bar from my first visit earlier in the year.

Mark turned around at the end of the long street, the little trailer behind us rattling as it jumped on its single axle.

"There was a parking spot back there," I said, twisting around in my seat.

"We need to find a place to stay," Mark said. "I saw a sign for a caravan park back on the main road."

I chose my words with care. "You don't want to stay in one of these central backpackers?"

"The caravan park will be better for our camping setup. And cheaper."

Nicole said nothing. Mark took the highway and headed north. Glimpses of the occasional sign enabled us to navigate to Lake Placid. We found the caravan park hidden in abundant foliage, set back from a large sheltered lake. Mark parked the car and went and inquired at the small office. Nicole and I walked down to the lake.

"It's very pretty here," she said.

I was seething. It was one thing for Mark to make all the decisions on the drive across Australia. It was another thing entirely for it to continue once we'd arrived in Cairns.

"How far out of town are we?" I said. "Twenty minutes? And I didn't see any public transport."

"But we have the car."

I looked at her. "Mark has the car."

I was fucked if I was going to sit out here miles from town and having to beg Mark for a lift every time I needed to get somewhere. I needed the freedom to make my own decisions and act on them when required. I also sensed that there was no point trying to explain this. Besides, in my current emotional state there was a very good chance it might come out the wrong way.

Mark came back and said he'd secured a good caravan for not too much money. I wished them both luck and then asked if he could drop me off in town.

"It's too out of the way here," I said. "And I don't want you to become a taxi service." I was doing my best to be generous.

There was a short silence. "Okay," Mark said, and he walked back to the car.

"Sorry to be leaving you like this," I said to Nicole. "I've got Mark's number. I'll call you guys when I'm settled somewhere."

I stayed for a few nights in a cute little bed & breakfast while I looked for a new place to live. Since I had no wheels, I concentrated on the streets bordering the central business district, itself a mishmash of hotels, bars, restaurants, tacky gift shops, and tour booking agencies. A flyer on a notice-board in a hippie café caught my eye. It advertised rooms in a share-house, and I called the number from a public pay phone.

"Hello, the Wilderness Society, this is John."

"I'm sorry," I said. "I must have the wrong number. I was calling about rooms in a share house." The Wilderness Society was a radical environmental group that made Greenpeace look like a bunch of conservatives. I must have dialed their office by mistake.

"Oh, you have the right number." He had a North American accent. "There's, ah, there's a room available in the house. It's upstairs above the office. We have the office downstairs." There was a pause. "I run the office."

He gave me directions and I hurried over. The house was set back from the road in a broad confusion of banana and mango trees. It would have been a beauty in its day, a classic turn of the century Queenslander, but now it was somewhat dilapidated. A hand-painted sign on the low front fence identified the house as the headquarters of The Wilderness Society. The open space underneath the house had been bricked up, and from an open door I heard the sounds of Nick Drake coming from a cheap stereo. I knocked on the side of the door and a young man of about my own age looked up at me from a computer.

"John?" I said. "I've come about the room."

He smiled. "We spoke on the phone, hello." He stood up and extended his hand. His white face was plastered with a scattering of freckles and his hair had a reddish hue. He was Canadian and he spoke in hushed tones with emphasis on long drawn out vowels. But it was his eyes that demanded attention; they held my gaze with a look of intensity beyond what was comfortable. He rolled a cigarette as we spoke, his fingers dancing a rhythm over paper and tobacco. He led me up a steep flight of outside stairs at the rear of the house.

"It's a great house, a great house," he said. "It's been falling apart for years...years and years. Sometimes we have sporadic attempts to halt the inevitable decline."

"So do you live here?" I surveyed the kitchen with its long counter down one wall, a battered and ancient white stove, and two fridges that squatted side by side at the opposite wall.

"No, no. I run the office downstairs. We lease the house and we get tenants in who live here upstairs and subsidize the rent for the office."

"How many people live here?"

John looked up at the ceiling as he pondered this. "Four or five. Maybe four. I'd say four if they're looking for someone."

We walked through the house, its inhabitants away for the day. The bedrooms were arranged on the outer part of the building around a central common room that was large and empty. The bedroom sizes ranged from regal to one that would have been better served as some sort of storage closet. At the end of the kitchen was a covered balcony that looked over the fruit trees. John made some tea and we sat out there to talk details.

"The small room is the one that's available," he said. "What happens is that people leave and everyone shuffles up a room depending on where the vacancy was. The rent is fifty bucks a week."

I had simple needs. The place had to be cheap and within walking distance of the town center. I hadn't stipulated anything about not having to live with tree-hugging hippies. "I'll take it," I said. "If that's okay."

"It's fine by me, but I have to run it past the house committee first. They get final say on who comes in, which is only fair I suppose."

I agreed that this was reasonable and we enjoyed a pleasant conversation while drinking our tea. The balcony was superb, big enough to hold a large table and chairs as well as a mismatched set of lounges and arm chairs. It was cool under the shade of the mango trees, and I pictured myself drinking a coffee here on early mornings.

"Dammit," John said without warning. "You're a good guy, we're getting on great. I'll tell you what—the room is yours. I'm sure the others will be ah, just fine with the idea. When do you want to move in?"

"Tomorrow if I can."

"Bring your stuff around in the morning when you're ready. I'll be here."

In the crisp early morning air I hauled my bags around the corner to my new abode. John met me at the office door. His face showed an uncomfortable concern and my optimism began to recede at a dangerous rate.

"Hey man, there's been an issue with one of the housemates. He got really annoyed that I took the liberty of agreeing to let you move in, and it's caused a bit of a ruckus in the house."

"Damn, that's not so good."

"Yeah, he's a bit of a goofball, but ah, he kind of sees himself as the executive decision maker in the house, more because nobody else can be bothered arguing with him. And because I don't even live in the house he had a kind of hysterical outburst last night when I told him that you were moving in."

"That doesn't sound good."

"Yeah, he went on a bit of a rant. Anyway ah, the upshot is that we just have to let him 'make the decision,' if you know what I mean, but he's at work right now."

"What does he do?"

"He's a high school teacher. So what I reckon is that you leave your stuff here and just go and hang out somewhere for the day, and ah, come back say around six tonight, and then we can all sit down and have a chat about the situation."

So I came back that evening and presented myself. John took me upstairs and introduced me to Warren. He was in his early thirties, tall, and painfully thin. His close cropped dark hair sat high on his skull, receding away from a massive forehead. His skin was tanned to the color of leather and his face looked gaunt and unhealthy. He resembled photos of soldiers who had emerged from the jungle after months of fighting the Japanese. A peculiar smell emanated from the pores of his body. It wasn't an offensive odor, merely unusual.

He shook my hand in a guarded manner while he eyed me with what seemed like hostile intent. I apologized for the misunderstanding and he made a little speech concerning his rights and how they had been violated, but once he got what he wanted to say off his chest we managed to settle on terms and I got the room.

We were moving through the kitchen towards the balcony when Warren stopped and indicated one of the fridges. "Just so you know, that's my fridge."

"You have your own fridge?"

He regarded me with fatigued disdain. "Yes, I do. Everyone else in the house is required to use the other fridge." He indicated it with his finger in case I might have confused his instructions.

"Are you afraid someone might drink your milk?" I joked.

He sighed. "Hardly. I'm a fruitarian."

"I don't think I know what that means," I said.

"It means he only eats fruit," John called out from where he sat on the balcony.

Warren opened his fridge door with a flourish. I stared with amazement at shelves packed with all manner of fruit in varying stages of decay. Almost a third of the space seemed to be taken up by bananas, the rest by fruit I'd never seen before.

"What's that?" I pointed at a very large spiny fruit, about the size of a watermelon. It smelled terrible.

Warren folded his arms and sighed. "Jackfruit," was all he volunteered.

"And what do you do with it?"

"You eat it."

We joined John on the balcony, where Warren subjected us to a long tutorial on how the human body was specifically designed only to eat fruit. He finished off by urging me to join him and become an advanced individual. I said that I would think about it. Over the next half hour the other housemates arrived home from their daily routines. They were mostly in their mid-twenties, had a wide range of jobs, and were all in varying degrees of vegetarianism. My announcement that I had worked for a meditation guru in Sydney got me immediately onside, and they were convinced that they had found a fellow hippie in arms.

The next day I accompanied John to the weekly Saturday market at Rusty's Market, an open-air affair spread out over half a city block in the center of town. Long metal trestle tables were set up in rows and protected by a gigantic tin roof, while a vast crowd meandered through the area inspecting the fruit and vegetables piled high on display. Most of the men sported long, unkempt hair and beards, their clothing a mismatch of op-shop throwaways and pieces that should have been discarded long ago. Bare feet were the order of the day, or at most a pair of flip flops or sandals. The women favored flowing dresses and an absence of bra support, with hair being either long and out of control or cropped close to their skull. I spotted my fruitarian housemate engaged in a heated discussion with one of the vendors as he haggled over some produce.

We seated ourselves at an outside table on a raised walkway overlooking the action.

"This is 'Le Pastry'," John said. "It's run by this crazy French couple, Sabine and Fabian. He makes the pastries out the back and she runs the front of house."

Wondrous smells wafted from the rear of the establishment. The café was crowded with customers, and I realized we'd been fortunate to secure a table.

"Here's Sabine now," John said. "She's the one throwing out that customer."

She was middle aged, short and stocky. Her frizzled black hair hung around a fleshy face proportioned by a pair of heavy black spectacles. Her voice commanded respect as she marched a foul smelling individual past our table and down onto the street. Then she turned her attention to us.

"Zey think zey can come in here with zeir unwashed bodies and foul feet and take up one of my tables for hours while zey drinks a single glass of water. I vill ave none of it!" She held up a finger in the air. "Now mister John, who is zis? Another one of your foul hippies?"

"No, I'm not a hippy," I said. "Definitely not a hippy."

She eyed me up and down. "Vell you look like a hippy to me. Or are you going to order somezing?"

We ordered coffee and cake and she marched away. In front of us a man was selling coconuts. He was stripped to the waist, and his large muscles flexed as he wielded a lethal machete. He filleted each coconut with a few short strokes in the top, placed a straw through the hole and then handed it to a customer while his long dreadlocks shined with sweat.

"So what's your plan for a job?" John asked.

"I don't know," I said. "I mean, I know what I don't want. I don't want to slip back into a hospitality job. I had this idea about starting some meditation classes but I don't know if that's what I really want to do. I have noticed lots of posters advertising rafting trips around town."

John looked surprised. "You're a rafting guide?"

"Well, no, not exactly. But I did a hell of a lot of white-water kayaking when I was a kid. And when I was back in Perth recently, an old family friend mentioned to me that there was a lot of rafting in Cairns and I should check it out. But I hadn't really thought about what he said until now."

"But if you've never guided a raft ..."

"It can't be that much different to kayaking."

"Really?" John looked doubtful.

I said, "It's all white-water in the end. I just don't know where to start."

"Well, I know a guy who is ah, familiar with the industry in Cairns," John said. "I could ask him how you could go about getting in."

"That would be great," I said.

Warren the fruitarian walked up to our table, his arms weighed down by plastic bags bulging with produce. "I think I have too much for my fridge."

John and I looked at him. I considered the best response. "That's too bad," I said. "What are you going to do?"

"I don't know. I may have to throw some of my old fruit out."

We all looked at the bags laden with fruit. And then he turned and walked down the street towards the house.

After a few days I grew tired of mung beans, lentil soup, and tofu stir fry, so I bought some thick juicy steaks for a nice protein hit. I was cooking the steaks when Warren's head emerged at the top of the rear stairs.

"What are you doing?" he said with outrage in his voice.

"I'm cooking some steaks."

"This is a vegetarian house!" Warren was beside himself with indignation.

"Well nobody told me."

"It was *implied*," he said as he wrung his hands in the air. "Do you think a fruitarian would live in a house where animal products are consumed?"

"Yeah, well I never lived with a fruitarian before," I said. "Are there any other rules that I'm not aware of?"

Warren stormed off to his room. There was the sound of footsteps on the rear stairs and John came into the kitchen followed by an older guy that I hadn't seen before. He was short and stocky and wore a loud floral shirt that exposed a great mass of grey chest hair. His name was Greg and I introduced myself.

Greg's eyes lit up at the sight of the cooking meat. "Steaks," he pronounced. "I never thought I'd see that lovely sight in this house."

There was enough for three people so I plated up meals for everyone and we sat out on the balcony with some beers that Greg had brought. I asked him what he did for a living.

"I run the local government employment agency. Hand out your hard-earned taxes to ne'er-do-wells and malcontents. Aside from that I do a bit of advisory work for *The Wilderness Society*."

"Greg's a hardcore activist from way back," John said.

"How hardcore is hardcore?" I asked.

"Well, I did invent the McHurl,'" Greg said.

"What's that?"

"You walk into a McDonalds and order a happy meal—you know, the standard burger, fries, and shake. Then what you do is you scoff down the lot right there at the counter, and then you stick your fingers down your throat and spew it all over their cash register."

"Jesus."

He took a long drink from his beer can. "The key to the whole performance is the nonchalant walk out of the building."

Warren came onto the balcony. "I can't believe this! All of you? You're all eating this poison?"

Greg let out a healthy burp.

Little more than a week after moving into my new abode I received a phone call from Nicole. She'd had enough of the caravan park and its remoteness from the center of town.

She asked, "Is there any more room in your house?"

My battle with Warren over allowable food products was at a stalemate, so the idea of a new ally pushed me to explore the possibilities of constructing another bedroom out of the front space of the house. Warren immediately tried to veto the idea, but another housemate meant more funds for the local Wilderness Society branch, and this more than anything swung the result in Nicole's favor.

John gave me a hand sectioning off the space, using plywood as temporary walls. We worked hard for most of the day while Warren loomed at irregular intervals, scowling at us as he chewed on a banana.

Mark dropped off Nicole that evening. I introduced them both to John and we ended up sharing a tofu-laden meal with the rest of the household. Mark was a little nervous around me but I did my best to make him comfortable. I had no interest in prolonging our disagreement, and I was hopeful that we could patch things up.

He and Nicole got on well with everyone and we enjoyed a fine evening. Nicole and I saw him out at the end of the night.

"Let me know if a room comes up for me," he said.

I smiled. "I'll work on it. I just have to tread carefully around Warren. He feels that I'm taking over the place."

"You *are* taking over the place," Nicole said.

"I know, but it's got to be a gradual victory. I don't want to hit him with a blitzkrieg. That would just play into his hands. I have to make him seem unreasonable."

Mark got into his car. "Yeah, well I don't think that's going to be too hard."

6

John made good on his promise to discover some background on the local rafting industry. There were two major rafting companies and a single small one. His contact's advice was to go for one of the larger companies.

"Why that one?" I said, in response to the name.

"He just said that it had better management. But I got the feeling that's a changeable thing. He said something else too—apparently they call themselves riverguides, not rafting guides."

The following day I sat in a busy office, waiting to see the manager. Her name was Dianne. Early thirties, brisk and efficient manner. She walked over to me with her hand held out and I scrambled to my feet.

"Come this way," she said and led me to her office in the bowels of the building. She indicated a chair and I sat down. My largely fictitious résumé lay on the desk in front of her. "So you worked for *Rivergods* in Perth?" she said.

"That's right," I replied. "I'm a riverguide." I'd been repeating that phrase to anybody who'd looked in my general direction since I walked into the building.

"What experience do you have?"

"Well, I've been white-water kayaking ever since I was thirteen, I placed well in a few races, and I worked on and off as a guide for a couple of years." This was essentially a big fat lie grounded in a smothering of half-truths.

"Not full-time?"

"No, just casual." This seemed the safer option.

"Well, you couldn't have come at a better time; we're desperate for guides at the moment. I want you to go down the Tully River tomorrow to check it out. The girls at the front desk will give you all the arrangements. Then come and let me know how you get on."

She stood up and I followed her out to the front desk, where she gave one of the booking girls instructions on how I was to proceed. Then she shook my hand and strode away. The girl smiled at me.

"We'll see you here tomorrow morning at six o'clock."

I rose early and walked down the Esplanade to the office as the sun rose over the inner harbor. The scale of the operation was impressive—there was a fleet of buses, drivers, and guides who were getting ready to collect over 150 clients for the day's rafting adventure. There was another prospective guide on a similar mission to my own, and we sat together on the large double decker coach as it swung out of Cairns south towards Tully. I asked him where he had been rafting before this.

"In WA," he said. "I worked for this company called *Rivergods*."

I pondered the chances of this happening while I frantically tried to work out what I was going to say. He asked where I had rafted and I spun some rubbish that seemed to satisfy him while dropping some names that we both knew. I resolved to be on my guard.

With a stop off on the way for morning tea, we didn't reach the top of the Tully River gorge until 10am. A line of guides were waiting to pass out life-jackets and helmets to the customers as they alighted from the buses.

One of them handed me a bright red helmet. "Here ya go, mate," he said.

"Thanks," I said, and then I added, "I'm not a customer. I'm a riverguide."

He looked surprised and amused. "Oh are you? Well, good for you, bloke."

The guides stood around in a relaxed and confident pose, their muscular physiques deeply tanned from long exposure to the sun. They wore old and tattered lifejackets in a variety of colors. These were festooned with knives and carabineers, ropes and lines, throw-bags and whistles. I had no real idea of the purpose for most of this gear. Then they herded the customers together like sheep-dogs collecting a flock and moved us down a track that wound through steep rainforest to where the river rushed below.

Clear pure water flowed through a tropical gorge. Ferns clung in patches to sections of the sheer rock wall and water dripped and fell from every nook and ledge. A fleet of rafts was tied up along the bank, grey and somber in contrast to the surrounding expanse of brilliant color. The trip leader placed the two of us with three company trainee guides; the five of us were to take our own raft and follow the trip. This was a nice way for me to see the river for the first time as it allowed me to learn its secrets from other would-be guides.

I sat in the front so as to get a good look at the action. The first rapid of the day was called Alarm Clock, and after passing through it I began to realise that I was out of my depth. The rest of the day was a confusion of complex rapids and safety systems, and all of it far more difficult than anything I'd seen in the past. Except for a stop for a barbeque lunch, we didn't get off the river until 3 o'clock. The five of us helped to load the other rafts, and then we went with the guides back to a large shed where we unloaded and stored all the equipment.

I kept my head down. I was terrified of being asked a question. The operations manager's name was Jason, and he gave a few of us a lift in his car to the country club where the customers were enjoying a meal and a drink. He had a gruff and unapproachable manner. He questioned us on our backgrounds and white-water experience. Our answers did nothing to quell his evident disdain for our potential as riverguides. He announced that he expected us to fail in a miserable manner. I had trouble disagreeing with his assessment.

It was early evening by the time I got home. John was still working in the downstairs office.

"How was the trip?" he said, leaning back in his chair.

"It was a very big day."

"So how long until you're a riverguide?"

"I think it's going to take a while."

I collapsed on my bed. The room was hot and humid and smelt of mold. The ceiling fan moved the stale air around my head. I was too tired to be demoralised, but deep down I could not hide from the reality of my situation. It made sense to stop this foolishness now. But I truly wanted this job. Becoming a riverguide had somehow become the embodiment of everything I had ever desired. I couldn't explain it, not even to myself. I just knew that I wanted this and would do whatever it took to achieve this new goal.

The next day I went to the office to speak to Dianne. I told her that the Tully was a little beyond my abilities and I felt that I would need some time to get my skills up to the required level. She said that she appreciated my sincerity and that I was to get on the river as much as possible. She also told me to start doing trips on the Barron River, which was run commercially a short distance from Cairns. The company did up to three trips on the Barron each day.

"I'll get on it tomorrow." I got up to leave.

Dianne stopped me. "My door is always open, Adam. Keep me informed on how you're progressing. If you need anything, just let me know."

I thanked her and went out to arrange my trip on the Barron. A young Kiwi guide called Josh was in the office. I had met him on my trip down the Tully the day before. He invited me for a drink and we went and had a beer at a little bar overlooking the Cairns Inlet. He was not commercial on the Tully yet, and he explained that he had been here for a month trying to pass his shotgun.

"What's a shotgun?" I asked.

"A shotgun is like a driving exam but on the river; that's what they call it over here. The Tully is a tough river bro, much harder than the ones I pushed rubber on back home. It's taking me ages to get my head around it."

"So what have you been doing for money?"

"I'm commercial on the Barron, but I don't want to get trapped on it and not get on the Tully. The Barron's just a shitty little river full of March flies that bite you all the time. I also clean tables at this food hall around the corner from the office, but I'm ready to give that away. I reckon I'll pass my shottie on the Tully next week."

My ears prickled at this information. "Do you reckon I could swing onto that job when you give it up? I'm running a bit low on funds and I don't know how long it's going to take me to get commercial."

"Sure bro. I'm working there tomorrow night. Why don't you come around with me and I'll introduce you to the manager."

Apart from one challenging rapid, the Barron lived up to Josh's description. Most of the trip consisted of squeezing and maneuvering the rafts through tight passages of rock baking under the hard tropical sun. But I stood a much better chance of getting commercial there than on the Tully, so I immediately shifted my focus onto it. The rafting office was also happy with this idea as they were desperate for guides to work on that river.

That night I accompanied Josh to the food-hall where he cleaned tables. He introduced me to the manager and we agreed that I would take over the job the following night. The money I earned would just cover food and rent.

My cash reserves were too low to purchase my own rafting gear, but without it I was not a serious contender—riverguides did not use customer equipment. My old kayaking gear was back in Perth, so I rang my father and asked him to box it up and send it over. He came through and a few days later I reacquainted myself with my old blue lifejacket, my battle-scarred helmet, and a few other bits and pieces. I scraped together the cash to buy some carabineers, a river-knife, and a few prussic lines, and with this I managed at least to look the part on the river.

But pretending to be a guide meant that I'd trapped myself in a position where I couldn't ask questions without showing my hand. And being a guide was not just about steering a raft down a river. There were complicated knots and recovery systems, rescue procedures, river signaling, and basic crew instruction and direction. Even the act of throwing a rescue line to a swimmer in a rushing river took hours of practice, hours I didn't have. I was supposed to know all this.

It might have been manageable if I was able to steer a raft, but I was having trouble just keeping it in a straight line on a flat body of water. Heaven knows what the other guides thought of me. I kept my head down and went on as many trips as I could. I wasn't so much learning how to raft as I was memorizing the river. I got to know every rock, passage, stone, and current. And each evening, after a day spent toiling under the hot sun, I cleaned tables in the food hall until late into the night.

By this stage Mark had moved into the house with us and we'd been in Cairns for a month. He got a job working casual hours in a bar, and Nicole managed to get a few shifts at an Italian restaurant. But this little bit of work wasn't enough.

In theory, the money I made from the food-hall was enough to survive on, but money management wasn't one of my strong points. As the wet season erupted over the Far North and the days turned dark from the sheer force of water falling from the sky, I was teetering on the edge of ruin. Mark wasn't doing much better.

We'd been purchasing a weekly lottery ticket together since he moved into the house, but it became apparent that we couldn't afford even that small expense. We agreed to scrape the money together for one last ticket.

That weekend, some of our numbers came up. It was only two hundred dollars, but we couldn't have asked for better. We headed straight for the local supermarket, dancing down the aisles while chanting, "We won two hundred doll-ars!' We spent it all on tinned food, frozen vegetables, rice, and pasta, only allowing ourselves the small luxury of a carton of beer and a few kilos of cooked prawns. The awful pressure of impending financial calamity and starvation had temporarily lifted.

I had already attempted a shotgun on the Barron with predictably disastrous results. But a party put on by one of the guides saved me. His family owned a farm not far from Tully, and the festivities began in the late afternoon after the day's rafting customers went back to Cairns. The house stood in the midst of sugar cane fields and we started drinking as the sun sank in a tropical haze of stark reds and oranges.

A bunch of them were keen amateur musicians, and there was a mixed assortment of musical instruments and equipment set up on a small stage. At a certain point I decided to get up and have a go on the guitar. They were wildly enthusiastic at my playing and we jammed for many hours. For the first time I felt accepted by my peers. It wasn't for my skills on the river, but I was willing to take any social allowance I could get.

My prowess on the guitar saved me in the eyes of the senior guides. Before the party, they'd considered me to be a useless waste of space. Now I was still essentially useless, but I was a good guy who played the guitar really well. I began to socialize more with the other guides. My house became a standard meeting point when people had free time, and the corner balcony filled with beer guzzling, pot smoking, and prawn devouring hard men of the river.

I arranged for my guitar and other belongings to come up from my grandmother's house down near Sydney. Then I approached the owner of a cool little bar with an offer to play some funky jazz in his establishment. He gave me Monday nights, and after a few solo performances I began to gather other musicians to my cause. Soon we had a seven piece band, which I christened *Purple Ghetto*.

I was also reveling in the status of being a would-be riverguide in the tourist mecca that was Cairns. The riverguides owned the town. Every bar and restaurant that catered to the tourist trade courted the guides at every opportunity. The guides enjoyed discounted meals, cheap drinks, and free entry to the late night bars and clubs. Then there were the girls. Whether they were backpackers from Europe, lithe Japanese girls on a five day holiday, college students from the US, or just secretaries on a break from some Australian city, they wanted to party and hang out with the riverguides. And in their eyes I was a guide, even if technically that wasn't accurate. The hedonism and pure debauchery was out of this world. Any good looking girl that came rafting was fair game. A guide had a sacred duty to prime any hot women on his raft for a night out on the town. And the destination of choice was the *Woolshed*.

I usually arrived around 10pm, after I'd finished my shift at the food hall. There was a long line of people waiting to get in, but I just gave a nod to the door staff and walked straight up the stairs. By this stage the bar was finishing its final food orders, and the patrons seated at the long wooden bench tables were starting to get rowdy. I got a drink and quickly located the group of guides surrounded by a healthy display of global beauties. They were all on the pull and guaranteed to get their socks off tonight. If you worked this job, in this town, and you couldn't get laid, you may as well go out and have your dick chopped off to save yourself future misery.

Milo was in the center of it. He wasn't the best looking guide, and he didn't have the best physique. As a matter of fact, he didn't have much of a physique at all. But he had the gift of the gab and he was a very funny man. His bus hosting skills were legendary. We would sit downstairs and listen to him on the microphone as he entertained the clients on the upper deck with a broad mixture of gags, misinformation, and anecdotes. Even the bus drivers, who'd heard it all, occasionally broke down in tears as they hunched over the steering wheel.

The chicks loved that shtick. Milo and I had become good buddies, partly for the fact that we shared a similar sense of humor, and partly because he never stopped giving me shit about me taking so long to become a riverguide. I took it well and returned the abuse in kind. I liked his straight talking. It was better than people whispering behind my back.

After a few drinks we got talking. "Dude," he said. "What were you doing out there today? You knocked me straight out of the eddy above Rooster Tail."

I knew what he was talking about. In the high water level I'd come into the top approach of the rapid too fast and careened off his raft, pushing it out of the safety of the eddy and into the main current. He had scrambled to find another place to stop before being swept over the main drop.

"I know. That was total rubbish."

"How long have you been training up to be a guide now?" he said.

"About two months," I said. "I've had two shotguns. The last one I thought I did okay. I don't even know why Muzza failed me."

Milo pondered for a moment. "I'll tell you why you're not getting passed, even if technically you look okay. Right now we can't count on you. You're a liability. You're all wrapped up in getting your raft down the river, but you're not seeing the bigger picture."

"And what's that?"

"The fact that we're only as strong as the weakest guy out on the river. If there's a trip of only two boats and it's you and me, then if something happens and I'm in trouble, the only person I can count on to save my ass in that situation is the other guide. You've got to start looking up and seeing what's going on around you. Otherwise you may as well not be there. You've got to be more onto it."

"And this is the part I'm missing?"

"This is the part you've got to get your head around. Riverguides have died because the rest of the trip wasn't onto it. Until we can be sure that we can count on you to be a solid team member, you're just not going to get passed."

The DJ amped up the volume level and suddenly the room underwent a complete metamorphosis as people scrambled off the bench seats and onto the long tables. Soon the bar was a mass of drunken revelers dancing on the long tables, their heads inches from the roof, with a mass of laser lights scything through the smoke-filled darkness. Techno beats alternated with current pop trash, but the overwhelming image was of a collective mass of hot and dirty and sweaty young nubile bodies, gyrating and jumping and pumping and humping as drinks spilled through the air and we howled in animalistic orgies of intent.

A few weeks later I felt ready to give the shotgun another go. It was an afternoon trip on the Barron, and Kelvin was my examiner. But for some reason I was off my game. I was guiding mechanically, my movements disjointed and out of sync with what was happening around me. The raft felt sluggish and unresponsive. I got stuck on silly little rocks as I made careless errors. The more I tried to think my way out of the situation, the more of a hole I dug myself into.

We floated down the final pool in the late afternoon light, joking with the customers and enjoying the coolness of the air and the stillness of the water. Then we went and unpacked the gear back at the shed. I didn't have much hope, and I wondered if three failures would see them showing me the door.

We finished unloading the gear and then Kelvin sat me down next to where the rafts lay stacked neatly on their sides.

"I'm going to pass you," he said. "Your lines were a bit off and you got stuck a few times but I think your main problem is having a guide sitting at your shoulder, watching you all the time. I think if you get a bit of time on your own it'll come together pretty quickly for you."

I just stared at him. "So, I'm a guide?"

He laughed. "Yeah, you're a guide."

I called Milo and gave him the good news, and he came around for some celebratory drinks on the balcony. Greg and John came up as well, and soon with Mark, Nicole, and the other housemates, we had a regular little impromptu party happening. It was just over a year since I had left Perth chasing a girl and already I'd found my new calling. So far I was liking the randomness of it all.

7

Becoming commercial didn't magically result in me blossoming into a solid guide. If anything, I got worse. I struggled to keep up with the other guides, and my anxiety resulted in some truly spectacular misadventures. The official photographer delighted in my exploits, as my wayward guiding resulted in customers being catapulted out of the raft in all directions, some landing on slippery rocks before tumbling into the seething white water.

Kelvin discovered that he was never to assess another shotgun again, and this gave me an inkling that my name was in danger of becoming a byword for ineptitude. At any other time I wouldn't have made it. The company would have sent me on my way. But I'd lucked into the busiest period ever seen in Cairns. They were screaming for guides and they couldn't afford to listen to what the trip leaders were telling them about my serious lack of ability.

I wasn't stupid. I knew what was going on. But I kept my head down, and I worked hard. If the office rang me out of the blue to see if I could work, my response was always yes. I watched the other guides, I asked questions, and I learned from them. I wanted the trip leader to be happy to see my name on the roster. I didn't want to be a liability; I wanted to be an asset.

The wet season continued, the rivers rose again, and I got my first taste of big water. It was a twelve boat trip, the maximum load. There were a bunch of us who hadn't seen this water level before, as at least half the guides were new to the game. We stared out the window of the guide's bus, catching glimpses of the brown water that roared behind a screen of rainforest.

One of the guides that day was an old timer called Rocket. He was in his forties and he sported an impressive beard that framed a pair of shrewd eyes. He regarded our awed mutterings with obvious contempt.

"Gonna be a big day today lads," he said to nobody in particular. "Gonna be a lot of carnage out there. No more taxi driving your raft down a little river. People are going to have to read water and if they don't know how, then we're gonna find out."

We all did our best to ignore him.

He said, "There's gonna be flips. Every-fucking-where. A sea of little red helmets getting swept towards their doom. Towards the big sieve at Rooster Tail. You go in there and you'll never come out. Yep, it's gonna be carnage."

And he leaned back in his seat with his hands behind his head and he began to laugh. Thankfully there weren't any customers on the bus. The experienced guides shook their heads and laughed with him. The rest of us eyed one another on the sly. Our looks said it all; we weren't going to let this lot have the satisfaction of seeing Rocket's words come to pass.

At the top of the short valley we unloaded the rafts and organized the customers. Safety talks completed, we set off towards the first rapid. Normally a small drop next to a large boulder, it was now a river wide hole that spat plumes of brown spray. The boulder had disappeared under water. The river swept us at frightening speed towards the hole.

I concentrated on trying to keep space between myself and the rafts front and back of me. And all the time I watched the first guide, waiting to see where he would try to punch through the gigantic stopper. I needed to see how he went before I committed my position. The river's speed would give me a few seconds to adjust. The boats in front of me didn't have that luxury.

The first raft dropped into the hole, its entire crew submerged in churning brown water. And then it was through. I memorized the angle the guide had taken and then I positioned my raft and followed the others into the drop. We went over and hit the hole and I felt my boat stop dead, the river clawing us back upstream into the stopper. My paddle was set hard in the water, and then we punched past it and I was looking behind to check the other guides' lines. There was a large pool after the rapid that was flowing hard with the high water. We floated across and looked at each other and I could see my own relief mirrored on their faces. We got to the end of the run in record time. Nobody flipped and there had been no swimmers. As we loaded the rafts, Rocket came around and called us disparaging names, but the grin on his face was genuine and we knew that we had done a good job. It was the first day I really felt part of the team.

Now that I was working as a guide I no longer needed the job wiping tables in the food court. I passed it off to some other poor shmuck that'd just arrived in the big tourist town. Warren the fruitarian gave up trying to fight the new regime and moved out. He tried to leave his fridge, but we made him take it. Milo promptly moved in and we found space for a guide called Kiwi Shane. We separated the new rooms and spruced it up with a lick of paint.

There were now seven people living in the house. The large middle room however, was still empty. We used it as an access point to all the peripheral bedrooms. It was dark and somewhat gloomy and one day we decided to give it a coat of paint. Due to the room's large size and a general lack of desire to spend any money, we painted it with a combination of every tin of paint we could find. The effect was an erratic tripped-out acid tone, a riot of random color splashed down timber paneling in odd combinations of pastiche. We finished the day with a beer as we sat on the floor and regarded our new room.

"It'd be a great spot to have a party," John said.

"We could invite heaps of girls," Kiwi Shane added.

"I'm a girl," Nicole said.

"You're not heaps," I said. "There are some basic rules for a good party that need to be followed if we're going to do this."

"What are they?"

"Put as many people as possible into as small a space as possible. The girl to guy ratio needs to be at least three to one, and you have to stagger the arrivals. Having a few people who hate each for entertainment value isn't bad either."

"Your band could play," John said. "And Steve could DJ." Steve played bass in my band.

Mark nodded. He was now working a good job in one of the major hotels. "I could make a poster; put it in every hotel staff room in town. That'd ensure some staggered arrivals, plus a cool hotel industry crowd."

"The guides will be easy," Milo said. "If you get a hot girl on your boat in the next few weeks then you invite her."

"What'll we call it?" I asked.

"The Hoffa Bar," Milo said.

"The what?" Nicole looked confused.

Milo reached over for another beer. "We once tried to organize a union for the riverguides. Our call sign was Hoffa. After Jimmy Hoffa, who got fed to the fishes. It all amounted to nothing, but this'll be a nice way to remember it."

"It's a good name," Mark said.

I looked at Milo. "Hoffa," I said.

He raised his beer. "Hoffa."

Two weeks later we were sitting on the rear balcony waiting to see if anyone would arrive when a group of young statuesque Nordic women came into view. They stood at the bottom of the stairs and looked around.

"Are you here for the party?" I called down.

They held up some vodka bottles.

In a few hours the house was heaving. My band had already played two sets and Steve was busy spinning tunes in the middle room as a smoke machine and laser lights created a realistic disco effect. The crowd was packed in so tight it took almost twenty minutes to move from one end of the kitchen to the other. So many revelers were sitting on the rear wooden stairs that I worried they might collapse.

The amount of beautiful women was staggering, and they hailed from every corner of the globe. The vibe was a wonderfully electric mix of happiness and dancing. I sat on the rear steps and marveled at the constant stream of new arrivals. We got a surge when the town's many hotel facilities closed for the night and all the staff headed straight for our place.

"Are you here on holiday?" I asked an English couple sitting next to me.

"Yeah," the guy said. "We got to Cairns a few days ago. It's a great town."

"How did you hear about this party? Did you go rafting with us?"

"No, we were at the Woolshed and it was a bit boring, so we left and got a taxi, and we asked the driver to take us somewhere that was happening. So he brought us here."

"Are you serious?"

"There's a whole line out of taxis out the front. I've never seen anything like it at a private party."

I forced my way down the stairs. Sure enough, a bunch of taxis were parked outside the house, all in a nice little line. I went back inside and found Mark.

"I've discovered how we can measure a party's success," I shouted to him above the din.

"How's that?" he shouted back.

"You go and count how many taxis are parked out the front. The benchmark so far is eight."

His eyes went wide and he raised his glass. "To the improvised taxi rank," he yelled, and we danced around with our glasses above our heads, Nordic vodka cascading on the bodies pressed against us.

The busy period lasted until May and then died in the ass. I had free time on my hands and I knew I needed to face the Tully. It was time to get commercial on my personal hoodoo monkey. It sucked to have a guide sitting at my shoulder again, but at least I was now reasonably competent. I was also an accepted part of the guiding community. It still took some time, as I could only go down a few times a week. Jason failed me on my first shotgun, but I had the feeling that was simply for appearances.

My second shotgun coincided with the farewell trip for Corey, a long-time guide. He was heading back to New Zealand, and he baked a special magic cake for the occasion. Unbeknownst to Jason, the other guides eagerly consumed a few pieces before walking down to the river. One of the guides stumbled on the path, and I put out a hand to steady him.

"Darren, are you okay?"

He peered at me. "This shit is unbelievable," he gasped. "What's Corey done to us?"

Jason stepped onto a boulder to divide up the crews and pair them with a guide. My colleagues stood apart, their heads down, some mumbling to themselves. Corey had a look of benign happiness. He swayed from side to side, his hands leaning on his paddle. I saw Gavin set himself down on the ground where he brushed some fallen leaves into a comfortable cushion. Milo gazed at Corey and mimed cutting his throat.

I grabbed my crew and Jason followed me down to our raft. We got through the first few rapids, and then I parked the boat at the top of a section of the river known as The Theatre. Gavin's raft was parked in front of me, waiting its turn to be called. Jason jumped off my raft and went down to see how everything was going. Gavin took this opportunity to collapse in a fetal position. He rocked back and forth, moaning that he couldn't go on.

I watched this with some alarm. One of his customers complained to me that he hadn't paid for this shit. Milo stepped in and tried to sooth the situation, but this diplomatic attempt was hampered when he fell into the river and had to be rescued by Gavin's crew.

Somehow we all managed to get through The Theater, but the next rapid was even more daunting, particularly to those of an altered state of mind. The Staircase was a two hundred meter run of confused mayhem with several large drops, the first of these being aptly named, Coming Home Sweet Jesus. Immediately after this first drop came a cover position that was the most difficult to put a raft into on the entire river. Darren was the first boat through, and we watched him spin crazily down the entire length of the rapid. Before he had reached the bottom, the next guide took the first drop and attempted to hit the eddy, but he too failed in a most abysmal way.

Jason and I watched this with varying levels of bemusement.

"What the fuck's going on?" he said as Gavin took the drop and sailed past the vacant cover position, his head between his knees. Jason turned and fixed me with his rigid gaze. "You better make this fucking cover spot. I don't know what these other clowns are up to, but if you don't hit it then you can kiss this shotgun goodbye."

If ever I was going to look good, this was the day. I called a forward paddle and then got my crew down on the floor as we went over the first hit. Even before we were through, I screamed for my crew to get up, and as they furiously back-paddled I stretched out behind the raft, my paddle digging into the white water as I attempted to claw the boat into the miniscule eddy by force alone. But force would never solve this problem; the only thing that counted was the correct angle to the eddy…and my angle was true. We shot into the calm water and I jumped out of the raft and took up position on a boulder, my arm raised high as I signaled the next raft through. I risked a glance down at Jason, but his attention was transfixed on the total calamity downstream as raft after raft careened off boulders and spun out of control to the bottom of the rapid.

Hours later at the end of the trip we packed up the rafts in a little clearing beside the river. Jason came to me and shook my hand and announced that I had indeed passed my shotgun. I was commercial on the Tully. The other guides broke into a muted cheer and I stood in a haze of happiness and relief.

Jason was very aware that it would reflect badly on him if I made a mess of my new responsibilities. He took me aside and gave me a stern look.

"You know your own history," he told me. "I'm taking a risk passing you. So don't let me down."

I promised him that I wouldn't, and then Corey came up with a big smile and handed me a large piece of cake. "I don't know if I want that," I said warily, but he shook his head and insisted that I take it.

"You're a real guide now," he said. "So get this into you."

Darren came up on unsteady feet and slapped me on the back. "Now you start learning," he said. "Now you'll be on a real river and having to back us up. It's a steep learning curve from here."

I ate the cake and we headed to the shed in the trucks. I felt the effect hit me like a brick, and then Jason came up and handed me a long length of rope.

"I forgot about this," he said. "Part of the shottie is that you need to set up a Z-Drag."

I peered at the rope and contemplated the prospect of having to construct a complicated equalizing rigging system while in the background the other guides collapsed in hysterics.

8

Girls, girls, girls. There were a lot of them, and I was having a fine time. Single girls on holiday wanted to go home with a story to tell around the coffee machine on Monday morning. And what better story than a passionate five day affair with their hunky riverguide? No one worried about commitments. They were here for a good time, not a long time.

Mind you, compared to most of the other guides, I was a glorified altar boy. Stories abounded and legends grew. One guide had a predilection for Japanese girls. On arriving in Japan to work the summer rafting season, he was greeted at the airport by half a dozen ex-conquests, each convinced that she would be the one to garner his permanent affection. Realizing that there was a fair bit of competition, the girls began screaming at each other. It was even rumored that fisticuffs were used. This all ended, however, when they realized that the object of their affections had walked off in disgust, and the small group of beautiful girls chased after him through the crowded airport, yelling out his name in high-pitched desperation.

We all got laid, well, most of us did. But there were some guides who not only scored all the time, they scored with any girl they fancied. One guide even scored with a chick on her honeymoon. Maybe not such a big deal when done on the sly, but this guy seduced her at the end of a rafting trip in full view of her new and very temporary husband. Lots of these Casanova guides weren't even particularly good looking. I tried to work out what they did, and by observation I came to the mistaken conclusion that they treated women badly. Not something I was prepared to do, so my own love life continued in its scattered way.

Years later I learned the truth. It wasn't that they treated women badly. Well, most of them didn't. The real secret to their success was that they didn't put up with any nonsense. They were secure with who they were and didn't tolerate anyone trying to change that. At the other end of the spectrum were guys who didn't value themselves at all and were willing to change anything and become anyone in order to score with a girl. The first is attractive, the second is not.

Not only were these confident guys able to attract scores of women, they also attracted truly great women, women who were also confident and secure in themselves. Like attracts like. And so these guys often ended up in a long-term relationship with a woman who was so far out of my own league at the time, it was impossible to imagine myself with one of them. In the politically correct world of pathetic pseudo-men, sensitive-new-age-guys, and whimpering would-be males running behind their girls on Ikea shopping expeditions, these guys stood out. They were comfortable with themselves and confident.

My confidence was better, but not by much. I hadn't had a relationship since Jodi. Either I wanted them and they didn't want me, or they wanted me and I was running for the hills. I was in limbo land. I'd cast off my earlier willingness to be anything a girl wanted me to be, but I hadn't yet become a strong, secure, and confident person. But that didn't stop me from getting into bucket-loads of trouble.

Every Saturday morning John headed down to Rusty's Market to organize the weekly fundraising activity for The Wilderness Society. From the balcony at Le Pastry, he directed swarms of backpackers around the town. They collected money in tins while dressed in a furry koala outfit. The suit was hot and heavy in the best conditions. It must have been a nightmare in the stinking heat and humidity of the tropics. Even in my most desperate financial moments, I'd never surrendered and donned one of the koala suits.

One Friday evening John came home in an exuberant mood. He told me about a gorgeous Canadian girl he'd met who agreed to work the next day as a koala. His enthusiasm was such that I was curious to see her. The next day I decided to go with him to Le Pastry. John didn't seem too pleased at this development. With the morning's paper in hand I ordered some breakfast from a suitably irate Sabine, and then I sat with John at his usual table on the front terrace.

Before too long a small group of would-be wearers of koala costumes gathered. The Canadian girl was funny, vivacious, and cute. While John was distracted I engaged her in a quick and dynamic conversation. I did my best to be as interesting as possible before she had to don the suit and trudge off into the vibrant heat. As she left she turned and fixed me with a playful gaze and announced that she expected to find me at Le Pastry when she returned.

Sabine banged some coffees down on the table. "John, I 'ope that you were not expecting to woo that girl, because I think she has fixed her sights on young Mr. Adam here."

John was fatalistic at his chances. "Yes, they did seem to ah, have some chemistry there. I could well try, but I think it would be better to cede my ground."

"It's because you're Canadian," I said. "She didn't come all the way to Australia to get it on with a fellow countryman. She needs someone more exotic than that."

"And you are exotic?" Sabine snorted in derision. "If she wanted exotic then she would go for the French! There is nobody more exotic than that." She stomped back into her café.

A few hours later the koalas staggered back to our table. I helped Sara remove her suit. Her long hair was drenched with sweat and she collapsed into a chair. I ordered her a large glass of orange juice, which she drank in moments. After some food she was back in fine form, and while John paid off the other workers and counted their takings, Sara and I played an enjoyable flirting game.

"So what do you do?" she said.

"I'm a riverguide," I said in as depreciating a tone as possible.

"Oh, that rafting thing! I've seen that. I'd love to go."

"Why don't you come down tomorrow?" I said.

"How much does it cost?"

"About a hundred and twenty dollars."

She looked at me. "I just spent three hours walking around in a koala suit. You think I can afford that sort of money?"

I made a quick decision. "Stay here," I said, and I hurried across town to the rafting office, where I charmed, bullied, and corralled the booking girls into giving me a freebie on the next day's trip.

"You're on for tomorrow," I said to Sara once I had sprinted back to Le Pastry.

She thanked me and gave me a big hug.

"You've never got me a free rafting trip," John said.

I made a threatening gesture in his general direction.

Getting Sara to the top of the river was somewhat of a challenge. I roused her from her bed, watched her immediately fall asleep on the bus, and then guided the bleary-eyed girl to the bathrooms once we stopped for morning tea. She emerged some time later looking a little better.

"Did you have a late night?" I said.

She shook her head. "I was in bed really early."

As I completed my safety talk on the raft, I asked if anyone had any personal medication they wanted me to hold for them. Sara approached me with a zip-lock bag bursting with multi-colored pills.

"What are all these for?" I said as I peered into the bag.

"They stop me falling asleep," she said. "I'm a narcoleptic."

I had never heard the term before. "You're a what?"

"Narcoleptics fall asleep without drugs to keep them awake. I sometimes lose muscle control as well, especially if I laugh too much."

"In a raft? You'd fall asleep in a raft?"

"I fell asleep skydiving once."

"Of course you did."

Sara perked up as we went down the river. She was witty, intelligent, respectful, and a whole lot of fun. But though I enjoyed her beauty and personality, a little part of me was wondering what I was getting into. At the lunch spot, she swallowed an impressive plethora of drugs, but her ability to remain awake had passed and she spent the remainder of the afternoon snoozing on one of the buses.

That night we had dinner together in a cozy pub near my house. She laughed and ate and drank with gusto, and at a certain point I managed to place my hand on her knee. Her eyes went wide and she turned to me in an exaggerated manner.

"Well it's about time," she said, and we laughed and I thought that I had finally found a good one.

Cairns was the starting point of Sara's six month Australian holiday. She never got any further. Although she found a room somewhere else, she spent most of her time at our house on Lake Street, and she soon became a permanent fixture. I couldn't keep up with her partying lifestyle, and she often crawled into bed just a short time before I was due to get up and go to work. Then she regaled me with her evening antics, which typically involved her talking about me all night to whoever would listen.

For the first time I felt like I was in a relationship of equals. But as the months passed, I felt a mounting unease at the thought of her returning to Canada. I tried to convince her to stay, but she was determined to go home and finish her university degree. I toyed with the idea of living in Canada, but it was easier to not think about the problem. And besides, she still had four months on her visa, so there was plenty of time to see how our relationship went.

There was some dissatisfaction among the senior guides regarding the company management. In late September things came to ahead, and half a dozen trip leaders quit and went to work in New Zealand. This threw the management into complete turmoil, which was most of the point. None of the guides in question had any intention of coming back, so they didn't care about burning bridges or causing total chaos in the head office. Milo was one of the chief instigators of this dastardly plot, and he'd kept it secret even from me.

"Couldn't risk word getting out, nothing personal, dude."

Milo had been a big support and I was sorry to see him go. By this stage I was an intermediate guide, which meant slightly better pay and an acknowledgement that I was no longer a danger to myself and others. But I figured there was a long way to go before I reached the heady heights of senior guide status, let alone the dream of being a trip leader.

I was wrong. Desperate times call for desperate measures, and Milo's sabotaging efforts merely resulted in some very hasty promotions. Before I knew it I'd accepted a trip leader position on the Barron River. Apparently this news caused much derision when it reached the boys in New Zealand. I didn't blame them. I had private doubts that I could pull it off. But in public I put my head down and led by example.

My approach was to let the trips run themselves. There was no need for me to come on all strong as the "new leader." The boys knew what they were doing; I just had to make sure that they didn't get too out of line. I was scrupulously fair when giving out the crews, and I often gave myself the fat, the lame, and the ugly. I kept the trips on time and dealt with all grievances before they became a problem. Ultimately I had two goals: be a trip leader that the guides looked forward to working with, and cover my own butt.

By the end of 1996, things were going swimmingly. In less than a year I'd gone from knowing nothing about rafting to being a trip leader. I lived in a cool house and had a fantastic circle of close friends. And I had a wonderful relationship with a girl I loved. I even had money in the bank. We had a New Year's Eve dinner on the balcony, and I felt a lot of satisfaction at how things had fallen my way. I suppose I assumed that this would always be the case.

The New Year brought a setback. Sara's grandmother fell ill, requiring an immediate return home to Canada to spend time with her. I'd been coasting along and putting off any decisions about our relationship. Within a week I went from having Sara in the country for at least another three months to waving goodbye to her at the airport. Now the decision was out of my hands.

One of the guides I worked with, Malcolm, went to Canada every year to work the summer season. I asked him what my options were for getting a job close to Vancouver.

"Well it's early January now, and the season starts in May, so you'll need to get cracking on a work visa. I'd put an application in yesterday if I were you." Malcolm gave me the contact for the Canadian embassy in Australia. "As for work, the company I've done a few seasons for is pretty close to Vancouver. It's about a two hour drive."

"That sounds perfect," I said.

He grimaced. "Yeah...well the owner is a bit particular. Some guides have had a lot of problems with him over the years. Me, I get on with him fine, but you'd want to walk in with your eyes open."

"What sort of problems?"

"Oh, I don't want to go into details. Just make sure your contract is nice and clear before you start."

I didn't even have a passport, let alone a visa to work in Canada, so I moved as quickly as petty bureaucracy would let me. I also had to arrange a ticket and find out all I could about the British Columbian rafting licenses and how to sit the required exams.

Which left me no time to sit down and really wonder if this was a good idea. I was chucking away everything I'd worked for to fly halfway around the world and start the process anew with a girl I'd known for about three months. If I'd bothered to look closely I might have discovered vague and troubling clues that my personal history was beginning to repeat itself.

We got a new housemate named Suzy. She'd started working with me after a stint with the competition ended badly. Suzy was one of only two female riverguides rafting the local rivers, and although a seemingly demure and petite brunette, she had a fearsome reputation as a rock solid guide. She was a relaxed and interesting presence in the house and we quickly became firm friends.

I got home late one afternoon after a day spent working on the Tully. I dumped my rafting gear in my room, grabbed a beer from the fridge, and collapsed into a chair on the balcony. Suzy flicked me a couple of letters.

"From your Canadian girlie," she said.

I reached over and picked them up. "Thanks."

"You two write a lot to each other. How often do you get them? Every week?"

"About that. It's too expensive to talk on the phone, so we save that for every month or so."

She smiled. "I love getting letters. It's like a tangible link with the other person. Something that they touched and put into a letterbox far away."

"When I post mine I wish it was me going into the letterbox."

"Aren't you going to open them?"

"I like to take my time. Settle in and savor the moment."

"Well I'll give you some space to enjoy them." She patted my arm and went to her room.

Sara had been gone for a couple of months by this stage, and I was discovering that a long distance relationship didn't offer much in the way of comfort. She was there and I was here, and a bunch of letters was all we had. It didn't add up to much. The other problem was Suzy. This girl was hot. She was cheeky, she was sassy, she was fun, and more to the point, she had my full attention. The occasional letter didn't really stack up against this onslaught. Somehow she was always around when I went to sit on the balcony, and if I heard her walk past my bedroom door, I inevitably left the room to see what she was doing. The whole situation was starting to seriously fuck with my head, because being faithful was very important to me. I had never cheated on a girl, and I didn't want to start now, but I sensed that my noble values were ready to crumble.

A few days later the phone rang and John picked it up in the office. I heard his feet on the back stairs and he came in to tell me that Sara was on the line. I jumped up and grabbed the other phone from next to the fridge.

"Hey baby," I said.

"Hi." Her voice sounded strained. I sensed something was wrong.

"How come you're calling?" I said. "Not that I'm unhappy, but we're not due to talk for a couple of weeks."

"I wanted to talk to you," she said. We spoke for a few minutes about nothing in particular, and then she summoned her courage and came to the point. "There's something I need to tell you," she said. "I've got to get it off my chest and it's been on my mind for over a week now."

My gut feeling was to stop her from telling me what the issue was. I didn't understand why I took this stance, but it seemed the right thing to do. "Don't tell me," I said. "It can wait until I get over there with you."

"But I have to tell you."

"It's all right. Whatever it is it can wait until I get there. Unless you're breaking up with me." My stomach felt like a stone.

"No, no," she reassured me. "I'm not breaking up with you."

I let out the air from my chest. "Then whatever is cutting you up like this can wait until I get there. Nothing's more important than us being together."

I could feel her relief. "Are you sure? Are you sure that's okay?"

"I'm sure. Whatever it is, we'll be fine."

I hung up wondering what she had wanted to say, and trying to understand why on earth I had stopped her telling it to me.

I got home one afternoon after a trip on the Barron. I lowered myself into a lounge chair on the balcony beside Suzy.

"Bad day?" she said.

"I had seven rugby union players in my boat. They were huge. I think the total weight of the raft must have been around a ton."

"Water level?"

"The lowest runnable."

"Ouch."

"More than ouch; my back is killing me."

There was a short silence, and then she said, "I can give you a massage if you want."

"No, that's okay," I said quickly. "I'll be all right."

She leaned over and felt my shoulders. "Your shoulders are tighter than a basketball. Come on, I won't take no for an answer." She took my hand and pulled me out of the chair and I followed her back to her room. She shut the door.

"Lie down on the mattress and take off your shirt."

I removed my shirt and lay down on my stomach. Her hands moved over my back and shoulders and I felt a surge of energy run through my body. The tropical sun was bright in the windows. I heard cars passing on the road. They came from a distance and I tried to concentrate on the sound to take my mind off the growing tension between us. Suzy moved her hands in a long and slow manner, up and down my back, from my shoulders to the base of my tailbone. Up and down. I tried to time her movements with my breathing, but the slower her hands moved the faster my breathing became.

"You're really tight," she said in a soft voice.

"Yeah."

"You should try guiding on the left side."

"I'm not good at the other side." I breathed in involuntarily as she hit a sore spot.

She moved her tanned legs over mine and straddled my lower body, her torso over my back. Her hands went up and down, and it came to me that she wasn't massaging as much as she was stroking. And then I realized all I had to do was roll over. She wasn't going to make the move. I was in a relationship, so it had to be me. What had Sara wanted to say to me on the phone? Why hadn't I let her speak her mind? The tension in the room was reaching its peak. If I was going to do anything, it had to be now.

Her hands stopped. "Is that better?" she asked.

"That's great," I said.

Maybe it was the neutral tone in my voice, but the end result was that she got to her feet. I rolled over and put on my shirt. "Thanks a lot," I said to her.

She leaned forward and kissed me on the cheek. "Any time."

9

Canada. What did I know about Canada? I knew it was big. I knew most Canadians I'd met were friendly. I knew I liked maple syrup. I knew ice hockey was pretty cool. At least it looked cool.

All in all, I knew fuck-all about Canada. But let's face it, what else did I *need* to know? I was going on my first overseas adventure. The excitement, the joy, the sheer anticipation of touching down in a place on the other side of the world was giddying. Plus I was going to see my girl, and on top of that, I was going to raft on the famous rivers that hurtled out of the steep peaks in British Columbia. I was going to see real mountains and possibly even snow for the very first time.

All I had to do was get through immigration. Standing there in the line with my two overladen bags containing everything I owned, my guitar, my passport, and a sheet of paper that stated I could stay in Canada and work for a year, I figured that my chances were fifty-fifty at best. While I'd managed to conquer every obstacle on my quest to reach this cold northern clime, I'd failed to satisfy a final requirement of my visa application. That requirement stated that I was to arrive in Canada with sufficient funds for the duration of my stay. I needed five grand in my bank account to get into the country, but I was about four grand short.

I'd been sweating this moment all the way on the eighteen hour flight. The line shuffled forward and I moved a little bit closer towards my doom. I'd heard stories of people being turned around and sent straight back to Australia for failing to pass the five grand test. I was supposed to have a printed bank statement, which of course I didn't have. There was also the acute awareness that Sara was somewhere in this very building right now at this moment, but I might not even get to see her.

My turn came and I presented myself at the counter. The official was young, brunette, and attractive. She smiled at me, I smiled at her, and then she spoke to me in an Australian accent.

Get-the-fuck-outta-here.

And she was originally from Perth!

We compared schools we'd gone to, we spoke about favorite bars, and all the while she smiled and her fingers clicked away at her keyboard, and then she did some stamping and I was on my way.

Nice. I moved my small mountain of belongings towards the exit sign, deftly maneuvering the trolley through the lines of visa hopefuls. The automatic doors slid open as travelers approached and passed through, giving tantalizing glimpses of the crowd of friends and relatives waiting on the other side. I was about ten meters away when a smiling official stepped into my path. He scanned me with a practiced eye, taking in my curling shoulder length hair, my beard, my casual appearance. It dawned on me that I was a prime candidate as a drug smuggler or something similarly criminal. But I was so happy to have my visa and to be in his country that I chatted away with enthusiastic detail about my planned work activities and my impending reunion with my girlfriend. He gradually became convinced of my total innocence to the point that he personally escorted me through the crowd, even lifting the barrier tape for me to pass under.

I thanked him and he wished me a successful stay, and then the doors opened and I emerged into a brightly lit hall that was crowded with people hoping to catch a glimpse of their loved ones, and then I heard some excited voices and Sara flew into my arms and we held each other for the first time in over four months.

A blonde girl was hovering in the background. Sara grabbed her by the arm and propelled her forward.

"This is Thea," she said. "She drove me down as I can't get a license, what with me falling asleep all the time."

I shook Thea's hand. She gazed at me with some intensity, which was a tad uncomfortable. The two of them led me outside into the coldest conditions I had ever encountered. I'd just arrived from spending eighteen months living in the tropics, so the driving rain and freezing temperature of early April in Vancouver was somewhat of a shock. The girls mocked my undisguised softness, teasing me with the knowledge that it would be much colder high up in the mountains where I would be working.

I was tired and my body was screaming at me that I should be in bed, but I dutifully followed the girls as they took me on a downtown tour of various bars and restaurants. The city was loud and big and resembled an American movie set. We had lunch in a tall building with large windows that overlooked the harbor towards where Grouse Mountain lay behind a thick covering of cloud. The girls explained the intricacies of tipping to me, and we sampled many delicious examples of Canadian beer.

By the time we got home to Sara's small apartment, it was all I could do to kiss her on the cheek as I collapsed onto her bed. Not the scene of reunited bliss I'd imagined.

We were lazing around in bed the following morning when the phone rang. Sara answered it and then held it out to me. I took it, trying to figure out who was calling me. No one knew where I was or how to get the number.

I said, "Hello?"

"Is that Adam?" It was a man's voice with a strong Canadian accent. He introduced himself as the owner of a rafting outfit up in Clearwater.

I had almost taken a job with his company before choosing to work for Hobson. "How on earth did you track me down here?" I said.

"I called your number in Australia and they gave me this contact to call."

"I got into Vancouver yesterday," I said. "What can I do for you?"

"Well, I wanted to know if you've truly made your mind up about where you want to work. I have a great need for your services up here this season and I reckon I can make it worth your while. I know you've already made an agreement with Hobson, but I have to be sure that I've tried hard enough to get you."

"Yeah, it was tough choosing between the two companies. But Hobson is hosting a five-day Advanced Wilderness first aid course up there, and I'll also have the opportunity to go and do the Rescue 3 course, and I need both of those for my Canadian trip leader's license."

"We can do both of those up here also," he replied. "Where has Hobson got you on the roster?"

"Second guide."

"I can match that too."

"It's tricky for me," I said. "I've committed to the first aid course, and he only got it up because of the numbers. Pulling out of that could hurt him."

"It's your season, son. I just want to make sure you've explored all the options."

"Well, I really appreciate your call and the effort into tracking me down. But I feel like it's better if I honor my original agreement."

"I respect that. But if you change your mind or something happens, then you have my number."

I thanked him and gave the receiver back to Sara.

"I can't believe he tracked you down here," she said. "Where is his company?"

"Up in Clearwater."

She thought about that. "That's around five hours away."

"And Hobson's outfit is two hours. So if I'm there then we see each other more often."

Sara put her arms around me. "Then that's a good decision."

"I sure hope so," I said.

I spent the afternoon at an enormous outdoor equipment store where I purchased all the rafting gear I thought I would need to survive in a cold water environment. My budget, however, was pretty limited, and I gazed wistfully at a full dry-suit that was way out of my price range.

On the third day, Sara took me out to the Greyhound bus station in the late afternoon. My destination was the Fraser River canyon. I hugged her goodbye and then jumped on the silver bus. We headed southeast out of the city and emerged onto a broad low plain covered in healthy green fields. I sat at the front of the bus where I could get the best view. The other passengers slept around me. I stared at the mountains rising out of the plains. They were bigger than anything I'd ever seen. I couldn't take my eyes off them.

The highway penetrated into the forested foothills and I caught a glimpse of the Fraser River flowing high and fast against its banks. The forest was thick pine, broken on occasion by a cluster of houses or a small store, their existence dominated by the surrounding wilderness. It began to get dark and I strained to see the names of the small towns as we approached.

I leaned over towards the driver to tell him where I was getting off. "At the rafting company at the end of the town," I added.

"Yeah, I knows it. It's the one with the yellow roof. Big yellow roof there, you can't miss it."

I thanked him and settled back in my seat. After another hour we came around a tight bend and the bus slowed and pulled over to the side of the highway. The driver gave me a nod and I scrambled to my feet and gathered my belongings. It was very cold. The bus moved away towards a scattering of lights in the far distance. I could hear the noise of the river.

There was a sign advertising rafting trips and I headed down a steep driveway towards some lights. Dogs barked at my approach, until a man's voice silenced them with a command. They came running at me from the darkness, two medium sized dogs with short coats, tails wagging in greeting. Behind them came a stocky man in his early forties. He held out his hand and gruffly introduced himself as Hobson.

I followed him into the house. It was warm and comforting, constructed of thick beams of wood that created intriguing nooks and crannies. A fire blazed in a large hearth and I instinctively moved towards it. A scattering of young children emerged from their hiding places screaming with delight at the excitement of my arrival.

Hobson introduced me to his wife Kay, a tall and lithe woman with a big smile and a friendly manner. She shooed the children away and sat me down at a large table.

"I've got a nice stew here to warm you up," she said. "We've already eaten, but you tuck in now. Hobson will show you up to the sleeping quarters after."

I thanked them for their kindness and began to eat. Kay and I spoke about my trip while Hobson drank from a large mug of tea.

"Is this your first trip overseas?" Kay asked.

I confirmed that it was and she spoke at length about her dream of going to Australia.

When I finished I thanked them again. "There is one thing," I said. "I'm mostly a vegetarian, but I eat meat now and then."

Hobson and Kay exchanged a look. "How long have you been a vegetarian?" Kay said.

"About six months."

"Is that because you're against harming animals?"

"No, it's a health thing. I just think it's better for you in the long run."

Hobson surprised me by speaking. "Gets cold up here, even colder on the rivers. You need some fat layers to keep you warm." He eyed me up and down.

"Malcolm is here already," Kay said. "He's up in the bunkhouse sleeping. Crashed out as soon as he got here."

"I'm ready to do the same."

I grabbed my bags and followed Hobson outside. He led me over towards a large shed. We walked up a steep stairway on the side of the building. He opened the door and flicked on a light. There was a large space that appeared to be still under construction, and the bare walls lacked any form of insulation. Partitions provided some degree of privacy, but it was pretty rough compared to the main house.

Hobson said, "There's beds and blankets and everything else you need. Find yourself a spot and that'll be you for the summer." He glanced at my bags. "Lotta stuff you got there." And then he turned and I listened to the sound of his feet thumping down the stairs.

I saw a mound of blankets move and groan in the light. I gave them a prod. "Care to give me a hand to sort a bed out?" I asked.

Malcolm's response was muffled by the bed coverings. "Not really."

I prodded him some more and with some cursing he emerged and helped me pull a large bed around into a secluded position.

"It's fucking freezing up here," I said.

"Get used to it. The rivers are even colder. Did you get some cold weather gear?"

"Yeah."

"We'll see if it's any good tomorrow." He crawled back into bed and I followed suit, if only to escape the freezing temperature. I made a pile of blankets and burrowed in underneath. My breath caused the air to steam above me. I fell asleep to the ominous sound of the nearby Fraser River.

I woke early. Malcolm's nose poked out of his covers but he gave no sign of being conscious. I pulled on as many clothes as possible, and then I went outside onto the landing at the top of the stairs. The view was spectacular. Immense mountain peaks rose all around the tiny rafting base, their slopes crowded with dense forest. The river thundered past a few hundred meters away across a line of train tracks. There was a matching train line across the river, and a memory came to me of a train's horn sounding in the night as I'd slept.

The two dogs met me at the bottom of the stairs and trotted behind me as I walked to the family house. Smoke rose in a straight line from one of the chimneys, and I saw a woman collecting firewood from a large pile.

"Hi, I'm Jenny, I'm the cook for the summer. You must be Adam. Come and check out the kittens. They were born a few days ago."

I followed her into the far recesses of the garage where a female tom kept a lazy watch over her new charges. She let us give them a rub behind the ear.

"I hear you're a vegetarian," Jenny said.

I grimaced. "Sorry about that. I'm thinking I should have mentioned that earlier."

She smiled. "No, no, it's fine—great even. I'm a vegetarian too, so now I have an excuse to cook something nice for myself for once." She was a big woman, with curly hair that framed a face that had seen its fair share of living. I had trouble determining her age. "Now, you look as if you could do with a coffee, am I right?"

"You're not kidding," I said with eagerness in my voice, and I followed her into the warm house.

I sat by the fire with my hands wrapped around a hot mug, chatting with Jenny as she prepared breakfast. Soon the entire family had gathered around the table. The children asked me many questions about my trip, and I did my best to keep them entertained. Malcolm put in an appearance as Jenny was collecting the plates, and he received a good-natured ribbing for his late arrival.

After breakfast Hobson outlined the plans for the day. "The rivers are huge at the moment. We had a big winter and it's just started warming up in the last week or so; there's a lotta snow up there. I want to test out Adam's skills, so we're going to do a run on the Coke. It's normally a pretty easy run, but today it'll be high which will be a good test. There's a couple of local boys for weight in the boat and a seventeen year old girl from around here who's been training up as a guide over the last couple of seasons."

Malcolm nodded. "She's good," he told me. "Paddles really nice."

"Tonight the others'll be arriving for the first aid course which starts tomorrow. That's five days, all day, every day. The woman who runs it takes no prisoners, so keep your wits about you. She's known to fail people on it pretty regular."

"Do you get your five hundred back if she fails you?" I asked.

"Nope. Let's get the boat loaded."

We followed Hobson out to the shed where he slid back the big roller door to reveal the rafts. They were good quality and appeared to have done only a few seasons. I liked the nice high lines. They would come in handy for punching through big holes. Malcolm took me deep into the rear of the shed to show me the giant J-rig rafts. Each was constructed of two massive grey tubes that curled up at the front, hence the name. These were lashed together with enormous chains with a wooden platform running down the middle. They were leftover army surplus from the Korean War.

"Hope to get my motor rig license this year," Malcolm said.

"What are they like to guide?"

"You stand at the back with the motor tiller in one hand, and with your other hand you hold on to that short bit of rope. The customers sit in two rows, one down each side. All they do is hang on."

"What happens if the motor dies?"

"There's a backup that sits there on the side. It's pretty useless though."

"How would you re-flip it if you went upside down?"

"You wouldn't. You'd need a crane to get it back over again."

"Well fuck me."

After shuttling a vehicle to the bottom of the run we reached the put-in and unloaded the raft. The water was a strange milky-blue color.

We pushed off and Hobson got me to guide right away. I settled in and called some commands to test the crew to make sure we were all on the same page. The water was freezing and I was glad to have five paddlers between myself and the breaking waves. The raft felt good and I enjoyed the experience of running a river blind, not knowing what was behind each bend and having to pick my lines with care.

The noise of the river was punctuated by the crackling sound of rocks being swept along the river bottom by the force of the water. I commented on this to Malcolm, who was sitting just in front of me and he told me that the river was exceptionally high.

Hobson gave me the occasional direction when the line was confused, but apart from this, I guided the whole way. The run took us a couple of hours and we pulled out of the water at the town of Hope.

"Nice run," Hobson said, and then we packed up the raft and headed back to the base.

"They shot *Rambo* in this town," Malcolm told me as we drove through Hope. "That's the fuel station that they blew up in the movie."

"Cool. Do we raft this river a lot?"

"No, only at the start of the season, and then it gets too low. After this one we switch over to the Nahatlatch, and when that gets low we finish the season on the Thompson. We run the J-rigs on the Fraser and the Thompson at the start of the season."

As we crossed the Fraser, Hobson said, "But not now. It must be running over half a million cubic feet a second. If it keeps rising like this, the water'll be in the trees."

We passed numerous small creeks and streams running under the road. We scanned each with interest as we crossed over, our practiced eyes taking in the possibility of being able to navigate the tumbled and narrow watercourses. Without fail, each was gorged with water, the tributaries of the Fraser doing their part to push the level of the big river higher.

Later that day, several people arrived for the first aid course. We found room for everyone in the sleeping area above the shed, and that evening we ate dinner together in the main house. The course was in-depth and required our participation from early morning until late afternoon. Our teacher was ruthless in keeping the course on track, informing us that she wouldn't put up with any irrelevant questions. She was true to her word as a few university students found to their discomfort.

We were having dinner on the third day when Hobson came into the kitchen and, in a low voice, informed us of a serious car accident above the house on the highway. As we made our way up to the road, our first aid instructor talked to me about random things. I think we both were afraid of what we'd find at the top of the road.

We discovered a crumpled car lying on its roof, the driver trapped inside and the other passenger lying a short distance away. We split into two groups and administered the first aid techniques we'd studied that very day. While the driver's injuries were serious but not life-threatening, his passenger was in a very bad way. The driver pleaded through alcohol-tainted breath to know his friend's condition. We assured him that everything was being done, but he knew the truth. Two ambulances arrived and I helped to direct traffic in the evening gloom as the paramedics went to work. As the police cleaned up the scene, we walked back down to the house, where conversation was muted over the remainder of the meal. Our first aid instructor returned a few hours later and reported that the second man hadn't made it.

Five days later I received my certificate. Not everyone was so fortunate. I said goodbye to the instructor and she wished me the best for the season ahead. I was five hundred dollars poorer, but the first crucial obstacle had been surmounted.

A few nights later, Malcolm and I took the company van and drove down to the town of Chilliwack for the written riverguide exams which were held in the public hall. I had to take three in total; a general exam, one for paddle guiding, and the trip leader component. Malcolm was there doing his motor exam. While I waited for him to finish, I got to chatting with a few other Australian guides who were working for different companies.

I found Malcolm at the end of the proceedings. "How'd you go?" I asked him.

"Yeah, passed no problem. You?"

"All good, except I failed the trip leader exam by one mark." I wasn't impressed with myself.

"I told you it was a hard one." Malcolm laughed. "Never mind, you get two chances for each exam every year, so you can do it again next time you're down in Vancouver. Think of it as an excuse to see your girl."

"When are the practicals?"

"The paddle and oar exams are this weekend here on the Chilliwack River. My motor exam is in a few weeks. They need to wait for the Fraser to drop."

The site of the practical exams was one of total confusion, with hundreds of participants spread out on a grassy field that fronted a small, fast-moving river. Hobson and I had come down together as he was an examiner for the day. I went off and passed all the various tests, such as swimming across the river and delivering a safety talk. That left me with the actual guiding part. There was some pressure since you only got two chances, and if I failed it meant that my Canadian rafting adventure was over, at least for this year. But after taking a trip down with some other hopefuls, I didn't think it would be much of a problem.

Things were going fine on my run until I missed an eddy due to the river surging at a most unfortunate moment. I finished the rest of the run well, but as I sat in the boat and waited for the examiner to add up his total, I had a bad feeling in the pit of my stomach.

The examiner said, "You lost points for the first eddy; you exited it too high. Obviously zero points for the one that you missed, although a bit of bad luck there. And I deducted a couple of points at number six for making the crew paddle in backwards."

"I did that to show you I could catch an eddy in reverse after missing that other one."

"Fair enough, but you didn't need to flog them." He smiled at me. "Apart from that, pretty damn good. You got 89—that's a pass."

The crew whooped and patted me on the back, and I felt pretty good about how things had turned out. After a few more runs helping out the others, I sat on the side of the bank to watch the rest of the day. Another guide joined me. He was from the local area and had just been successful on his second year trying. I congratulated him on his achievement, and then I commented about the poor general skill level I'd seen in the other guides. He explained that with the new licensing system, a lot of rafting companies were offering expensive courses for people interested in river guiding. The courses usually lasted five days. There was no way anybody could learn to guide in five days. I knew, after all I had tried.

"The worst thing," he said, "is that the companies imply that if you pass they'll get a job. They don't *say* it, but it's implied."

"So even if they do pass by some sort of miracle, there's no way that they'll get a job?"

"Yep. I've heard of it happening a few times, but those are really rare cases."

We watched a girl burst into tears as someone told her that she hadn't passed. Acrimony and recriminations flew back and forth as failed guides confronted the people who had encouraged them to try the exam. In the background, I watched a raft spin out of control on its way down the river, the guide struggling to react to what was happening around him.

Hobson found me when he'd finished and we headed back to the rafting base. I made a careful observation at the general lack of skills I had seen that day.

"Yeah, some were pretty shocking today," he said. "I failed a fair few. They sure weren't happy about it."

"Do you run these training courses for people who want to be guides?" I asked.

He shook his head. "Not on your life."

10

The following weekend I had my first commercial rafting run in Canada, a five boat trip on the Cochquihala. It was a bitterly cold day with the river running high and fast. As we came around a bend, my view was obstructed by Malcolm's boat in front. He moved to the left and I caught sight of a small rock sticking up in the middle of the river. I tried to steer away from it but only succeeded in hitting the rock side-on. With an awful slow certainty, the raft tipped up and over.

The cold water didn't just take my breath away; it slammed the air from my lungs, leaving me gasping in the knee-deep river. I was starting to think that my thin wetsuit and water jacket weren't doing much for me in these conditions. I scrambled on top of the inverted raft, and as I began pulling people up with me, I blew hard on my whistle. The other guides reacted well and we managed to collect everyone before the bottom of the next bend. Although I was pissed off at flipping on my first commercial run, I was happy with how quickly we got it cleaned up.

The rest of the trip was straightforward, and we headed back to the base where we washed the wet suits and dry tops in tubs of disinfectant. Most of my crew were camping at the base for the night. They attempted to pull me down to the fire pit, where they had already begun drinking from an impressive pile of beer cans.

Hobson stepped in and steered me away. "He'll be with you guys in a bit," he said, and then he indicated for Malcolm and the two Argentinean guides to follow him. The Argentineans worked for a rival company but he had called them in to help on this trip. We went into the shed. He looked at me and folded his arms. "So what happened out there today?" His tone was unfriendly.

I told him about the boat, or as much as he would let me. I had had two extra people in my boat, and the added weight had caused me to run faster than Malcolm—

"This isn't about Malcolm," Hobson said. "It's about you."

"Is it?" I was starting to feel uncomfortable. "I thought we were talking about what happened on the trip. We're all a part of the same team, I thought. And to be honest, that was a great clean-up. We got that flip sorted in under two hundred meters." I looked around. "I thought we did a really good job, and thanks for helping me, guys."

Nobody met my gaze. I turned back to Hobson. "First trip and you flip," he said. "It's not good enough. You're not getting paid for today. I won't put up with sub-standard guiding."

I stared at him while struggling to comprehend what he'd just said. "You're not paying me? Since when does flipping cancel out payment for a trip?"

"That's the way I'm calling it." His tone indicated no discussion was to be had.

"Is this a blanket rule or are you just throwing it out there?" I said, but I was speaking to his back as he walked out the door. I looked at Malcolm for some support. "What the hell's going on?"

He shook his head. "I don't want to get involved with this," he said. "I just want to do my season."

"Get involved with what? I don't even know what's going on."

But Malcolm was gone and I was alone in the big shed. I heard Hobson's voice calling to the customers to come and get some food. There were loud catcalls of excited laughter. I stood in the gloom trying to work out what had just happened.

The next morning Hobson had us get the J-rigs ready for the first motor-raft trips. I wanted to say something about yesterday, but I didn't feel comfortable bringing it up, and Malcolm sure as hell wasn't going to mention it.

If we weren't on the river, Hobson had a long list of tasks for us to complete. He paid us in food and lodging. I didn't like this arrangement. I wanted to be paid in cash and have an agreed sum deducted for expenses. I finally said this to Malcolm, but he shrugged his shoulders and told me that's the way it was.

In the late afternoon Hobson's wife came out and told me I had a phone call. I followed her into the small office and picked up the phone. It was Sara.

"Hi. How's it going up there?"

I closed the door into the office. "Pretty shit, actually. I flipped on the river yesterday and Hobson decided not to pay me as punishment."

"Is that normal?"

"No, it's not. How's it going down there?"

"Oh, it's okay. Look, there's something I have to tell you."

I could hear the nervousness in her voice, and I suddenly felt very anxious indeed. "What's up?" I said.

"Do you remember when you were back in Australia and I called you really upset and I wanted to tell you something?"

A vision of Suzy flashed across my mind. "Yeah, I remember it."

"And you told me not to worry about it and that if anything was wrong we could sort it out when you were here?"

"I remember." I wondered what she was going to tell me.

"There was this party. We were all fucked up. It was a university party, and there were lots of people there."

"What happened, Sara?"

"I didn't want to do it. I was just so out of it and the next day I felt so bad and I called you and you calmed me down but now I can't keep it in any longer." She was crying.

"Did you sleep with someone else?" I said. The words felt unnatural in my mouth.

"Yes." And then she broke down into the phone and I did my best to calm her.

"It's okay," I said. "You've told me, and you're sorry, and what's important is that we can go on from this. I'm not happy about it, but I forgive you. You're the reason I came over here, and we can work through this together."

She couldn't believe I reacted so well. I couldn't believe it either. Eventually I had to end the call, aware of the fact that Kay wouldn't be happy that the company line was being tied up for so long. I put down the phone and sat in the chair, staring out at the yard where Hobson and Malcolm were working. I felt numb. I leaned forward with my head in my hands and wondered how it was possible to feel so bad.

There was a knock on the door and Kay popped her head around the door. "Everything okay?" she asked.

I stood up and managed a smile. "Yeah, everything's fine." I walked out to where the others were working. "Are we done for the day?" I said.

Hobson caught something in my tone. He looked at Malcolm and then he put down his brush. "Yeah, sure. We can finish this off tomorrow."

"Do you mind if Malcolm and I take the van?" I said. "I need a drink."

Later that week we had a visit from the two Argentinean guides. They spent a few hours talking to Hobson and then they left. Malcolm and I observed this as we worked at some mundane task. Hobson strolled over towards us.

"The rafting outfit they're working for has gone bust," he said. Malcolm and I exchanged looks. "They're in a tight spot so I've given them jobs. They're going back now to get their stuff. You guys might want to go up to the sleeping quarters and make some space for them."

"What does this mean?" I asked Malcolm as we moved beds around the space. "Is there enough work for four guides this early in the season?"

"Doubt it. But they'll be handy to have around if we get some big trips, and that can happen this early on. Perfect situation for Hobson; they're in no position to negotiate."

A three boat trip was scheduled for that Friday on the Nahatlatch. On Thursday afternoon, Hobson got us together and said that he and the two Argentinean guides would be running it. Malcolm would be the safety kayaker. I was to take a raft down with the trainees.

"It's big water. It's about the limits of what can we raft the Nahatlatch, and you've only seen it a couple of times," he said, indicating me. "The Argentinean lads have plenty of experience at this level."

I didn't say anything, but my mind was going into overdrive. The Argentineans had more experience than me at *any* water level on these rivers. Hobson had employed me as the second guide on the roster knowing that I would be seeing these rivers for the first time. Now he was changing his tune.

We ran the trip. I liked the Nahatlatch; a challenging, express train ride with a couple of hair-raising moments. But this was a long, cold, wet day. The rain arrived in early morning and remained at a constant drizzle. On our second run of the river section for the day I found my legs shivering uncontrollably. I watched with envy as Malcolm paddled the river in his expensive new dry-suit.

The afternoon was shrouded in gloom by the time we arrived back at the rafting base. Kay hurried out to meet us as we picked our way down the bus stairs. The rain increased in intensity.

She gestured at Hobson and me. "You and Adam have to leave immediately. There's a Rescue 3 course happening up at Whistler starting tomorrow morning, and two spots have just opened up."

It was the last course I had to complete for my trip leader's licence, and Hobson needed to renew his own. I looked at Hobson and he moaned.

He said, "Damn, that's over a three hour drive."

"There's some food on the table," Kay said. "Go and get changed, get something to eat, and then you can get going." She looked at our faces. "Was it a good trip on the river?"

Hobson grimaced. "It was long, and cold, and wet, and miserable, and it's just got a whole lot worse." He stomped off into the house.

I went up to the sleeping quarters and got changed. My river gear was dripping wet as I shoved it into a bag. I hurried past the other guides who were washing the customer equipment and wolfed down the hot meal that Jenny had prepared. It was after seven by the time we were ready to leave. Hobson tossed me the keys as we walked towards the big Ford truck.

"You can drive the first shift," he said. "Just go straight down to Vancouver and then follow the highway signs for Whistler. I'll pick it up once we're through the city." He got into the back of the truck, stretched out under some blankets, and fell asleep.

I had never driven in Canada, and here I was driving a big Ford F350 on a rainy night. I cranked up the heating to the maximum setting and headed down the dark two-lane highway, following its route as it bent and curved its way through the mountains. Hobson's snores soon echoed around the cabin. I kept to the speed limit since I didn't have an international driving license. As we came into Vancouver, I scanned back and forth for any directions to Whistler, a small panic rising in me as the highway increased to six lanes.

The sign appeared in the distance and I had to change two lanes to make the exit, struggling through the Friday evening traffic. After the darkness of the mountain roads the city light was intense, and I was dazzled by the surrounding brightness. It had been a fourteen hour day of intense activity and my head began to drop as I searched for a place to pull over and give Hobson his shift.

That was when I fell asleep driving. It could only have been for a couple of seconds, but I came awake as the truck was veering off the highway towards the barriers. I jerked on the wheel and pulled it back into line, the big vehicle swerving in protest. Hobson was thrown around and he came to in a groggy state.

"Your turn to drive," I said, my heart pounding like crazy.

He sat up and peered out a side window. "There's a truck stop just up here," he said. "Pull in there and I'll take over."

A few minutes later I pulled the Ford into the parking lot. I killed the engine and sat still for a moment, trying to comprehend in my dull mental state. Hobson jumped out and hurried through the rain to the truck-stop, coming back a few minutes later with a couple of coffees. I thanked him and wrapped my hands around the warm cup. We sipped our drinks as hundreds of vehicles swept past us.

"No problems on the drive?" Hobson asked.

"Apart from falling asleep at the wheel, no."

Hobson looked at me for a couple of seconds and then laughed and shook his head. "Yeah, funny."

I crawled into the back and settled myself in the blankets. The sound of the tires on the wet road lulled me to sleep and I came awake with a jerk as I felt the truck stop and the engine die. Hobson crawled in beside me and we rearranged the blankets as best we could.

The cold woke us. It was a clear day, the tops of the mountains a brilliant white in the morning sun. I sat up, my back aching from the unnatural sleeping position. After a fruitless search among shuttered ski resorts for a rejuvenating coffee, we made our way to the meeting point for the course. Several river junkies stood around, stamping their feet and muttering about the cold, their breath steaming in the frigid air. I got to talking with a few of them while Hobson greeted people he knew.

The course instructor was the same guy who had been my examiner on the guide test. Hobson spoke to him for a bit and then came over to me.

"Good news," he said. "We can stay at Ted's place for the next couple of nights."

We drove in convoy to the river. It was narrow, fast, and shallow, promising a good amount of bruising for all concerned. I got out my bag and began the frightful experience of changing into my cold and wet river gear. A fine drizzle began to fall and we trudged up to the top of the river section, where one by one we had to swim down for a few hundred meters, extricating ourselves on the slippery rocks below. We compared bruises while we took turns throwing a rope to Ted as he was swept down the mountain torrent.

The drizzle turned to sleet. Ted's shivering hands made it almost impossible for him to demonstrate a knot. I'd reached a point where I was beyond being cold. Hobson resembled a miserable, drowned bear. By mid-afternoon, even Ted had had enough, and he called a halt for the day. Nobody was in the mood to go for a drink; we were all fixated on a hot shower and a warm meal. Hobson and I followed Ted through the small town of Squamish to where his house stood in isolation, encircled by a vast bowl of mountain peaks with thick forest at the margins of roughly fenced fields.

A troop of young children tore through the house at our arrival, hard on the heels of a pack of border collies. Ted's wife showed us to a large guest bedroom, and after steaming hot showers we gathered around the table in their open mezzanine kitchen. I tore into the thick beef stew with relish. After the children went to bed, we gathered around the fireplace. Ted broke out good whiskey and cigars, and we spoke about rafting until I felt my head begin to nod.

After another two days of similar weather, we climbed into the truck and headed back, our course certificates in hand. Even though Hobson and I had spent the last three days in close proximity, I couldn't bring myself to talk to him about my place in the guide hierarchy. The drive home was in a somewhat uncomfortable silence, alleviated by small conversations leading nowhere. As we passed Vancouver I felt a great need to jump out and see Sara, while another part of me preferred to stay where I was.

Malcolm and the Argentineans had completed two full days of rafting in our absence, and the South Americans seemed to have established a clear position above my own. I waited a couple of days and then got up the courage to approach Hobson. He listened to my argument in silence. When I'd finished, he simply shook his head.

"I'm not convinced about your ability," he said. "You indicated on your CV that you were a safety kayaker, but you're nowhere near that ability level."

"I thought I was hired as a riverguide," I said.

"I need guys who are flexible and can do a whole bunch of roles."

"I haven't seen the Argentineans safety kayak once," I protested. "How can you tell me that I'm bumped down the list for not being a safety kayaker when the guys who jump in front of me never do that job?"

"But they can if I want them to," he replied.

"This wouldn't be an issue if that company hadn't gone bust and they hadn't become available. You wouldn't have been out looking for guides to bump me down; this was just served up to you on a plate and you took it."

"That's your opinion."

"We had an agreement. And based on that agreement I turned down other jobs and came to work for you. Are you going to honor that agreement or not?"

He pointed a finger at me. "This isn't just some little holiday operation. The money we make this summer has to see us through for a whole year. You're not up to being the second guide. That's my call, and that's how it's going to be. End of story." He stared at me, daring me to say anything else.

I held up my hands. "Fair enough," I said. "It's your company. I can't argue with that. Just don't expect me to like it."

"I've got more important things to worry about than that."

Malcolm had recommended me in the first place, so he was busy enough dodging any fallout from being associated with me. The Argentineans were sympathetic to my situation, but they weren't going to position themselves to take a loss. I was comfortable hanging out with them, and we regularly went out together for drinks, but I couldn't use them as a sounding board. Jenny commiserated with me and I had several talks with her, but she wasn't a riverguide. I needed an objective and informed opinion of how I should proceed, but there was nobody I could talk to.

I took a bus down to Vancouver to visit Sara for a few days. It was the first time I'd seen her since we'd talked on the phone. I was still hurt by her betrayal, but I didn't have the energy to argue. We smoothed things over and I convinced myself that everything was fine, but I knew that things weren't fine at all. I just didn't have anything left in the tank to deal with my personal problems.

I got a few trips here and there and I made sure that I was rock solid on the river, but Hobson had made his mind up about me. Mostly I took the trainee guides down in a separate raft. On one of these trips, the trainee guiding the raft made a big mistake, and the resulting force catapulted her through the raft and onto me. My right knee collected the full force of her impact.

It left me in the bottom of the raft with a feeling that my leg had been torn apart. I tried to get up, but my leg buckled beneath me. This was a potentially season destroying injury, and I felt despair and rage surge through my head to match the pain in my leg. I yelled at her to stop the raft on the side of the river. In her panic she'd lost all ability, and I called out instructions through a haze of fine agony. The other trainees sat in their positions, unable or unwilling to take command of the situation. She managed to get the raft to the bank. I yelled at one of the others to get out and hold the raft. He moved with ineptness and I propelled him up the bank with a barrage of expletives.

That evening I sat on the couch in the family house, my leg propped up in front of me. Jenny, a self-proclaimed "faith healer," was tending to my knee. It looked like mumbo-jumbo to me, but I gritted my teeth through the pain. Truth be told, I would have preferred an actual doctor.

Whatever she was doing didn't feel like it was helping at all, but somehow I felt my emotional defenses crumbling. Everything that had happened to me since arriving in Canada chose this moment to come out, and I felt tears coursing down my cheeks. Jenny looked at me knowingly, and then I glanced up and saw Hobson staring at the two of us from the doorway. I felt embarrassed and tried to regain my composure, but then he turned and walked away.

11

I spent the next two weeks hobbling around with my knee wrapped in a brace. It rained every day, which only added to my misery. Sometimes the clouds opened for a brief moment, giving me a glimpse of the mountaintops covered in fresh snow. I'd never touched snow before, but there was no chance I'd crawl up and take a look. The local bears would have me for breakfast in no time anyway.

Time off my knee seemed to help it heal, but two weeks was a long time to sit and do nothing while watching your job disappear into thin air. Weak knee or not, I needed to get back on the river and show that I was still up to the task, otherwise I risked Hobson replacing me with some other South American guide. There was a four boat trip on the Cochquihala, and with Malcolm in a safety kayak, I was a guaranteed a spot if my knee could manage it. I didn't hesitate in putting my hand up.

On the day itself, a large group of customers arrived in a bus. It turned out that a loose associate of Hobson had organized the entire group himself. I figured the guy was getting a cut of the action, but I didn't expect him to get a shot guiding a raft as well. *My* raft, as it turned out. So I was dropped and this old fart was getting my day's work.

He was in his fifties and had a craggy face hidden behind a lump of messy grey hair. He boasted that he'd fought in Vietnam, and from listening to him, you'd think he could have won the war all on his own. He strutted around the base, talking it up while the rest of us struggled to load all the gear and get the customers kitted up and ready.

"Have you seen this guy raft before?" I asked Malcolm.

He tugged down on a rope. "Not before today." We looked over at The Vet as he laughed loudly with a group of customers. "I hope he knows what he's doing though. This is going to be a big water trip."

Even though I'd been bumped, I still wanted to go on the trip to show I was up for it, so I volunteered to sit in Hobson's raft as an extra hand. We got to the river only to find it out of control. The force of water thundering past had made the put-in point unrecognizable. Hobson got the guides together on the side of the bank and gave a pep talk for the run. The Vet's face had a white sheen and he made an effort not to look at the river.

From the outset, it was clear that The Vet was out of his depth, the river level way beyond his abilities. The other guides quickly assessed the situation and moved to damage control, shepherding him down the river while showing him a clear line for each rapid. I was ready to take over from The Vet if needed, but I refused to speak up about the situation. Hobson knew I was there, but I wasn't going to point out the bleeding obvious.

We stopped for lunch, eating sandwiches prepared earlier. The Vet didn't say a word. He just sat off to the side watching the river with a vacant stare. At the end of lunch, Hobson gathered the guides around him once again.

"We've got through most of the hard stuff," he said. "It's almost a clear run from here. Just watch out for that huge hole in the middle of the river a few clicks down. Malcolm, I want you to give it a very wide skirt. I don't want us anywhere near that thing today. Make the line really obvious well before it, and I'll give a blast on my whistle when we're getting near. After that it's only three clicks to the takeout."

I called that rapid the *Monster Hole*. I had run it a few times on previous trips, but only with very good crews who wouldn't stop paddling when they got scared. It would be unthinkable to go anywhere near it today.

We came over a large rise of water to see the *Monster Hole* in the distance. It was enormous, and the main current surged towards it. Malcolm pointed his raft with an extreme left angle to compensate for the massive water flow. Hobson and I watched and waited for The Vet to turn his raft. His angle was weak and ineffective, and I realized he wasn't going to make it.

"Oh shit," Hobson said in a low voice.

"At least straighten up," I said out loud. "Straighten up if you're going to hit it."

He hit the hole with his raft still pointing left. It was such a violent flip that the front of the raft twisted upside down before the rear got around to joining it. Hobson blew hard on his whistle, but there was no need. Everyone had seen it coming.

The rest of us made it around the hole and went into damage control. The river was fast and broad at this point, and we were confronted with swimmers spread over a wide area. They were experiencing very nasty swims, the waves pounding them from one hole to the next, the water freezing cold, and the river unrelenting in its ferocity. This was a potentially killer swim.

The Vet pulled himself up onto his inverted raft, and there he lay, spread-eagled and holding on for dear life while his crew was getting thrashed around him. I saw Malcolm jump out of his kayak and run back upstream to where a swimmer was clinging to a rock. Malcolm had to pry the man's fingers away from the rock one finger at a time.

At the speed we were travelling, we weren't far from the takeout. A little further on, the river entered a spectacular series of unnavigable gorges, certain death for anyone unlucky enough to be swept down. The Vet continued to lie unmoving on his upturned raft. Hobson had spent the better part of a kilometer attempting the highly difficult task of maneuvering his raft as close to him as possible. As he rowed against the river, I stood at the rear, ready to jump. At the first opportunity, with our raft lifted up by a large wave, I launched myself across and down towards where The Vet lay.

I hit hard but managed to stay on the pitching surface. Without a word, I pushed The Vet over to one side, clipped my flip line onto the raft, stood up, and leaned back, bringing the boat over on top of me. The freezing water pulled hard, but I hauled myself up and onto the righted boat. I launched a rope to Hobson who was struggling to stay in close proximity, and then we pulled the two rafts together and secured them. The Vet managed to haul himself into the bottom of his boat, and there he stayed, making strange noises to himself.

We rounded the next bend, and there before us was the takeout, the rafting vehicles parked close to the rushing water. All the customers were accounted for, although some were in a mild state of shock. Others were visibly angry, and we had to keep them separated from The Vet. He made no effort to explain himself. As we reassured the customers and packed up the rafts, he shut himself away in one of the vans.

Later, Hobson called a guides meeting in the big shed. I knew what he was going to say. I'd heard it from him before. But I was in shock when he began talking. He concentrated on the positives and how we had reacted to the emergency. I stood in silence, not trusting myself to open my mouth. When the meeting had finished, I turned and left without a word. Malcolm caught me at the foot of the stairs.

"Pretty crazy day, eh?" he said tentatively.

I turned with anger. "That was fucking bullshit in there," I said. "I flip and we clean it up in a hundred meters, and then he chews me out and refuses to pay me. This clown flips in the worst possible place after being specifically told not to go there, and then he lies on top of his raft, crying like a baby while we all risk our necks saving his punter's lives. And then we get a pep talk about our general awesomeness. Fuck this shit."

I turned and walked up the stairs to get changed. Malcolm paused for a moment and then slowly followed behind me.

We were doing some repair work on a couple of boats when word came through that someone in the town had been hit by a train. A few of us walked down to the railway line that ran below the rafting base. In the distance towards the town, a freight train sat motionless on the tracks. We stared at it for some time and then walked back up to where the others were waiting. Hobson, Kay, and Jenny were visibly distressed. Nobody was a stranger in a small town.

A short time later, a police vehicle pulled slowly into the base. We watched its arrival with a sense of unreality and disbelief. We were all distanced around the yard, perhaps in the hope that some space would protect us from unwelcome news. Two young officers got out of the car and Hobson walked towards them. They spoke only a few words, and then Hobson turned towards Jenny. He walked over to her with a look of profound sadness on his face. Jenny shook her head from side to side, determined to refuse the unwanted tragedy, and the female officer moved and took her arm, and then Jenny fell to her knees in the brilliance of the morning sun, her long wailing cry echoing around the stillness of the yard.

Kay was instantly by her side. I didn't know what to do. Nobody else did, either. We stood in the peaceful morning air as they told Jenny how her mother had been killed by the train. Details emerged over the next few days. The driver had seen the elderly woman at the side road and had sounded his horn as he moved slowly through the little town. He'd been convinced that she had seen the train, and then she'd looked in the opposite direction and stepped directly into the locomotive's path. Jenny went to comfort the devastated driver the same day she received the news of her mother's death.

After the trauma of the funeral, she threw herself back into her work. Kay tried to give her some time off, but Jenny would have none of it. For her, work was better than grief. I had a few long evening chats with her over bottles of red wine, where she tried to unburden her shattered emotions.

It was mid-June and I had only been there a couple of months, but I already felt emotionally exhausted and the main part of the season hadn't even begun. I couldn't shake the mounting sensation that I was in the wrong place.

Hobson was still the only guide at the base with a motor-rig license, so he had to scramble and find another guide when a big trip came in. The guide was Australian and had been working in Canada for a number of years. He didn't say much to the rest of us, but I happened to notice Hobson paying him before the start of the trip. I shuttled one of the vehicles to the takeout point, a sandy beach under a high bridge where the Thompson joined the Fraser River, and I took some sun while I waited for the two big rafts to arrive.

A few hours passed, and then I saw them nosing around the bend. Hobson jumped off his boat while I held the line, and then he reversed the trailer down into the water from where the Australian drove his raft straight up and onto it. We shuttled the remaining vehicles, loaded the other raft, and made our way back to the base.

I was driving one of the trucks and the only passenger was the Aussie guide. He offered me a cigarette and I accepted, removing the filter before I lit the other end. He watched with some amusement.

"Pretty strong taste you've got going there."

"I'm not a fan of filters," I said as I blew out some smoke. "I haven't had a cigarette for months, so this is nice."

He leaned back in his seat. "Is this your first season out here?" he asked.

"Yeah, and I got stuck with Hobson."

He grunted. "Yeah, I've been there. He's what I call a unique individual."

"I noticed that you got paid for the trip up front."

"Let's just say I've learned from past experiences."

We drove a little way in silence, and then I decided to trust that this guy could keep his mouth shut. He listened as I recounted all that had happened and my dilemma at finding myself bumped down the guide roster. He punctuated various moments with small snorts of derision and the occasional wry chuckle, but otherwise he refrained from commenting.

"So what do you think?" I said.

He lit another cigarette. "Oh I reckon you've been well and truly shafted. No doubt about that."

"Thank fuck for that. I thought I was going crazy there for a while. So what would you do?"

"That's not for me to say. You know your situation better than anyone. You'll still make pretty good coin as fourth guide on the roster. But he's taking liberties with you, and that's never a place that I like to find myself in."

"I've been thinking about leaving," I said.

"It's still early in the season, so you have a good shot at getting another position."

I sighed. "It's just the idea of starting all over again. Having to re-establish myself, learn the rivers, go through all the shit. I just don't know if I have the energy for it."

I asked him for another cigarette and he passed one over, the filter already removed. It felt good to talk about the situation with someone who understood and commiserated, but I was no closer to resolving anything. We pulled into the base and I went to get out of the cab. He stopped me with a hand on my arm.

"Up to now it's been pretty quiet for you guys on the work front, yeah?" I nodded my head. "Then you need to wait for a moment when he needs you. And I mean when he really needs you. Then you hit him up. Tell him what you want, lay it all out there. Force him to make a straight decision. Even if you don't get anywhere, at least he'll tread a bit more carefully around you from then on."

"There's a fifteen day trip on the Fraser leaving next Saturday."

"Is that the one he runs every year?"

"I think so. Malcolm is going with him. Me and the Argentineans are holding the fort while they're away. And there are a bunch of trips booked all through those two weeks. There's even one the same day that they're leaving." I smiled. "So yeah, he needs me."

He opened the door. "Then that's your moment."

As the weekend approached I thought about my options. Everyone was busy prepping for the long trip, and things got even more hectic with the added complication of some media coverage for a long distance swimmer who was going to attempt to swim with the rafts down the length of the Fraser. As I helped with the many tasks, I managed to narrow the problem down to two key questions. Was I going to confront Hobson at all? And if so, when was the best time?

I decided Friday evening would be the perfect moment. Hobson would have all the final tasks to complete before he left the next day, and he would have very few options, if any, to replace me at such short notice. But even though I knew I had problems that deserved to be addressed, I still felt uncomfortable cornering my boss when he was at his most vulnerable. It wasn't my style to start a total shit-storm.

I thought about letting it go, just doing the season. Put my head down, keep my mouth shut, and take my money at the end. But this wasn't about the money. This was about who I was and what I was willing to stand up for.

I realized that there was another possibility. If I confronted Hobson and he didn't give me what I wanted, I could end up in an even worse situation. I tried to imagine backing down and living with that humiliation, but I knew that'd never happen. If he didn't play along, my only remaining option was to walk out.

The customers for the two week trip arrived on Friday afternoon. Despite detailed instructions on the space limitations, many of them had brought far too much gear, and it was a frenzy of activity trying to pack everything into watertight barrels. Hobson was forced to sit down with each of them and go through their baggage piece by piece. Jenny cooked up a huge dinner and we squeezed around a large trestle table set up outside. I found that I had no appetite. My guts were knotted tight from tension. It was dark by the time we'd finished eating, and the compound lights were turned on as there were still many tasks to be done before morning.

I still hadn't decided one way or another if I was going to go through with this or not. I watched Hobson hurrying from one small problem to the next. I was looking for a break in his activity where I could go up and talk to him, but no such moment presented itself. If I was going to do this, it looked like I'd have to do it the hard way. Malcolm asked me to help him with some barrels, but as we stacked the gear, I decided to go through with my plan.

"Sorry," I said. "There's something else I need to do." And I walked over to where Hobson was directing three different tasks at once.

"Where are you going?" Malcolm said, but I didn't respond.

Hobson looked up as I stood in front of him. "This had better be important," he said.

"We have to talk."

"You've got to be kidding me. Whatever it is it can wait." He back to the task at hand.

"We need to speak, right now."

Perhaps it was my tone, or the nervous tension radiating from my body. Whatever the reason, he looked up in surprise, and then he straightened. He glanced around and indicated for me to follow him. We sat side by side on a low stone wall. He made no effort to speak.

I outlined my grievances, making sure to stick to the bare facts. He listened with one eye on all the surrounding activity, and when I had finished, he leaned back on his hands.

"So what do you want?" he said.

I kept my voice flat and I made sure to look him hard in the eye. "I want all the money owed to me so far, including for the trip where you refused to pay me for flipping."

"I can do that."

"And I want to be reinstated as the second guide on the roster. Effective immediately."

"That's not going to happen," he said. I had his full attention now.

"Well then we've got a major problem."

We talked the issue round and round. Someone came to ask Hobson some questions and he waved them away with a look of irritation. I saw the staff in the background talking amongst themselves and looking in our direction. We sat on that stone wall for over an hour and argued it back and forth. There was no anger in our voices or in our bearing. We were both very calm, akin to a couple of lawyers discussing a legal brief.

Hobson acknowledged that I had genuine grievances, but this didn't alter the fact that for him the circumstances had changed. And I realized that even if my case was overwhelming, it made little difference if he was unwilling to change his mind. The reality was that it was his company, and his decision was going to stand. I was fourth guide on the roster, no matter what I said or did. My tactic of putting him in a tight spot had failed. He'd met some of my demands, but not the most important one.

I stood up. "I don't think we can say any more. I'll pack my bags. I'll be leaving in the morning."

His eyes went wide. "Don't be stupid," he said. "You'll still make a lot of money here this season. If you leave now you'll have a tough time finding other work. You're a part of the team. I admit that you haven't had it easy, but I'll make sure it's a different story from now on."

"Then reinstate me as second guide."

He looked desperate. "I can't do that," he said.

"I don't know what you promised the Argentineans, but they came to you, not the other way around. You've got the position of power, not them."

"I can't, I genuinely can't. I made a deal with them…"

"No," I interrupted, using my finger to emphasize the point. "You made a deal with me."

We stood in silence for some moments, and then he said, "I can't."

I nodded my head. "We'll settle up tomorrow morning before you go?"

He agreed and I climbed the stairs to the sleeping quarters to pack my gear. The other guides followed me up. I told them what had happened as I packed my bags. They commiserated with me, but I got the feeling that they wouldn't have taken my stance.

"What are you going to do?" Malcolm said.

I shrugged. "Head down to Vancouver I suppose."

"And then what?"

"Find a job. And if that doesn't work, I suppose it'll be back to Australia."

"You can't do that. I know a guy who runs sea kayaking trips out of Vancouver Island. I'll give you his number; you can give him a call."

"Thanks mate," I said. "That's big of you to put me forward again after what happened here."

"Yeah, well, you got a rough deal. It was shitty. It's the least I can do."

We turned in as it was very late and tomorrow was a big day. I slept well for the first time in a long while.

The next day I walked down the stairs with my bags. The morning bus to Vancouver was due in a short time. The yard was a mess of crazy activity as a swirling mass of people attempted to sort out the remaining problems. The staff did their best to avoid eye contact with me. Jenny handed me a coffee and I thanked her. I went into the office and listened as Hobson went through the money with me, his voice flat. I signed the sheet of paper and he handed me a little over five hundred dollars. It was all I had to show for my time there.

He stood up, shook my hand, and wished me luck. And then he hurried off to get the group underway for the long drive in front of them. I said goodbye to the others. Jenny gave me a big hug and thanked me for my support. I took it all with as much calm as I could muster. But when Kay came up with moist eyes and wrapped her arms around me, I felt my defenses crumble. She held me for not a little time, and tears slid down my face. Even if things hadn't worked out, it was a family operation, and I'd been a part of the family.

I walked up the steep drive and dropped my belongings at my feet. I stood at the side of the highway and waited for the bus to arrive, willing it to come before the rafting vehicles came up the drive. To my relief, I saw the silver Greyhound approaching from down the road. It pulled to a stop beside me. I threw my bags and guitar in the storage bin, and then I climbed on board and paid for a one way ticket to Vancouver. As we pulled away, I saw the rafting bus coming up the drive, but then we were around the bend and they were lost from sight.

And as I settled back into my chair a feeling of relief washed over me, and I felt all the accumulated stress that I had been holding down for all this time begin to release in a flooding wave of energy. I was jobless and my funds wouldn't last long. But it was the first time in my life that I'd stood up for myself like this, and even though the outcome wasn't the one I'd wanted, I'd done the right thing.

12

I had just over two hours until the bus arrived in Vancouver, and the doubts settled in quick and fast. That voice in the head that second guesses your every move. I thought I'd left that voice behind in Perth, but here it was, as loud and insistent as ever.

Sara had moved apartments, so it took me a while to find her new address. It was a smallish apartment with three bedrooms and four housemates. The numbers didn't add up. Which one was her room? I soon found out. It turned out that she was saving money by sleeping on the couch. Everyone did their best to make me feel welcome, even bothering to pretend enthusiasm at my arrival, but how enthusiastic could any of us be when the place was barely big enough for them? And now they were supposed to let in a fifth roommate. Suddenly, that voice in the back of my head sounded a lot more persuasive. Maybe this hadn't been such a good idea.

But I was here, and I'd be damned if I turned back after coming this far. I dug out the number that Malcolm had scribbled down for me and made the call. I introduced myself to the company owner and explained my circumstances and why I was calling. We spoke for a while, and then I hung up the phone.

"Well?" Sara said.

Her flatmates hovered within earshot. Their only chance of me getting out of their hair depending on if I got the job. But looking at Sara, I saw the mixed feelings on her face.

I said, "Good news and bad news. The bad news is he has his guides for the season. The good news is that he has a five day trip leaving tomorrow that he's a guide short for. Pays a hundred and fifty a day, plus tips. Which means I stand to make more in five days than I have in the last ten weeks busting my butt up the Fraser valley."

Sara looked upset. "So you're going now?"

I picked up my bags. "I need this money. So what's the best way to get to the ferry out in North Vancouver?"

I stood on the top rail and admired the scenery as the big ferry churned its way across the sound to Nanaimo harbor. Earlier in the day I'd had doubts about quitting my job. Now I was having doubts that I was capable of leading a five day sea kayaking trip in unfamiliar waters. At least that was some sort of progress. After docking in the picturesque port of Nanaimo, I took a ten minute ride on a much smaller ferry across Departure Bay to Gabriola Island. Waiting for me at the little loading dock was a large bear of a man. This was Peter, the owner of the sea kayaking outfit. His hand enveloped my own in an easy grip and he patted me on the back and thanked me for coming.

"There's a little camping spot over here," he said as we got into his four wheel drive. "The guests are arriving on the evening boat. If you could meet them and walk them up to the camp spot and show them where to camp, I'd appreciate it very much. Have you got a tent with you?"

"Yep, so I'll camp there with them?"

"Great. They should have their own food, so you don't have to worry about cooking them anything."

"Where can I get some dinner?" I asked.

"There's a general store a little way up the road. I can drop you there and then you can walk back. It's not too far."

After showing me the clearing that doubled as a camping area, he drove me up the road to the small store. I grabbed my pack and jumped out of the vehicle. Peter wound down his window and told me to wait. He struggled to get his wallet out of his rear pocket and then he pulled out a fifty dollar note and handed it to me.

"A little advance for the trip," he said.

I purchased some food and grabbed a six-pack of Dos Equis. The shopkeeper ran it up on an old fashioned till with a lever. I cracked a beer and slowly drank it as I walked back to the clearing. A small truck pulled up and a man leaned across and stared at me.

"Do you want a lift, fella?"

"No thanks. It's a lovely day for a walk."

"That may be, but not so lovely a day if the good sheriff sees you drinking that on the road."

I looked at the bottle of beer. "That's not allowed around here?"

"No sir, I dare say that it is not."

"Maybe I'll take that lift," I said and got into his truck.

We moved away with a shuddering of gears and I tore off a beer and handed it across to him.

"Ha! It's a bit early in the day for me, but thank you anyways for your offer."

He dropped me at the clearing and I pitched my tent and sorted out my gear. I had a change of clothes, a sleeping bag, a thermal mat, and a little cooking stove. I got set up, drank another beer, and then wandered down to meet the last ferry of the day. A few people stood around with me and we exchanged pleasantries.

The ferry arrived and the locals moved on and off with a minimum of fuss. I watched a group of a dozen or so people dressed in brightly colored adventure-wear struggle off while dragging a fair amount of gear. After introducing myself, I led them up to the clearing and helped them to put up their tents. We made small talk into the night as I drank the rest of my beers, and then I crawled into my tent and fell into a contented sleep.

Peter arrived at the camp in the early morning. Most of the guests were still in their tents. I left them to arrange their breakfast while we went to load the kayaks. He had a lovely house set back in the forest, and his wife and young daughter came out to meet me. She handed each of us a steaming mug of coffee and we stood around for a few moments and talked about how the trip would run. Peter led me into his shed where a large number of kayaks were stored. I helped him load them on a purpose-built trailer.

"These are beautiful boats," I said.

He grinned. "Whenever I get some extra cash I invest in a new boat. My wife gets mad at me sometimes, but I can't help myself."

We loaded up the kayaks, doubles for the customers, singles for me and the other guide.

"She'll be coming in this morning on the ferry," Peter said. "You have to make sure the clients look after these boats. They're the best quality glass boat on the market. The thing you have to watch out for is them grounding the rudder. If they sit back in the boat while it's grounded, they can snap it right off."

After we'd finished, we went back into the house. While we drank more coffee, Peter explained the charts and tides to me.

"The tides are pretty radical this time of year," he said. "If you leave it just a bit late, you can find yourself high and dry, literally. These customers are all experienced paddlers, so hopefully you won't have any problems. I've packed the food for the trip, and it's ready to go in the truck. So let's finish off this coffee and go and rouse up those sleepy-heads."

Beating the tide turned out to be a race against the clock and the customers' preference for paddling in a large circle, but somehow we managed it. The group of islands that we were paddling through were protected on one side by Vancouver Island, and on the other by a series of long narrow islands that framed the Georgia Strait. Apart from the occasional swell from a passing pleasure boat, the sea conditions were innocuous in the extreme. This didn't stop the customers from capsizing on regular intervals, and we spent a great deal of time fishing them out of the water.

That evening I sat on a weathered log that perched on the edge of the water. We'd cleaned up for the night, and I was drinking a glass of red wine and smoking a cigar courtesy of one of the customers. It was close to mid-summer and the sun was still low in the sky, creating vivid hues of purple, orange, and red, all outlined against the deep green of the forest backdrop. A few mountains on the mainland jutted white-topped peaks into the evening sky. A few more days spent pleasantly plodding from one island to another and the trip would be finished. Soon I'd need to figure out what to do next. I decided my best course of action was to call my contact up at Clearwater and see if his offer was still open.

At the end of the trip, we met Peter at the original departure point. The customers helped us to unload and pack the boats, and then we drove them down to the ferry. The other guide and I each received a generous tip. We headed back to Peter's house and unloaded and cleaned all the gear, and then he paid us over a glass of beer.

"I'm sorry I can't give you any more work," he said to me.

"That's all right. I enjoyed it a lot though. I've got a contact up at Clearwater, so I'm hoping to get some rafting work up there."

"Actually, I heard that there's a job going for another sea kayaking operation that works out of Nanaimo."

"Really?" I said.

He grimaced. "They're not as professional as I'd like, and their boats are definitely inferior, but I heard they're in a tight spot." He handed me a sheet of paper. "Here are the owner's contact details. You can give her a call from here if you like."

I dialed the number and received an instantly enthusiastic response.

"Where are you calling from?" the woman said.

"I'm on Gabriola Island. I can be in Nanaimo on the next ferry if you like."

"I'll meet you there," she said.

I thanked Peter and his wife, said goodbye to the other guide, and then Peter gave me a lift down to the ferry. He shook my hand and wished me luck and then got back into his four wheel drive and drove away. I felt sorry to see him go, but at least I had a reason to tell the voice in my head to shut up.

Two days later I was leading a three day trip on my own. We were paddling through the same area of islands in cheap plastic kayaks. The one advantage the new company had over Peter's was that we only had to carry each day's lunch with us. Every evening when we arrived at our camping island, the company owner had already been there before us and set up all the tents, leaving a fully stocked cooler of food and alcohol. All I had to do was get a fire going and cook dinner.

There were certain rules and regulations covering the area in which we were kayaking, and one of them had to do with the disposal of human waste. Many of the islands were quite small and lacked toilet facilities, meaning that taking a crap involved walking out at low tide, digging a little hole with a stick, and squatting down in full view of anyone from the shoreline or a passing boat. Most of the customers chose to walk through the trees to the far side of the island, after loudly announcing their intention to do so.

Eventually I too had to succumb to nature's call and I wandered out over the tidal flats, stick and toilet roll in hand. The receding tide had left an eighty meter length of exposed rock and shingle. Tiny crabs scurried around my feet, and I did my best not to cover them in something nasty. As I was digging a hole my bowels felt strange, and I only just managed to squat down in time before my backside exploded in an unfamiliar series of bursts and noises.

But when I wiped myself I discovered that it wasn't fecal matter on the tissue. I was looking at some unidentifiable pale yellow mucus. And there was blood, a lot of blood. My stomach went cold with fear and apprehension, and I felt a sense of unreality come over me. After all I'd been through on this trip, now I got dealt something like this?

I got up and proceeded to walk to shore when the overpowering urge to crap came over me again, and it was all I could do to get my pants down in time before the explosive bursts began anew. I didn't know whether to stay there squatting on my haunches or risk walking, but eventually things calmed down and I moved cautiously back over the rocks. I arrived back at the fire where the customers were drinking red wine and finishing their meal.

"Feels a bit like being in a spotlight out there," one of them laughed at me.

"Yeah, it's a real pain in the butt."

They laughed and one of them handed me a glass, but as I sat with them my mind was in a state of barely controlled panic.

As the trip went on, my condition became much worse. The explosive bursts of blood and mucus left me little time to find a toilet. The next time I was sitting in my kayak, terror came over me and I looked to the shore, but I could do nothing except let my bowels go right there. The only redeeming feature was that it didn't smell.

After a few more trips, I headed back to Vancouver for a couple of days. Sara commented on how pale I looked, but I told her it was just a bug, and she accepted my explanation. Her housemates tried to be accommodating, but we'd known since I arrived that the living arrangements in the apartment were strained at best.

I felt ashamed at my sickness, but it was the inconvenience that affected me the most. Each time I made landfall I'd scurry into the trees in a desperate rush before my bowels took over. On occasion I'd relieve myself, wait a few moments and start walking back to the group, when I'd feel the urge again and have to drop my pants where I stood or risk soiling my clothes.

At least the sea kayaking job was great fun, due in no small part to the extraordinary characters that came on the trips. One of my more outlandish trips had me leading a group of female school teachers who took great offence at me addressing them as ladies at our first meeting. They instructed me that I was to address them as women, which I did as often as I could in the most grammatically inappropriate moments, beginning the day with, 'Good morning, women,' and leading on from there. After spending five days together, I dropped each of them at their homes on Nanaimo Island, where they showered me with hugs and enthusiastic farewells as their frail husbands waited timidly by their respective front doors.

Often I slept under the stars and listened to the wind whistle through the tall pine trees. I came to know where the sea eagles nested and hunted for food, and where was a good spot to locate schools of porpoises. I learned how to handle a small runabout on the water after the initial shock of discovering that motorboats don't have brakes.

The clients appreciated my cooking skills, my sense of humor, my ability to make everyone feel welcome, and my skill at handling any sort of unforeseen problem. But lurking behind every moment of the day was the knowledge that I was very unwell. I pushed it down, and in my attempts to hide it, I learned to live with it. By the end of the summer, I thought nothing of going to the bathroom and seeing a mass of blood in the toilet bowl. Maybe I should have gone to see a doctor, but by then being sick seemed almost normal, and when it didn't, part of me hoped that denying the problem would make it disappear.

I did my last sea kayaking trip in the second week of August, and then my boss handed me a check for the remaining money she owed me. I hung out in Vancouver with Sara while I tried to figure out my next move. I'd only been in Canada for five months, and I still had over half a year remaining on my work permit. There was a good chance of getting a job in one of the ski resorts, but with the winter season over three months away, I didn't fancy the idea of spending it on Sara's couch. I figured her flatmates weren't too keen on the idea either. I was sick, I was tired, I was worried about what to do, and I was becoming increasingly irritable.

Suzy was also in Canada to do the rafting season, and we met up one afternoon in Vancouver. She looked great. We spent a nice time together, and since the next day was my birthday, she purchased a bunch of birthday balloons and made me carry them down the street wherever we went. When we said goodbye, she kissed me on the cheek, and I wondered if maybe she hadn't come all this way just a little bit because of me.

Two weeks later the check still hadn't cleared, so I went down to the bank to find out what the problem was.

The teller looked up my account details on his computer and then frowned. "How much was the check for?" he said.

"Just over six hundred dollars," I told him.

He tapped away for a moment and then raised his eyebrows. "It bounced," he said in a not unfriendly manner.

I didn't understand what I was hearing. "Bounced?"

"Like a rubber ball."

I got on the phone to one of the administration girls in the company office. I was desperate for the money and unwilling to risk not being paid. I explained the situation to them in a garbled rush and embellished it with a fanciful story of my brother being injured in an accident back in Australia. In other words, I had to get out, and I had to have the money. The girls bought my story and, after a frantic collection of funds from the office, they deposited the money in my account.

That money was all that I had to my name, and I knew that I wouldn't be around to see December in Vancouver. The longer I stayed the less money I would have to restart somewhere else. Towards the end of August, I woke up one morning, looked outside at a grey and miserable day, and decided that I just wanted to go back to Cairns. I called my old number for the Lake street house in Cairns and spoke to John. There was a room free, and I told him to keep it for me. Next I called the airline and organized the first available seat back to Australia. After all of this, I realized it would probably be a good idea to inform Sara of my new plans.

It didn't go down that well, and I think deep down we both knew that this was it, but we each promised eternal devotion forever and ever, and maybe we really believed it, too. I didn't feel a sense of relief as the plane took off, I simply felt tired. I landed in Cairns after an overnight stopover in Tokyo, where I spent the night watching Japanese television.

I took a taxi home from the airport. The familiar scenery had a comforting effect, and I felt a bit better as I pulled open the rusty gate and walked down the flagstone path. John was at his place in the office. We exchanged greetings, and then I dragged my bags and guitar up to one of the rooms. It felt like I'd never left.

I walked into town to the rafting office and got my old job back, but I had to wait almost two weeks for the new roster to come out. A few people asked me how my trip had gone, and I did my best to put a positive spin on things. I went to Le Pastry and sat at my favorite table on the outside walkway. Sabine served me coffee and cake and remarked that I looked thin. On the way home I stopped at the bank to get some money. The machine ate my card.

13

It didn't take me long to get back on my feet financially, although there were a few short periods of eating nothing but packet noodles and rice. I assumed that this wasn't good for my chaotic digestion and horrifying bowel movements, but I put all that on the back-burner, so to speak. And even though my Canadian trip had been an epic disaster, it did place me in the camp of riverguides who had worked internationally on different types of rivers. In short, it gave me some valued street cred. I began to get work on the exclusive North Johnston River trips, five-day rafting excursions in wilderness rainforest accessible only by helicopter. Only the most experienced and trusted guides got to go on these trips, so in a professional sense, I was doing very well.

Sara and I were in constant contact and towards the end of the year I came up with the brilliant idea of flying her to Perth to spend Christmas with my family. I flew over a week earlier, and my father and an old school friend met me at the airport. As I came out of the arrivals gate, they exchanged a worried look. They asked if everything was fine with me, and I assured them that it was.

I caught up with my mother the next day. She took one look at me and flew into hysterics. "Jesus mother of Christ," she said. "You look like a concentration camp victim."

After a hasty meeting with my father, the two of them got me to reveal the true extent of my health condition. It was weird to speak about it with someone else after spending so much time keeping it a secret. From their reactions, I began to understand how much I was risking by ignoring the illness and hoping it would go away. They frog-marched me off to see the family doctor, and after a series of unpleasant tests and mildly disturbing personal questions, the doctor booked me into the local hospital for a colonoscopy.

"What's that, exactly?" I said.

"It's Latin for 'not a friend.'"

It was a few days before Christmas, and the hospital was running with a skeleton staff. They put me under for the operation, and when I woke up in the bed, I felt a large box lying on my foot.

"What's in that?" I asked a nurse as she moved to leave the room.

"Your drugs."

"What drugs?" The size of the box was alarming.

"It's all on the attached paper," she said with irritation.

I read the script. It said something about steroids. I didn't like the sound of that, and I pressed the button to see the nurse again. She returned in a very bad mood.

"Why do I need to take these steroids?" I said.

She looked at me as if I was a moron. "Because the doctor prescribed it."

"Well, I want to see the doctor."

She folded her arms. "That's not possible."

"Why not?"

"He's very busy. It's just before Christmas, you know. We have lots of things to do."

"If I can't see him then I want to speak with him. Surely he can pick up a phone."

"It's not possible," she said, shaking her head.

"You don't understand," I said. "I'm going to keep pressing this button and calling out to every passing nurse and make as much trouble for you as I can until I get to speak to the doctor. I've got nothing else to do. So do you want to go through all of that, or do you want to get the great man to take a few minutes out of his precious time to talk to me on the phone?"

She stared at me for a moment, and then she walked out of the room. I settled back in my bed, and a few minutes later the phone rang.

"Hello?" I said innocently.

"You wanted to speak to me?" I pictured an older man in a white coat sitting at a big desk with a gigantic sense of self-importance.

"Yes, it's about these steroids that have been left on the end of my bed."

"What about them?" Through the phone, I heard the sound of tapping at a keyboard.

"Well, nobody has told me anything about what the operation came up with and why I have to take these drugs."

"Mr Piggott, you have ulcerative colitis," he said. I began to detect a sense of irritation in his tone.

"I don't even know what that means."

"It is an inflammatory disease of the bowel. It requires treatment, and that treatment is what I have provided you with. There is nothing else to talk about on this matter. It's a clear cut case. A first year medical student could diagnose it."

"So are there any other options or treatments available to me?"

"The treatment available to you is there in your room. You need to take the steroids. Now, if that's all I'd like to get back to work."

"For how long?" I said.

"I beg your pardon?"

"How long do I have to take the steroids for?"

"Until they run out, then use the prescription to get some more."

"No, I mean how long in total will I have to take these drugs? Will they clear it up in a few months?"

There was a pause. "You need to take them for the rest of your life."

Mark had also come back to Perth to be with his family over Christmas, and he came to the hospital with my father to pick me up. I explained the steroid situation to them. Mark opened the box and pulled out a large packet of drugs. There were many similar packets packed inside. He inspected the information attached with the steroids.

"Well, at least you'll have really big muscles," he said.

"I'm not happy about this," I grumbled. "The idiot doctor obliged my pestering by informing me that I have to take this shit for the rest of my life."

My father picked up the box. "Let's get you home and figure out what to do from there."

"My parents are doctors," Mark said as we were walking out of the hospital. "Child psychologists to be exact."

"What are you trying to tell me?"

He ignored my jibe. "They have a few drug lists at home. And they have the internet there, so I can look it up with their help and maybe find out some side effects of these drugs."

"They have that on the internet?"

"Apparently. I've just started using the internet a bit and you can find quite a bit of stuff on there."

We agreed to meet back at my father's house. Mark arrived a little later with some sheets of paper.

"Three pages of side effects," he said.

My father and I each took a sheet. "Osteoporosis," he announced. "That doesn't sound too good."

I read out some on my list. "Suicidal depression, personality changes…you have to be kidding me."

"Check out the one that says that your dick shrinks," Mark said.

"I'm not taking this crap," I said, throwing the sheet of paper on the table. "There has to be another option."

"I asked my parents about that," Mark said. "They have a contact for a very good doctor here in Perth. He's from India. He has a Western medical degree as well as an Eastern one. Apparently he uses Western medicine for diagnosis and Eastern for treatment. He's hard to get into though."

With Mark's help I managed to arrange an appointment for the following day. I had gone from doing nothing about my illness to attacking it on all fronts.

The doctor was a tall and distinguished man in his fifties, a turban wrapped neatly around his head. His office was large and comfortable, the colors muted rather than the usual antiseptic white.

He sat me in an arm-chair next to his desk and I waited while he inspected the surgery report. Satisfied with that, he began to ask me a wide ranging series of questions. As I spoke, he listened, only occasionally interrupting when something important needed to be clarified. I told him about my diet, about being a vegetarian, my lifestyle, physical activity, relationships, and stress. He asked about my medical history and any prior conditions or medications I had taken. I spoke about my trip to Canada and all it had entailed. It was very different from any other medical consultation I'd experienced. I'd never had a doctor really listen to me before.

He determined that the disease had been caused by a long series of antibiotics in my teenage years combined with the extra roughage in my diet from being a vegetarian. He showed me on the x-ray where the roughage was clearly visible.

"The stress that you experienced in Canada was the catalyst for these problems to manifest themselves in this disease. By treating the symptoms with steroids, you do nothing to help the deeper cause of the problem. Symptoms are merely a way for your body to let you know that something is wrong. We will forget treating the symptoms; they will disappear once the deeper problems are under control."

He began writing in a notebook. "The first thing you have to do is to start eating meat again. Your reason for being a vegetarian was your health, but ironically, in your case it has helped contribute to the disease. As there was no moral reasoning in your decision, I doubt that this will be a problem."

I resolved to eat a cheeseburger the moment I got out of there.

"However, we are not interested in any meat, particularly meat that is processed. All meat must be fresh and of the highest quality. There is an Italian butcher I can recommend."

"So no cheeseburger then?"

"That is correct. Next, I am putting you on a gluten free diet. This will help your body in its recovery. You will need to follow the diet for at least two months. There is to be no tinned or frozen food. Everything is to be fresh. Lastly, I have some supplements that you will need to take. There is a pharmacist down the road who handles all my prescriptions. You should only need the one order."

"I hope so. I'm flying back to Cairns in a couple of weeks."

"The other question is your mental attitude," he said. "Stress was a major cause of this problem, so you cannot let this impede your recovery. We are providing your body with the tools it needs to recover. You must let it get on with its job. Worry and stress will have an impact on its success."

While I waited for the pharmacist to prepare my prescription, I allowed myself to dare to hope that this would work. From what I had learned, ulcerative colitis wasn't going to kill me. But the effect that it had on my quality of life was enormous, and I wanted my life back.

He came out with two large glass containers of foul-looking liquid. "The Doc always gives me interesting stuff to prepare. Real apothecary shit this is."

"What the hell is it?"

"You don't want to know."

On the day of Sara's arrival, I went to pick her up at the airport. It was four months since I'd left Canada and I was pretty desperate to see her, to hold her, to have her give me some much needed comforting.

I stood at the arrivals gate, waiting for her to appear. I tried to act cool, but I was almost hopping from foot to foot. Each surge of people coming through the gate was a cruel mixture of hope, searching, and then sharp disappointment. Glancing at those around me, I took some small comfort in the fact that I wasn't alone in my pain.

Finally, I spotted her in the midst of a large group of arrivals, towering over the people around her. She saw me and her face broke into a large smile and she raised her hand. I stepped forward to greet her, a wave of positive energy surging through my body. This was it. Not only was I reunited with my girlfriend, not only was she here to help me through my ordeal, but I finally sensed that we had a future together after all.

I went to kiss her, but she turned her head away, and right there and then I experienced such a clash of emotions. I literally willed the floor to swallow me whole to save me from the rest of what was coming.

"What's going on?" I said stupidly.

She gave me a prim and uncomfortable smile, and then she leaned forward and pecked me on the cheek. "We have to talk," she said.

"We have to talk?" I was confused and becoming very angry.

"Can we not do it here and wait until we're outside?" she asked.

I gritted my teeth and led her to the car. A family friend had gone on holiday and left me her car and house to use while she was away.

"Nice car," Sara said as I put her bags in the Saab convertible. I didn't respond.

We pulled into the traffic.

I couldn't take it anymore. I said, "So do you want to tell me what the fuck is going on?"

She was silent.

"Look, you've had about ten thousand miles to work out what you're going to say, so you need to say something now or I'm going to drop you at the first hotel I see."

"I started university again out in Victoria on Vancouver Island," she said.

"Yes?"

"So I have to stay out there; I can't commute back to Vancouver."

"I know this. You sent me photos. I have photos of your apartment block."

"Let me get to the point in my own way," she said. I fumed at the traffic. "There's a guy there, a really lovely guy ..."

"I get it. You've been sleeping with him."

"No! I didn't do that. He wanted to, but I told him that anything between us had to wait until I saw you."

"You know, the thing I don't understand is why you couldn't have told me this over the phone, or in a letter, or by fucking courier pigeon. Why did I have to pay for a ticket for you to fly all the way out here to tell me this shit? And what are we going to do for the next two weeks? Just swan around with my friends and family and play make believe that everything is okay? I can tell you that right now I don't have the energy for that."

"You can drop me at a hotel if you want," she said in a small voice.

I should have done it. I should have left her at one of the crummy airport hotels that lined the street around us. But I didn't have it in me and she knew it. So I drove her to the house I was minding. She thought it was wonderful, and God help me, we made up as best as we could. But it was over, and not only that, I had to keep up a charade of happiness for the next two weeks around my friends and family.

The New Year's Eve party we went to was especially excruciating in its awfulness. We toasted a future that we didn't have as my drunken friends partied around us. I resolved to get real with my approach to women. I'd been told my entire life that a man had to make a woman happy by running behind her and providing for her every whim. It was time to put myself first for a change.

14

Back in Cairns, Greg celebrated my return to carnivore status with a welcoming dinner of T-bone steaks. Following my special diet was tough as it was almost impossible to find gluten-free food. I stocked the fridge with fresh fruit and vegetables while John watched with an amused look on his face.

"Warren would have been so proud," he said.

Six weeks later I sat down on the toilet and had my first real shit in almost nine months. I never thought that such an act could feel so wonderful. There was no blood or mucus, just a beautiful gigantic turd.

I began to put on weight and I found that I had a lot more energy. When I thought of what I'd been through in Canada and how low my energy levels had been, I realized I'd done a lot better than I'd previously thought. But most of all I was proud at beating the disease and not submitting to a life of steroid induced muscles, not to mention the shrinking penis.

1998 was the first year that I felt things were going well. All the hard work paid off, and I settled into a nice routine based around work and my core group of friends. Officially, I wasn't in a relationship. Unofficially, I was in several. Well, if you could call them relationships. There were a fair few girls who rotated through my room, each one carefully selected based on the fact that they were briefly passing through my part of the world.

The rafting company asked me to become the marketing representative for the coastal area down to Airlie Beach, in addition to my normal rafting duties. Every six weeks I drove a few thousand kilometers down the coast, stopping at various tourist hotspots and visiting key booking agencies. And then there was the best of my duties, running promotional nights at backpacker lodgings and hostels. Hordes of nubile young Scandinavian women competed for my attention as I awarded prizes for feats ranging from eating a banana in an erotic manner to slamming a jar of toothpicks into your own forehead, with the winner being the one with the most toothpicks staying imbedded in their own skull. The winners, who were often Japanese as it turned out, also obtained the coveted title of "Mr. Specklehead."

My employers were pleased with my efforts and I heard rumors that they were considering me for a future management role. I had visions of buying a house perched on one of the hillsides around Cairns where I could sit in the late afternoons and drink frosty gin and tonics while gazing over the tropical sea. Maybe I could convince one of the jaw-droopingly gorgeous Scandinavian beauties to fall in love with me. We could raise a troop of blue eyed, blonde headed angels.

The arrival of a video cassette from Uganda swept away my romantic dreams. I first saw the cassette at another guide's house. The video showed a package of rafting highlights from a river called the White Nile. I watched in total disbelief. The water volume was huge, the rafts barely able to survive the punishment. Bodies were flung in the air and pieces of raft buckled and tore under the immense pressure. Flip after flip, surf after surf, the footage was hypnotic in its destructive power. It was the craziest rafting I'd ever seen.

But the truly inspiring detail was seeing the familiar faces of Milo and Corey on the video. I knew these guys, I'd lived and worked with them. And now they were working on the other side of the world in deepest darkest Africa on the biggest and baddest river I'd ever seen.

I sent Milo an email and he replied with an enthusiastic run-down of the river and life in Uganda. I wanted to believe that I could get a job there, but my colleagues soon put me in my place.

"You don't apply to work for those guys," one guide told me. "They invite you to work for them."

The outfit was the top expedition rafting company at the time, and they specialized in pioneering rafting in new locations. They'd only been on the White Nile for a couple of years, which was about the length of my own rafting experience. I felt disappointed at not being able to get a job there, but deep down I was also relieved. The thought of rafting on such a monstrous river in such a dangerous location was daunting. I dared to dream, but I was happy to continue on with my life in Cairns.

Towards the end of the year, we received a notice to vacate our old and beloved house. The owners wanted to tear it down and build a small apartment complex. I did a bit of scouting and found another large Queenslander for rent a few kilometers away. Unlike where we had been living, this house had been renovated and boasted a separate flat downstairs, as well as an impressive swimming pool in the rear garden. Greg was also in the market for a new home, and together with John and Steve, the four of us put in an application and got the house. While sad at the demise of our old abode, we soon became used to the luxury of having a nice house. It was most enjoyable to take an afternoon swim in the baking tropical heat after a day spent toiling on a near-dry river.

One day late in the year, John came home from the Wilderness Society's new office and handed me a letter from Milo. I read it with astonishment. Milo was now the head guide in Uganda and needed to fill a vacancy. If I could get there within two months then the spot was mine. I had one week to give him an answer.

"Are you going to go?" John said.

I didn't know what to think. "I have no idea," I said. "It's a huge opportunity, but this is serious shit we're talking about here. You should see the footage of the river."

"You'd be good enough to handle it, wouldn't you?"

"You only really know when you get there. I handled Canada, and there were some big rivers there, but this is something else. I've heard that the Nile is currently the largest commercially run river in the world."

"And then you'd have to give up everything you've built up here."

"Yeah, there's that. And there's the fact that I just bought a new laptop and some other bits and pieces…"

"And you chased that Austrian girl down to Brisbane and hung out with her for a few weeks."

"Yeah, that cost me a bundle. I don't know if I'll be able to get the coin together in time."

"How much do you need?"

"I don't know. I better find out."

The ticket was expensive. I didn't have enough money, and there was no way I'd be able to save up enough in time. I could get some more cash together by selling some of my stuff, my guitar, my amplifier, and some furniture I had dragged around Australia. But that would close the door on my Cairns existence and send me to Africa with no way out.

I'd also have to give up my spot on the guide roster and any chance of promotion into management. All my previous departures had been easy when the journey promised more than what I was leaving behind. This time was different. If Uganda didn't work out, I risked losing everything I'd worked for in Cairns.

But if I didn't take this chance, I'd never know if I was good enough. Of course, the flip side was if I found out that I *wasn't* good enough. What was worse? Spending your life not knowing, or spending it knowing you didn't measure up?

That week I was roped into participating in a television pilot that featured a transvestite attempting to captain a raft down a river. Filming lasted well into the night as we shot a scene around a campfire. The transvestite was enamored with one of the Japanese river guides, and I watched as they filmed them dancing to some disco music. Jason, the operations manager, sat down next to me. I expected him to be his usual gruff self, but he was unusually relaxed. I needed advice but had been afraid to talk to anyone, afraid they'd rat me out to the rafting company. But I suddenly realized that if anyone wouldn't rat me out, it was the guy who'd kill you for breaking his trust.

"Milo has asked me to go and work on the White Nile," I said.

"And?"

"And what do you think?"

"What are you worried about?"

"A few things. That I'm not up to it for a start."

"You'll be fine."

"Okay. Then the other question is if I should take it. Am I mad for chucking away everything I've worked for here?"

Jason took his time. We sat side by side in silence for a little while and watched the flickering fire and the dancing lunatics.

"You've got nothing to lose," he said. "I wouldn't worry about any misplaced feelings of loyalty. Personally, I think the tourist numbers in Cairns have peaked. The Japanese numbers are going down very fast with their economic problems." He trailed off.

"So, you reckon I should go?"

"Yeah. I'd go if I were you."

"Thanks."

He stared at the fire. "Don't blame me though if it doesn't work out."

I sent Milo an email confirming that I wanted the job, and then I went on a selling spree. I needed to offload my gear fast, and the people buying smelled my desperation. When I added everything up I still didn't have enough for a return ticket, so I did the only thing I could; I purchased a one-way ticket to Africa.

I gave four weeks' notice as I didn't want to burn any bridges and I needed every cent I could get. One day on the Tully I came across a guide from the other company stumbling around on a track beside the river. He was incoherent, and I couldn't work out if he was drunk or insane. One of his mates came to give me a hand.

"What's wrong with him?" I said as we got him up to a standing position. We put his arms around our shoulders and helped him negotiate the rocky track.

"It's malaria," the other guide said. "He's having a relapse. His drugs are up in the bus. Let's set him down here and I'll dash up and get what he needs."

"Are you sure he's going to be all right?" The guy was making pitiful noises and was in great distress. I'd never seen anything like it.

"Yeah, as long as we get some of his drugs into him. I've seen it a few times now. He picked it up working in Africa."

I was suddenly cautious. "Whereabouts in Africa?"

"He was in Uganda."

A week before I was due to depart, a group of tourists were hacked to death in Uganda by Congolese rebels. It was all over the news reports, and I watched the updates with a growing despair.

The slaughter had occurred in an area of the country far from the rafting activities, but this was small comfort as I imagined grisly scenarios where armed Africans chased me through impenetrable jungle. And if I was thinking twice about going, how were future tourists reacting to the same news? I could be going all that way for nothing if all the work dried up. I emailed Milo, and he promptly replied that everything would be all right, but I couldn't ignore the fact that this was a sign, and the sign was screaming at me not to go.

I confided in Greg that I was going to Africa on a one-way ticket. The two of us were enjoying a beer around the pool, our chairs shaded by the mango trees. He roared with laughter at hearing this news, so much so that he snorted beer up his nose and dissolved into a coughing fit. I waited for him to recover, then asked him what was so funny.

"The fact that you're a total idiot," he said with a broad grin.

"It's a budget consideration," I said.

"It's an idiot consideration more like it." He cracked another couple of beers and handed me one. "What I want to know is why you even want to go to Kenya."

"Uganda," I corrected him.

"Whatever. Same shit, different border. What's the big attraction?"

I rubbed my face with my hands. I didn't feel like having to explain my motives. "It's the Nile," I said. "It's the longest river in the world. It has the most history attached to it. It's in the bible, for God's sake. It's a massive opportunity, and I'd be mad not to go."

"That's all very interesting, but I reckon you're mad to go."

"Why's that?"

"Well, leaving aside the dozen-odd tourists who got cut up with machetes, the AIDS rate, and the general chances of contracting malaria or some other horrible disease, look at what you're leaving here. You live in a great part of the world, you've got a job most blokes would kill for, you have a senior position in the company and prospects of going into management role, and you've got a bunch of very good friends. And you're just going to chuck all of that so you can go rafting in Africa."

"I'm not chucking my friends," I protested.

Greg leaned his considerable bulk back on his chair. Some cigarette ash spilled onto his tropical shirt and he rubbed it off absentmindedly. "Yes, you are. You're going on a one-way ticket, for fuck's sake. That's not just a budget consideration. It's like you have something to prove over there and you're willing to throw away everything else you have for a chance at being successful at it. You're not leaving yourself any outs."

"Because I can't give myself a chance for it not to work out. What am I supposed to do if it doesn't? Slink back here again with my tail between my legs? That's already happened once. This time it has to go right."

"So no pressure then?"

"This is a chance for me to do something great. I don't want to get stuck in a rut."

"A rut is independent of location."

"I've always done my best not to just go with the herd, the steps that everyone follows because they don't know any other possibility exists. Finish school, go to university and do some degree that you don't really have an interest in, get a job, get married, have kids, wake up at fifty and have a panic attack that it's all passed you by. I don't want to go down that same path."

"But isn't that a path in itself? The non-path? The refusal to follow the path? Maybe you're just deluding yourself into thinking that you're somehow different or special, when you've just swapped one rut for another. Is it possible that you're trapping yourself into always having to uproot yourself just when things start going well for you?"

I thought about what he said. I didn't want to hear this right now. I wanted people to give me pats on the back and wish me luck and tell me how awesome and brave I was for going over there. We'd been having a nice beer by the pool, and now I wanted to be somewhere else. "The type of person who does what I do, who does it seriously …"

"You're talking about rafting here?"

"Yeah, rafting. I mean, there are heaps of guides who do it for a little while or who are weekend warriors, but those don't count. I'm talking about the lifers, the hard-core guides, the international guides. These guys don't go down that path."

"Bullshit. This is about you, not them. You weren't even a guide before you rocked up to Cairns. It's you who can't go down that path. And the thing that worries me is that in your blind adherence to avoiding the straight and narrow you might wake up one day with nothing."

I cracked another beer and handed it to him. A slight breeze moved hot air over my bare shoulders. "You shouldn't have given me this advice."

"Why not?"

"Because nobody ever follows advice."

My friends saw me off at the airport, but Greg was not among them.

"He's hurt that you're going," Steve said. "He feels like there's a threat of our group of friends breaking up."

"I kind of understand how he feels," Bob said.

I put on a brave face and shrugged off his absence, but I was disappointed. My flight landed in Perth, where I spent a couple of days saying goodbye to my family. A family friend put on a farewell lunch for me. He was one of the top lawyers in Perth and not known for holding back his opinion.

"I think this will be a very good trip for you," he said to me.

"Why's that?" I said, suddenly curious.

"This trip will make or break you. You'll have to dig deep, find resources you don't know you have. It's a very good idea."

I felt reassured by his words. Afterwards I went to a clinic where I was due to receive my tropical immunization shots. The medic had a long list of boosters that I needed. I scanned the list.

"Yellow Fever?" I had never heard of it.

"That's an important one, and you'll need to carry this little vaccination booklet with you to prove that you've had it. Now, how many do you want first?"

"Just give me the lot of them," I said. He raised an eyebrow.

Several injections later and I sat up from the bench. My head began swimming and I felt myself being overcome by nausea. The medic took me by the shoulders and laid me back down.

"Just lie there for a bit," he said.

I didn't protest. He came back a little later and asked me what I wanted to do with regards to malaria.

"Is there a shot for it?" I asked.

"No, there isn't. There are a bunch of drugs you can take. Larium is the best one, although the side effects can start to mount up if you take it for a long time."

"I'm probably going to be there for a couple of years."

"In that case, it's probably best not to take anything. Just wear long clothes at night and make sure you sleep under a mosquito net."

In other words, take a few precautions and hope for the best. That about summed up my plan for Uganda in general.

My father and brother saw me off at the airport for the midnight flight to Johannesburg. I said my goodbyes and then took the long escalator up to the departure lounge. I kept telling myself that this was the start of a big adventure, but that did little to take away from the fact that I was close to shitting myself.

15

I woke from a restless sleep, my neck crushed against the cabin bulkhead. I opened the window shade and looked out over Africa. It stretched out into the dawn light, its hills and ridges colored a dark blue. I felt a sense of unreality, as if the past few months leading up to this moment hadn't really happened at all, and all I had to do was blink and I would be back in my old room in Cairns. Which obviously was a load of horseshit. I told myself I had to toughen-the-fuck-up, a mantra which I repeated often over the course of the next few days.

The flight path from Johannesburg to Kenya took us over an enormous slum. It stretched out from the edge of the city across a flat brown plain. Tin and wood seemed to be the main building materials and the sprawling mass of shacks and hovels were packed in so tightly against one another it was impossible to make out any streets. The size of the slum was immense, and the jet took a few minutes to clear it.

Finally we arrived at Nairobi airport, a haphazard construction that stretched in endless directions. The narrow corridors were jammed with people, and I was swept along with the crush as I tried to find the gate for Entebbe and my final connecting flight. The gate was a long and narrow room lined with hard plastic chairs and already crowded with travelers even though the flight wasn't due to leave for another eight hours.

I ordered a bottle of coke from a woman who scowled at me when I asked for my change. There was strange Arabic script on the bottle. I selected one of the hard plastic chairs. On my left sat a man in a long flowing robe. He wore a little fez tilted at an angle. The man on my right wore an unfashionable brown suit. He had very dark skin. I had never seen skin so black; it seemed to absorb the light. I was starting to feel a little out of place as the room's only resident white guy.

Both men were watching an American basketball game on a small television bolted high on the facing wall. The dark African's suit was stained with sweat. His tie was knotted high on his throat and his shoes made a creaking sound when he shifted his feet. The noise from the basketball game jarred the room, bouncing off the plastic chairs and the concrete walls. Nobody spoke. This was going to be a long eight hours.

It was late afternoon by the time the plane left for Entebbe. I was seated next to a European woman who worked for an NGO in Uganda. The flight was brief, and soon we were lining up for our final approach. As we came down I could just make out the shape of what appeared to be a burned out jumbo jet on the side of the runway. I asked the woman if she knew what it was.

"That's the old Israeli jet that was hijacked back in the seventies. It got stormed by their secret service when they were rescuing the passengers."

"And it's still here?"

She gave me a look. "Wait until you see the airport."

We walked across the tarmac through the dense humidity to the airport buildings. I felt insects hovering around my arms and shooed them away in panic. I noticed most of the foreigners were wearing long cotton shirts and trousers.

The buildings were riddled with hundreds of bullet holes, both inside and out. In places, ducting hung from the ceiling. The airport staff far outnumbered the arriving passengers, and as I set down my bags for inspection, a small group of them gathered around me. They had a common look of total boredom; in fact, they seemed to sway on their feet from mental fatigue.

One of them made me take out my laptop and turn it on to prove it was mine. The group swelled in numbers as they jostled for a glimpse of the computer. Somehow I satisfied the one in charge, and then I proceeded to customs, where a large woman made a brutal series of stamps in my passport. I had a visa for three months.

After a moment of indecision, I made my way over to the taxi stand. It was now quite dark, but the air was warm. I thought that someone would have come to the airport to pick me up. Maybe I'd given them the wrong date, or the wrong flight. Maybe I wasn't meant to come at all. Maybe while I'd been in the air Milo had sent me an email saying that it was all off and they'd left the country.

As bad as things were in my head, I couldn't have imagined what was really going on.

A Ugandan approached me with a sheepish look on his face. He handed me a note, and, until I read the note, I assumed that he was my lift into Kampala.

I opened the note.

"Run Adam run. It's all gone to shit. Get out while you still can."

There appeared to be dried blood on the paper. I looked around but couldn't see anyone familiar. I studied the note again and tried to work out where I was supposed to run.

The man attempted to steer me towards his taxi, and I decided that this was probably the best option. I would get him to take me to Kampala and then try and figure it out from there. He was stowing my bags when Milo and Corey appeared from behind a concrete pillar with large grins on their faces.

"You bastards," I said and clapped them on the back with relief. I hadn't seen them for over two years, but the old feeling of close friendship was immediately there.

Corey retrieved my bags from the taxi driver's vehicle, to the driver's many protestations.

"Where's your guitar?" Milo said as he told the taxi driver to go away with a jerk of his thumb.

"I sold it to get here," I said as I followed Corey over to a battered single-cab pickup.

"Sold it? The only reason we got you over here was for how you play the guitar."

"So, not for my guiding skills, then?"

"Not really, no."

"Is he serious?" I asked Corey.

He looked uncomfortable. "I have to say that the guitar playing did come up in conversation."

"Well, I'm here on a one-way ticket, so this'd better work out," I said.

"We're all here on one-way tickets," Milo said.

The three of us piled into the front seat, and Milo gunned the motor and swept out, scattering the group of taxi drivers who had followed us over to the car. I looked back to see if they were all right. Milo didn't take his eyes off the road.

Corey had a big smile on his face. He began repeating a mantra of how much I was going to love living in Uganda. He had his arm stretched out nonchalantly on the back of the seat and was turned to face me. Milo was weaving a constant path through a sea of moving obstacles. I tried to concentrate on what Corey was saying while I watched the road out of the corner of my eye. Milo swerved around a small motorbike while simultaneously dodging an oncoming van. My foot pressed down hard on an imaginary brake pedal.

"What's the river like?" I asked Corey.

He spread his arms wide apart with a big grin. "Huge," he said, and he began rattling off a bunch of unfamiliar rapid names.

Our vehicle swerved again and almost lifted onto two wheels. I stared at Milo in alarm.

"All you gotta know about driving here is that it's every prick for himself," he said. "You can't show any weakness; don't hesitate, just keep ploughing through the fuckers. You can't see a lane? You make a lane. This is how they drive over here and the nice rules from home don't count anymore."

We were on a dark two lane highway. Jungle crowded in from the sides. There was no obvious habitation, yet masses of people crowded the road, in vehicles, on foot, or balanced on precariously loaded bicycles. Little market stalls were set up at regular intervals, each scene illuminated by small fires.

"What's the plan?" I asked them.

They answered simultaneously. "Al's Bar."

"What's at Al's Bar?"

"Alcohol and chicks," Milo said. "It's where we hang."

Corey leaned towards me. "Every guide's first night is at Al's Bar."

"I can't wait," I said with scant enthusiasm. After over twenty four hours spent traveling, a drink sounded like a good idea, but I didn't trust these two not to play some heinous trick on me.

Milo was having trouble overtaking an open-back truck. It was packed with people dancing and drinking from large bottles of beer. The truck lurched from side to side, each movement throwing around the passengers. Somebody tossed out an empty bottle, and it sailed over our car.

"This is bullshit," Milo said.

He slowed down to get a better view of the road. The truck ran over a large pothole, jerking the vehicle and causing the tailgate to drop down with a bang. A long wooden box fell onto the road causing Milo to brake hard and swerve to avoid it. The revelers called for the truck driver to stop, and then some of them jumped down to retrieve the box. I leaned forward and saw that the impact had broken it open, revealing what appeared to be a dead body.

"Looks like they're off to a funeral," Corey said.

"A bit late to bury someone, isn't it?" Milo observed.

As a couple of them stuffed the body into the broken coffin, the others laughed and danced, the bottles raised above their heads. Smoke from nearby fires drifted across the road, casting the people with a burnt orange glow. Their faces appeared demonic in the gloom as they loaded their cargo back onto the truck.

Milo gave me a deadpan stare. "Welcome to Africa," he said, and we moved around the scene and continued on our way.

After about half an hour we came to the outskirts of Kampala. The city was pitch black, only the beams of car headlights providing any light. I gave up trying to orientate myself as we picked our way through what seemed to be an oversized slum. At last Milo pulled over and parked amongst a line of vehicles. Across the road stood a ramshackle building, a neon sign proclaiming its status as *Al's Bar*. The two of them made to get out.

"Shall I just leave my bags in the back?" I said innocently.

Corey and Milo looked at my luggage sitting on the open tray-back.

"We'll stick it in the front. It'll be fine," Milo said.

"And my laptop? Will that be okay inside the car as well?" Milo and Corey exchanged a dubious glance. "I mean," I continued in an innocent voice, "does stuff get stolen here?"

"All right," Milo said. "We'll run home and drop off your stuff and then come back. It's not far."

I remained silent as we continued down the road. All I knew was that as soon as we got inside the house they would have an impossible task getting me out again this evening. After another ten minutes careening down the main road, we turned off onto a dirt track lined with gated houses. We sped along this for a few minutes while turning down an endless series of branch roads until we came to a tall metal gate. It was painted bright blue and not dissimilar to the other fortifications around us. The gate was lined with razor wire, and broken glass was embedded into the tops of the walls. Milo leant on the horn and the gate was quickly opened by a young Ugandan carrying an AK47 assault rifle.

"Our Askari guard," Milo said as we swept past him and into a large courtyard. "He's pretty much useless."

"We also have a cook, a cleaner, and a garden boy," Corey said.

"Are they useless too?"

"Let's just say you won't be doing any cooking, cleaning, or washing for a long while."

"Or gardening," Milo added.

Two large dogs trotted up to greet us, and I squatted down and presented the back of my hand to them. They sniffed it in turn and then ambled back to the house, an enormous Colonial era mansion. The sound of several generators echoed around the surrounding neighborhood. I hauled my bags inside and followed Corey up to the second floor, where he presented me with a small room.

"This is you, bro."

The room had a four poster bed with a mosquito canopy. A large wardrobe jutted up against the bed, and there was a small desk and chair off to the side. The floor was a radiant blue tile. There was a large window with a wire screen, and a light breeze wafted the mosquito net. Outside I saw only an occasional light in the darkness. I inspected the net for any holes.

Downstairs in the large common room I somehow managed to convince the boys not to take me out that night. They agreed that it was late and that tomorrow would be a big day.

"You're gonna need all the sleep you can get," Milo told me. "'Cause tomorrow you're gonna get trashed."

I took a shower in the bathroom down the hall and then climbed into bed, Milo's words ringing in my ears.

We were up and gone early.

"There's three boats today," Milo said as we lurched down the road in a small bus. "Me and Corey are guiding, and Eddie is waiting out at the river for us. He'll be guiding the other one. We get one guide to stay out at Bujagali every week in case any overland trucks come in and want to raft the next day."

"Who am I going down the river with?" I asked.

"Me." Milo grinned, and Dave, the video kayaker, laughed.

I had known Dave in Cairns. He was a tall and lanky Kiwi with a passing resemblance to a blonde Clint Eastwood, complete with disdainful sneer.

"Milo's our trash champion," Dave said. "You'll probably get some mighty downtime today."

"What's downtime?" I said, unsure if I wanted to know the answer.

Dave smiled. "The length of time you get held underwater. What's your record, Milo?"

"About a minute," Milo said, deadpan.

Dave turned back to me. "Think you can hold your breath for that long?"

"He looks green," Milo said.

"Shut up, you two," I muttered.

Dave laughed and then stood up and got the driver to stop. We'd come to the intersection with the sealed road. Dave jumped out and walked over to a group of young men sitting on little motorbikes. They smiled, and one passed him a cigarette.

"This is Gabba Road," Milo explained. "The suburb we live in is called Gabba. By the way, the driver here is Isaac. He's a Ugandan who actually knows how to drive."

Isaac was a little round man of indeterminate age. He beamed at Milo's introduction and shook my hand with an extremely weak grip. "Is very nice to meet you, Mister Adams," he said.

We pulled onto Gabba Road, leaving Dave behind. "He's waiting for Corey," Milo said. "They'll go out to the river before us with the pickup. They need to buy lunch for the punters on the way."

"What's our job?" I asked.

"We're picking up the punters. Got some at the Kampala Backpackers and some at the Sheraton. The backpackers is run by an old crazy dude called Geoff. He once chased a bunch of local terrorists down the street after they threw a grenade into his garden."

"Did he catch them?"

"Lucky for them, no."

Driving was a more concerning prospect with the light of day. The road was single lane in each direction, but at times vehicles were three abreast. We swerved around gigantic potholes as Isaac waved breezily at various passers-by. Then we came down a long hill towards a very large roundabout that was packed with road users of every sort.

"Clock-tower roundabout," Milo said. "This will be an awful mess later on, but it's moving pretty well for this time of day. We'll go across this and up the other side and then swing back into the city to the Sheraton, and then from there it's about an hour run out to the river."

After stopping at the two pickup points, we headed east out of Kampala with enough clients to fill three boats. Traffic was heavy, and we passed a never-ending line of buildings and markets. After half an hour of this, we came over a rise, and Isaac slowed the bus.

Milo stood up. "Breakfast time," he said to me, and then he addressed the rest of the bus. "Okay everyone; this is the in-your-face-chicken-place. This chicken was running around having a good old time about an hour ago and now it's dead, cooked, and stuck on the end of a stick. It's the freshest chicken you'll ever get."

As the bus slowed, a line of young Ugandans, each wielding an array of thin sticks topped with flame-cooked chicken, ran beside the bus, yelling out Milo's name.

Milo continued. "Now just make sure that you don't open too many windows, because when you open a window, they stick in the chicken. Watch me and I'll show you how it's done."

The bus came to a halt, and Milo moved to open a window at the front of the vehicle. The crowd of chicken merchants pushed and shoved each other as they fought to get the prime position in front of Milo. He opened the window and had to duck his head as a phalanx of chicken-topped sticks were thrust into the little space. The boys were yelling and screaming the goodness of their wares as Milo tested each one with a slight touch of the finger.

"These are hot," he announced, and he purchased two of the sticks. He handed one to me as the more courageous punters opened their own windows, and soon the bus was awash with the noise of hasty breakfast transactions. Isaac selected his own and ate contentedly.

The chicken was covered with a scattering of salt and was unbelievably fresh and tender.

"Best chicken you'll ever get," Milo said.

We left the chicken stop behind and soon passed through a large section of forest. Milo dozed beside me as I stared out the window. After another half hour of travelling, Isaac got me to wake Milo. He stirred, looked around him, and then got to his feet.

"Okay everyone, time to wake up." He stifled a yawn. "We're coming up to the dam wall that separates Lake Victoria from the Nile. So you're about to pass the starting point of the world's longest river. The dam will have some of its release gates open. One gate is big, two gates are pretty terrifying…and I don't even want to think about three gates."

The bus followed the road out and onto the dam wall. A huge plume of water thundered out to the left, and we all crowded the side of the bus to look at it.

"Two gates," Milo announced. "It's going to be a big day."

"How big is big?" a customer asked him.

"Well, let's just say I'm not wearing the brown underwear for nothing."

I stared out the window at my first sight of the Nile. It moved quickly away from the dam wall, snaking a path through large cultivated hills. We turned north and followed a wide dirt road that wound up and down the hills. Mud hut villages were interspersed with dense banana plantations, and as always, there were crowds of people walking, cycling, or simply standing and staring at the passing bus full of white people.

The younger Ugandan men were dressed like American basketball players. At some point conservatism set in, as anyone above the age of thirty dressed in severe suits several decades out of fashion. The women either favored traditional long flowing dresses of intense color, or they dressed in Western clothing in what they imagined was a provocative style, but which had more of an effect of tawdry sleaze.

The road was muddy from recent rain, and Isaac had a bit of difficulty cresting the long final hill before the turn-off to the river. The bus slid around in an alarming fashion, but both he and Milo seemed unperturbed. After clearing the hill we trundled down a narrow track that ended in a large clearing. At the entrance to the park we passed a sign advertising rafting with a different company.

"Who are they?" I asked Milo.

"They're a South African mob that started up here about a year ago. There's no love lost between them and us."

Corey and Dave were waiting by the pickup. Next to them were a small crowd of local boys who were engaged in pumping up the rafts.

"This is Bujagali Falls," Milo said to the twenty-odd people on the bus. "Jump off and grab a life-jacket and helmet from the boys, and then we'll divide you into three groups."

I got off the bus. The river was a few hundred meters away at the bottom of a steep hill, but its power and intensity was formidable even at such a distance. It passed through a series of large jungle-covered islands. I could make out very large rapids, the white-water foaming and throwing spray high into the sky.

I met Eddie, the guide camping out here at the falls. He was small-statured, his face hidden by a large beard, and he possessed a very easygoing manner. There were also two Ugandan safety kayakers. Kato shook my hand with a broad smile, his large head bobbing from side to side. Musu had an impressively muscled physique, and he strode around like a shirtless peacock as he handed out helmets to the punters.

I changed into my own gear as well. Dave came up and fingered my new lifejacket with contempt.

"New one is it?" he said. "Don't think that's going to save you. Scrawny chap like you, you'll go straight to the bottom and stay there."

"That's mister scrawny chap to you," I said.

"Whatever. Have fun saying hello to the fishies. And you can forget about taking that throw-bag; that'll get ripped off you the first time you surf. Don't expect to keep that nice Gerber knife either. Let's face it; you're probably going to finish the trip naked."

"Actually," Milo said, "I wouldn't wear those Tevas if I were you. They will get ripped off for sure. Notice how everyone else has bare feet?"

"I did notice that, yeah."

"Just be careful of jiggers."

"What the fuck are jiggers?"

"These little worms that get into your feet and breed and hatch eggs between your toes."

I stared at Milo. "Are you taking the piss?"

He shrugged. "Ask Eddie about them. He spends most of his time digging them out with his knife."

Eddie showed me the wounds in his bare feet. "Nasty little buggers they are. Burning with a cigarette sometimes helps too."

I looked at them both in alarm, and then we went down to the river, the three of us walking behind the local village boys who were carrying the large rafts above their heads. They set down their burdens, and then Milo paid their leader with some small denomination notes he got out of a zipped pencil case.

"We don't carry boats here," he explained to me. "We don't pump boats, we don't fix boats, we don't dress punters, and we don't clean gear. All we do is guide. We employ about fifty locals at various points to do all this stuff for us. The trip leader has the job of paying them all throughout the day."

"Sounds pretty good to me," I said.

"It's how they can get away with paying us fuck-all," Milo retorted.

"I thought that was because we're living the dream," Corey said.

Dave snorted off a laugh, put away his video camera, and climbed into his kayak. "See you the other side of Bujagali. Try to flip, for fuck's sake," he said, and then he paddled away into the heaving whitewater.

We floated around in the large pool as each guide took his crew through their paces. Then we peeled off into the massive current, the raft shifting and moving around beneath us, gaining momentum through the confused line as we passed a small crowd of viewers standing on the bank by a large open pagoda, and then we dropped down into a chute that ended in a massive wall of white water. Most of the crew on the left side was sucked out in a moment, the force of water taking them under the raft and out the other side. The safety kayakers zipped around rescuing customers and retrieving lost paddles. We watched the progress of the other two rafts, both passing without incident. Dave had a sour look as he paddled away.

After a few smaller rapids, we eddied out in the middle of the river behind a large rock. Downstream was a chaotic maelstrom of holes and waves, white water being squeezed into the air, and currents running in confused directions.

Milo stood up and addressed the crew. "Okay folks, this is our first class five of the day: Total Gunga. What we have is a two hundred meter lead up through all of that shit, and then we're going to drop down into a trough and I'm going to get you down on the floor like little chickens, and then we'll hit a huge hole that'll knock your bathers around your ears. We'll probably flip there, and then you're facing a nasty three hundred meter swim through the rest of it. Good luck."

He sat down next to me at the rear of the raft. "We've gotta wait for Dave to give us the all clear." He pointed to a section running through trees on the river right side of the rapid. "The other mob run their boats down there. It's a class three dribbly shit run."

Dave had clambered on to a tiny rock off to the side of the main part of the rapid. He checked his video camera, then looked back up towards us and raised his hand in the air.

Milo pulled out from behind the rock. The surging current took the raft and swung us downstream, and we quickly left the other rafts far behind. The crew paddled hard as Milo angled his boat across the line of water towards the left. We came up and over a large mound, and I got a glimpse of a dangerous looking hole to our immediate left. And then we dropped down into a huge wall of water directly in front of us, and as I got on the floor we hit it dead center and I flew out of the raft.

I was gone, deep underwater, blackness enclosing me. I couldn't tell if I was moving or stationary in the water. The pressure on my ears became too much, and I blew hard on my nose to equalize. I scraped against something hard, a rock, and then it was gone as I was swept past. The black became a deep green, and then there was more light, and I willed myself to break the surface, until the water propelled me back into the chaotic turbulence, a harsh reality after the calmness of the deep gloom.

I sucked in great mouthfuls of air as I tried to work out how long I'd been under. Twenty, thirty seconds? Whatever the time, it'd felt like an age. I was in a large pool below the main rapid. I spied Milo kneeling on his upside-down raft, and I swum over as he re-flipped it. We both jumped in and proceeded to rescue the crew.

"Big hit that one," Milo said. "How was that for you?"

"I don't remember a thing. It all happened so fast."

"It does that, yeah."

"I went real deep though. I hit a rock."

"Bullshit. I don't know anyone who's hit the bottom here."

"Well I fucking did."

"What did you notice before we hit the hole?" he asked me.

His tone was serious, so I mentioned the large hole I'd seen towards the left.

He nodded. "Good. That's the class six part of the rapid. You don't want to go in there. So don't overcompensate at the top or you could find yourself in a bucket-load of pain."

We helped to clean up the mess from Corey and Eddie's flips, and then we headed downstream to another class five monster where Milo flipped me again. After a few more kilometers of negotiating channels through islands filled with chattering monkeys, we stopped for lunch on a small island next to an adjacent village. Afterwards we paddled along a series of long pools that culminated with a difficult portage around a waterfall that was only runnable when the river was low. It looked terrifying, but it was nothing compared to the truly awe-inspiring cataract that heaved and thundered on the other side of the river at the same point.

"That's called the Dead Dutchman," Milo told me. His voice was raised above the sound of the river. "Named after a Dutch dude who thought he could paddle it in an inflatable kayak rubber ducky thing."

"You can't be serious."

"They found a part of his lifejacket."

We ran a few more big but straightforward rapids, and then we paddled across another long pool. We pulled over to a small protected eddy on the river, right where some more local village boys were waiting for us. They hauled the rafts out of the river and carried them away on their heads. Beside us roared another impassable cataract. The clients followed the porters while Milo and Corey pointed out the features of Itanda rapid. Their tones were serious and their body language more subdued than before.

"We don't run that, do we?" I asked them.

"No," said Milo. "That would be silly. We run a tiny part of the bottom of it. It's the biggest hole of the trip."

"It's called The Bad Place," Corey said. He held my gaze for a moment, and then he walked off. Milo and I followed him down a hill to where the three rafts sat in a tiny eddy. We watched Eddie's crew climb into the raft. He gave them a pep talk, and then they paddled out of the eddy while keeping very close to the right hand bank. They passed an enormous hole in the middle of the river, and then they headed sharply to the left and out into a gigantic wave train.

"He missed the hole," Milo said. "Some clients you don't want to take in there. This isn't hero shit."

Corey brought his raft out of the eddy and followed the same line. But instead of heading out to the wave train, he squared his raft, which rose up and dropped out of sight.

"He's in there," Milo said. "Watch this."

I saw the raft reappear, its 18 foot length vertical as it attempted to claw its way out of the hole, and then it disappeared from sight as it was sucked back into the stopper, and then the raft was surfing, the hole flinging it in violent circles while bodies were thrown around like rag dolls, until at last the stopper released its grip, and the raft floated out with its main thwarts hanging in broken pieces.

"That's why the thwarts are clipped in," Milo said. "The clips blow out instead of the thing being ripped off in a surf like that. Corey will clip them back in once he has his crew together." He clapped me on the back. "Now it's our turn. We're going to go right in the guts."

"Lovely," I muttered

We swung out into the heaving water, passed close to an enormous stopper wave, and then we rode over a rising mound and dropped into the biggest hole I'd ever seen. It stretched far above our heads, and I had a brief moment to wonder how we would ever get out before we slammed into its fury and I was thrown into the violence of the Bad Place.

After suffering my second downtime of the day, we proceeded to the takeout point around the next bend. Another set of local boys man-handled the rafts up a steep and muddy track to a little village where our vehicles were waiting. The clients took photos of the village urchins as they played up for the cameras. I dumped my gear inside the bus and spotted a large cooler filled with beer and soft drink.

"We can drink beer on the bus?" I asked Corey in wonder.

"Welcome to Africa, bro," he said. We got the punters into the bus and headed home for Kampala. Milo was so generous with the beer that we had to stop for further supplies before reaching the city. The bus was a mobile party making its way through coffee and banana plantations, the sun dipping in front of us, orange and purple hues bathing the countryside and towns that we passed, Corey and Milo all smiles as we celebrated my first day on the Nile.

"I've never seen anything like this before," I said.

My comment roused Milo and Corey from their sleep. We were at the clock-tower roundabout, and the night was lit by the headlights of hundreds of vehicles crawling through the bumper to bumper madness stretched out before us. A solitary policeman attempted to direct traffic, but the drivers ignored his desperate signals as each vehicle inched forward to fill any immediate space that presented itself. Cars attempting to exit the roundabout sat face to face with those trying to gain entry.

"Holy shit," Corey muttered.

"Very bad stop this one is," Isaac observed.

Milo stared around in disbelief. "That idiot policeman is making things worse. We're never going to get through this carnage with him directing people into one another."

"Probably caused this mess himself," Corey said, laughing.

Milo opened a front window, leaned his body halfway out of the bus, and proceeded to abuse the startled officer. I glanced at Corey in alarm, but he placed a reassuring hand on my shoulder.

"Milo knows what he's doing," he said.

As Milo's invective increased to comparing the policeman with his own morning's bowel movement, I noticed that Isaac was inching us forward. He placed the bus with great skill, imploring those on his side to let him through while Milo continued his diatribe at anyone foolish enough to consider coming into our path from the other direction. We left the panicked policeman behind as we negotiated our way through the dust and light beams, clearing the roundabout almost twenty minutes later.

Isaac trundled along until Al's Bar came into view. He pulled to a stop and opened the automatic side door. I followed Milo and Corey off the bus and across the road to the entrance, leaving Isaac to drive away.

A couple of doormen armed with pump action shotguns stood guard outside. They nodded to Milo and Corey who presented me as the new guide. Inside was a large bar surrounded by tables and stools with a small stage set down the back. We made our way up a short set of stairs past a DJ booth suspended in the side of the wall to a long mezzanine area with a pool table and another small bar. Milo ordered a round of drinks.

"Waragi and tonic," he said with his mouth close to my ear. "It's the local gin; nice and rough."

Even at this early hour the place was getting crowded. Hendrix wailed from over-sized speakers hanging from the high ceiling. There were around twenty African women of various nationalities grouped around the pool table. They were all astoundingly beautiful and had a collective dress sense bordering on the pornographic. They converged on us as soon as we turned away from the bar.

"These are mosquito girls," Corey yelled. "They buzz around and never leave you alone."

"Are they working girls?" I asked, trying to be diplomatic.

"It depends on your definition of the term," Milo said. "They spend their time here playing pool and trying to hook up with a mazungu. You're a mazungu," he added on seeing my puzzled expression.

Corey leant across. "We think it means 'white honkey ass', but we could be a bit off on the translation."

The girls began a collective chorus of pleading to get our attention, chanting Milo and Corey's names in unison. "They don't always do this," Corey said. "But they've seen you, and they know they have a chance to get it on with a new guide."

Milo turned and spread his arms. "Girls, let me introduce you all to the new guide, just arrived yesterday and pure as the virgin snow. This is Adam!"

The girls erupted into wild cheering whilst simultaneously trying to maneuver themselves into my arms. Milo and Corey jumped back, and the other patrons observed my desperate struggles with amused indifference. I begged the boys for some help.

"You have to pick one!" Milo yelled.

The girls redoubled their efforts to be the chosen one. I pointed to one at random.

"Not her!" Corey shouted in warning.

I'd had enough. "You fucking pick one for me then!"

Corey shrugged and selected a cute girl hovering in the background. The rest of the women immediately ceased their clamoring and mooched back to their positions around the pool table. The girl hung on my arm. I tried to talk to her, but she looked at me in confusion.

"You're not supposed to talk to her," Milo said. "She's your protection."

"What do you mean?"

"If you have her next to you then the others will leave you alone."

"I don't get this country," I complained.

"Nobody gets this country," Corey laughed.

Dave arrived with Scott, another guide that I knew from the Tully. Scott was stocky, with long blonde hair and a missing front tooth. He'd worked in Cairns for the other company but our paths had crossed a few times when rescuing each other's customers from sticky situations. He clapped me on the back, welcomed me to Uganda, and purchased another round of drinks. Dave went to the bar and obtained a pack of smokes. He showed them to me; they were pre-rolled marijuana cigarettes.

"Cost two US dollars," he said, winking. He walked up another set of stairs to a secluded third level where he lit up.

The bar filled with a broad mix of Ugandans and expats. Some of the clients from the day's rafting trip arrived having followed Milo's directions. I played a game of pool against a guy who worked for the UN. The music blared, the mass of people surged around me, I drank from my glass with one of Dave's cigarettes in my other hand, I danced with my glass above my head, the Somalian girl clung to my side, I saw Milo dancing with his arms above his head and a crowd of girls around him, I danced and drank and smoked, the lights reflecting off the back of my head, Corey yelling in my face that I was here, I was here in Uganda, I was a mazungu in Africa.

16

I went down the river again the next day. I was on Corey's raft, but I took the stick and guided the whole trip. I didn't want to keep sitting in other guide's rafts and looking at the river. The thing to do was to face the task head on and not pussy around. I wanted to be passed as soon as possible, but I felt that Milo was reluctant to make me commercial. The last time he and Corey had seen me guide, my skills had been quite low, so I understood why they were cautious. Nevertheless, they'd asked me to come to Uganda, so they had to step up at some point and give me a chance.

After another week I was cleared to guide on the Nile, and I started to get some trips. The major difference on the Nile from other rivers was how we gave the customers value for money. With only twelve rapids spread over a twenty kilometer route and much paddling across flat pools, the onus was on giving them the most excitement possible at each rapid. The combination of warm water, very few rocks or obstacles, and long pools after each rapid meant that we as guides were not only able to comfortably flip the raft, it was a requirement. The real skill lay in consistently hitting a rapid's sweet spot. This meant having a perfect line-up sometimes hundreds of meters away.

Yet it was still possible to get into serious trouble if the river took you where you didn't want to go, and for this reason I favored taking crews who looked like they could paddle. To this end I started advertising myself as "the trash boat", attracting the customers who wanted to go hard, and thus ensuring that I had the power to stay out of harm's way. But this also meant that I had to live up to my word, and with the number of flips and surfs that I suffered, I began to sell a lot of videos for Dave.

The first couple of weeks were a steep learning curve for me. Not only did I have to adjust to living in Uganda, I soon became aware of an astounding level of political infighting in what was a very small rafting operation. Milo was barely on speaking terms with the two New Zealand women who ran the administration. The office was in the upstairs part of the house, and I did my best to stay out of the hostilities. Milo had a bedroom with its own ensúite across the hall from me, but most of the time he stayed with his girlfriend, an English girl who had grown up in the local expat community. He was also doing very few rafting trips, and there was a suspicion that he was setting up his own company. But due to the drop in tourist numbers we were only getting two trips a week, so his absence was better for us anyway.

On the surface, earning a hundred dollars a week seemed pitiful, but with the average Ugandan earning twenty dollars a month and going to the same establishments as we frequented, we actually had a lot of purchasing power. Plus we didn't have to pay for accommodation or food. But I had to send a certain amount of money home each month to cover the stupid loan I'd taken out to buy my laptop, which meant I had to keep some sense of control over how I spent money.

I thought I'd hit on a solution when some expats asked me to join their band. I met them my first week in the country when Milo and Corey took me down to the Musician's Club in downtown Kampala. Located on the top floor of a nondescript office building, the small room had a stage fronted by tight rows of chairs and a small bar in a hole in the wall off to one side. It was so crowded that patrons wanting a drink would relay their orders and money through the audience without leaving their seats.

The stage held a variety of instruments, and we sat and listened to a woman screeching a tortured version of Whitney Houston while a scattering of musicians struggled to stay in time.

"I can't wait to see what they think of you," Milo said as we drank our first beers.

I wasn't sure about playing, but I couldn't let down the boys seeing as this was the main reason they got me out to the country in the first place. I waited a few more songs, and then I made my way to the front and asked the guitarist if I could have a turn on the instrument.

I got them to play a standard blues riff, and then I started playing an acid jazz version over the top. The room went nothing short of wild. I'd never experienced anything like it. We jammed the same song for a good ten minutes while a group of young Ugandan men knelt in front of me, their eyes glued to the fret board as they tried to memorize what I was playing. At the back of the room I saw Milo and Corey exchanging high fives.

I finished playing, and the group of expats steered me to the side and offered me a spot in their band. I played a few gigs with them at upmarket hotels, but their policy was to give the gig money to the Ugandan band members due to their greater need. I told them that I also had need, but they couldn't comprehend this. It was assumed by everyone that white people had no money issues.

With so much free time at my disposal, I took to exploring the downtown area of Kampala. Corey became my willing accomplice, and we wandered down any lane or alley that took our fancy. The city was spread over a number of large hills, and the architecture in its more run-down areas was a curious mismatch of 1920's art deco with Arabic and Indian influences. Many buildings were in ruins or only half finished, supporting rods sticking out of concrete walls like the amputated limbs of robots in some alien cyborg conflict, while some of the tall office buildings were still scattered with bullet and shell holes, testimony to the futile last stand of Idi Amin's defeated army.

As white guys on the street, we were the target of continual curiosity. For most of the population, even in the city, we were a novelty, and their natural assumption was that we were immensely wealthy. Stories abounded of great hardship, of refugees fleeing persecution in neighboring countries, of whole families torn apart by the effects of war and disease.

A middle aged man approached us one day in the downtown area. He was dressed in rags, but spoke eloquently of his flight from Somalia, across Kenya, and into Uganda. The other lads were unmoved by his plight, but in my innocence I tried to give him some assistance. We gave him a lift across the city to where he needed to go, and I handed him a small amount of money. He had tears in his eyes when we left him, and I thought that I'd done a good thing, but over the next few weeks I spied him reciting similar tales to unsuspecting tourists.

Every second Ugandan I saw on the street wanted to be my immediate friend, and this soon wore thin. My body armor became my wraparound Arnett sunglasses, as they severed any possibility of eye contact, making first communication impossible.

Corey and I became experts on the Kampala bar scene. At night we frequented the expat spots in the central city and the suburb of Kabalagala, home to Al's Bar, Capital Pub, and many others. But by day we sought out city watering holes unknown to the expat community. The dingier the bar and the more out of place its location, the more it met our expectations. We played pool with local toughs and chanced our digestive systems on kitchens serving unidentifiable food.

Our exploration centered on a large area containing the crumbling soccer stadium, the vast Owino Markets, and the Taxi Park. From the Taxi Park it was possible to catch some form of transport to any point in the country. A taxi was actually a small Toyota van with a sliding door that acted as a bus service, known as a matatu. Designed to seat nine passengers, they were often overcrowded with twenty or more people and farmyard animals. A tout assisted the driver by hanging out the sliding door and seeking customers.

The Taxi Park was a chaotic assembly of hundreds of such vehicles parked nose to nose in a seemingly haphazard fashion and surrounded by market stalls selling food, produce, and various household necessities. Larger conventional buses sat on the periphery offering trips to neighboring countries. It was noisy and crowded, contaminated by dust and exhaust fumes, and preyed upon by street urchins, thieves, beggars, and conmen.

Standing out among the buildings that ringed this circus was a crumbling art deco tower rising five or six stories into the sky. One day I looked up at it and thought I spied people sitting and drinking on its open top.

"We have to find the entrance up to it," Corey said.

We walked to the surrounding alleys, stepping with care over sewerage dribbling down narrow open channels. I entered a door only to startle a woman breastfeeding her baby.

"Mazungu," she said.

"To the top?" I asked, my finger pointing to the roof.

"No, mazungu," she said, and she turned away.

After a few more attempts we discovered a faded beer advertisement at the bottom of a set of steep stairs. We made our way up several flights through grim scenes of poverty and desperation. The stairs terminated in a tiny room, the interior dominated by a makeshift serving space. The barman signaled his surprise with a startled exclamation at seeing a couple of white guys.

"Ei! Mazungus!"

"Two beers," I said. "Nile Special if you have it."

He cracked the ice cold bottles and settled for the regular payment after trying to extort us with the price. We took the beers and walked outside. Below us spread the Taxi Park in all its glory, and we took a table at the rail and watched the human drama unfold below in the quasi alien scene. It soon became one of our favorite spots.

My first turn came up to spend a week at Bujagali, but since there was no rafting trip that day, I had to make my own way out to the river. My plan was to get a matatu from the Taxi Park. To get to the Taxi Park I needed an actual taxi, known in Uganda as a "special hire".

I walked down to the Gabba Road intersection where a few special hire drivers were loitering around their vehicles. They rushed over en masse when they saw me walking with my bag. I selected one at random and got into the back seat, my backpack next to me. The driver drove the clattering vehicle to the closest gas station where, with my advance payment, he purchased enough fuel to cover the job. Then we headed off for downtown Kampala.

As we were coming down the hill towards the clock-tower roundabout, a pair of policeman standing on the side of the road waved us over. They made a pretense of inspecting the vehicle, and then one got into the front seat while his partner tried to get in the back with me. He pushed my backpack over to give him some room to get in the vehicle. I pushed it back. He exclaimed in surprise and again pushed my bag towards the middle of the seat. I once again pushed it back to its original position.

The policeman sitting in the front seat turned around to see what was happening. "Mazungu," he said. "You must let him have the space to sit inside."

"No, I don't," I said.

His partner standing by the rear door couldn't understand what was happening. "Of course you must," he continued in his most pleasant voice. "We are needing a journey on very important police business."

"And what important police business is that?" I demanded, returning my bag once again to the side of the seat.

He looked at me while he thought of an answer. "Secret police business. Very secret."

I wasn't impressed. "Yeah? Well, you can do your secret stuff on your own money. This is my special hire. I'm not paying for you two."

The driver remained in his seat, his head moving back and forth with rising panic. There was a line of perspiration on his forehead, and his suit jacket was stretched tight across his shoulders.

The second policeman reached the end of his patience and threw my bag onto the road. I moved across, blocking him from entering the vehicle, and then I got out to retrieve my bag. He and I stood face to face on the side of the busy road. The driver leapt out on seeing his fare exit the vehicle.

The first policeman sat for a moment by himself in the front and then slowly got out as well. He walked around to where the three of us were standing.

"Mazungu, I must explain to you how it is working here in our country. This man is a very bad driver of his special hire." The driver made suitable noises of contrition. "Mazungu, do you see the conditions of this special hire? It is very bad. Look at this very large break in the front glass." He pointed to a faint line on the windshield.

"You're full of shit," I said. "You saw a mazungu in the special hire who you thought was a stupid tourist, and you thought you could get a free ride."

"Mazungu, it is you who are the stupid," he sneered. "Of course you must be paying."

"What are you, corrupt?" I said.

"Aiyeeee!" exclaimed the driver as he threw his hands into the air in horror.

The first policeman tried to stare me down, but I lifted my jaw and met his gaze with clenched teeth. We stood like that for a little while as traffic and pedestrians streamed around us, and then he signaled to his partner, and the two of them walked off without another word.

The driver got hurriedly into his vehicle. I placed my bag on the rear seat and got in next to it. He fumbled for the keys and took off down the street without checking the traffic.

"Oh mazungu, mazungu, you are crazy," he stammered. "You cannot be speaking to the policemens like that. Oh my, you are crazy. Never have I seen before such a one as crazy as you."

I leaned back on the cracked vinyl seat as the worn shock absorbers pounded every bump and jolt through my spine. The driver continued to proclaim my general insanity as we trundled around the busy roundabout.

"Mazungu, do you know what will happens to you if you speak to the policemens like that?"

"Apparently nothing," I said. "Take this exit for the Taxi Park, and don't even think about taking me the long way."

I made the rookie mistake of being one of the first into the matatu, and I soon found myself wedged in the back with innumerable other passengers. The tout kept calling in more and more, and we left with the overladen vehicle swaying alarmingly on the highway. The minivan took almost two hours to sputter its way to Jinja. We crossed the dam wall, and I got out in front of a large gas station and Chinese restaurant. Sitting at the corner on their little motorbikes were a large group of boda-boda riders. They crowded around me and I negotiated a price with the one whose equipment seemed most in order. I shouldered my pack and climbed onto the pillion seat. The cost for the trip to Bujagali was five hundred shillings, around thirty cents.

"Sebo," I said. "I will pay you one thousand shillings if I don't have the fear."

He smiled and nodded his head, and we motored up the dirt road. My driver called out to people as we passed, evidently happy with the social status he got from carrying a mazungu. We bumped our way down the final track through a coffee plantation to the entrance to Bujagali Falls. I paid him the extra sum and arranged for him to be my permanent ride. He flashed his very white teeth and rode away.

On the side of the coffee plantation overlooking the Nile was a small ramshackle hut. I placed my bag inside and on the bed, peering with dismay at the holes in the mosquito netting.

Outside I sat on the covered porch and watched the river thunder through the island channels. After a while a blue raft made an appearance at the rapid above the pool where we started our trips. I figured it belonged to the other company, and I watched its line with interest as we didn't run that rapid due to the large tree that sat below it in the middle of the river. Another raft came into view as the first ran the drop hard to river-right, skirting around the tree where the river poured through its lower branches.

The second raft's line was different to that of the first. I noticed that it was further towards the center of the drop, and as it went over it was caught by the turbulent water, which spun the raft sideways, dumping the downstream passengers into the water.

I rose from my chair in alarm. I saw some swimmers being swept towards the tree, and then the hill hid my view. I grabbed my lifejacket and throw bag and sprinted down to the river.

As I crested the hill I saw that the raft had managed to reach the safety of the pool. Two kayakers were frantically attempting to reach the tree, but the dangerous strainer prevented their approach. If a swimmer had gone under the branches then they would be in serious trouble. Two swimmers had managed to reach the bank below me, and I helped them out of the water.

I caught a flash of color in the water at the base of the large tree, and then I saw a man pulling himself up the branches against the force of the water trying to rip him under the hazard. It must have taken the man a phenomenal amount of strength.

I signaled to one of the Ugandan kayakers until he understood what was happening, as their vision was blocked by the tree itself. The man had reached a position of relative safety and he hung there, exhausted by his ordeal. I got his attention and through signaling made him understand what needed to be done.

He climbed slowly through the middle of the maze of tangled branches, the rushing water snatching as his feet, until he was on the downstream side. I threw him my rope, and following my instructions, he placed it over his shoulder and jumped into the water. The sudden weight caused me to sink down into a sitting position, and I swung him over the main current and safely to the bank.

He was in no state to continue, but at this point it had nothing to do with me, and I backed away. The Ugandan kayakers thanked me for my help. The two Western guides ignored me, and I made my way back up to the hut.

A few hours later a small delegation from the rafting company approached my hut. I got up and went down to meet them. There were a few Ugandans as well as one of the two guides. They all shook my hand and thanked me for my help. I didn't make a big deal of it. I asked if the customer was okay, and they told me that he was.

"Maybe you can come to our base in Jinja for a beer," one of them said to me. The others agreed that this would be a great idea. Imagining that I had a chance to heal the great rift between our two rafting operations, I accepted. Their rafting base was just outside the main town. It had a small backpacker operation and a bar. We were enjoying a beer when a loud voice interrupted the scene.

I turned and saw a very small man with thick stocky legs and long unkempt hair. He spoke with a French accent, and as soon as he spotted my staff shirt he went berserk. The others had to hold him back from attempting to throttle me, but I was happy for them to let him take a shot.

He frothed at the mouth and hurled abuse, and I put down my beer, thanked my hosts, and said that perhaps it was better for me to be going. The others were very embarrassed, and they made profound apologies as I walked out the gate. I found my boda-boda boy waiting there for me.

"One thousand shillings, Mister Adams?"

"How'd you know I was here?" I said. He just laughed, and I got on the back of the bike. "Stop at that Chinese restaurant," I told him. "I need something to eat."

"Fang Fang Chinese?"

"That's the one."

The following afternoon an overland truck arrived at the campsite. I phoned through their rafting trip booking department to the office with the company mobile phone. The truck was a large enclosed vehicle designed to travel around Africa with tourists for extended periods. This group had been travelling together for two months. On the surface it seemed like a good way of seeing Africa close up, but after spending an evening socializing with the group, I questioned the wisdom of being stuck with some of these personalities for any length of time.

There were two Western drivers and an African cook with the truck, and I managed to score an invitation to eat dinner with them that evening. There were no facilities to buy or even store food at the site, something I had been unaware of before commencing my week sojourn. I managed to purchase chapatti bread from the locals each morning, but each day's dining was a challenge.

Milo arrived unannounced towards the end of the week, travelling on the back of the same boda-boda that I favored.

"How about a beer down in the bar?" he said.

"If you're buying," I said.

We headed down the hill to the large open pagoda-bar located at the side of the main falls. Milo got two bottles of beer from the surly Ugandan barman.

"A toast," he said, raising his bottle.

"What are we toasting?"

He winked at me. "My new bar."

Milo and his secret partner had purchased the lease on not only the bar, but the entire campsite. "I'm going to fix it up," he explained. "Put some nice one bedroom banda huts among the coffee plantation near the guide hut, as well as an amenities block with showers and toilets."

I agreed that this was needed. "What about the bar?" I asked him. "There's nothing to eat out here. It's a nightmare trying to scrounge up food. I got some rice and vegetables in Jinja, but it's pretty rough living."

"Going to get that sorted as well."

"So does this mean you've finished rafting with us?"

He grinned. "I resigned today, which means I'll be getting their payment each trip for entry into the campsite. Come to think of, that's something else we can toast." He signaled to the barman. "Two more of my beers, sebo."

Towards the late afternoon we were somewhat inebriated and unwilling to eat the remains of my moldy food supplies. Then Milo had the brilliant idea of sending one of the local boys down to the Fang Fang Chinese restaurant. We wrote down our order and gave it to him with the money. The boy took off on his bicycle, and we toasted our cleverness at solving the food issue.

Hours passed, and our delivery boy still hadn't returned. We drank more beer and tried to calculate a reasonable time to peddle down the dirt road to the highway, wait for the order to be completed, and then peddle back. The longest we could give it was two hours. Five hours later, with the assumption that the kid had stolen the money, we were resigned to going to bed hungry.

Suddenly we heard the sound of an approaching bicycle. "Oh dude, is that him?" said Milo.

The boy emerged from the darkness, and the two of us leapt into the air in celebration at his arrival.

"I can't believe you've come through with this," Milo said, taking the two large plastic bags from the boy. Milo opened one of the bags and looked inside. He stared into it for some moments.

"What is it?" I said.

Milo lifted his head and looked at me. "You're not going to believe this," he said in a measured tone.

I peered inside the bag. It contained a mishmash of chicken bones protruding from a dark brown gooey mess. "That doesn't look like Chinese takeaway," I said.

Milo regarded the somewhat nervous young lad. "I'll tell you what he's done. He's gone back to his house and said that the crazy mazungus want to spend all this money at Fang Fang, and his mother has taken a look at the list and decided that she can cook that shit no problem. That's why we've been waiting here so long. We've been waiting five hours for his mother to cook this slop. Isn't that right, Musaka?"

The kid bolted. Milo leaped after him in drunken fury, swinging the overladen bag around in the air until it burst, showering him with its contents. I was laughing so hard I fell over on the floor. Milo walked back and threw his soiled shirt into river. The barman watched us impassively from behind the counter.

"Well, at least we got a bike out of it," said Milo. "He sure as shit isn't getting that back."

Milo stayed for another couple of days, and then we got a matatu back to Kampala. His phone rang on the way, and after a few minutes talking he brought me up to speed on the conversation.

"That's a South African guy I know. He's selling his jeep, and I need some wheels. Going to go around and have a look at it as soon as we get into Kampala. Want to come?"

"Sure."

The vehicle was an old Land Rover without a roof. Milo could barely hide his glee as he walked around it.

"What do ya reckon?" he asked me.

I shrugged. "I suppose it's better than nothing."

"Dude, you must be joking. This is exactly like the one out of *The Gods Must be Crazy*. How cool is that? Can you imagine driving around in this?"

"I hope it doesn't only go in reverse."

"It goes forwards," the South African smiled.

We gave it a shot, and I had to admit that it was rather stylish in a bizarre African way. Milo settled terms on the spot, and then he gave me a lift back to the guides' house. He needed to pack his room.

17

Scott got the position of head guide and moved into Milo's old room. He had a local girlfriend, a lovely girl called Grace. She spent a lot of time at the house, and we enjoyed having her around as she came from a respectable Ugandan family and had no ulterior motives.

The office received a shakeup with the two managers departing for New Zealand. They were replaced by two more New Zealanders.

The new office manager, Kate, was ex-military. For some reason, she attempted to run roughshod over us with a dominating and aggressive management style. It didn't go down too well, and battle lines were drawn once again.

Tim was the new accountant. We had great hope for him as he was a dedicated kayaker, and we thought we'd found someone who could bridge the gap between those who worked on the river and those in the office.

Our hopes went unrealized, as Tim was an accountant first and a kayaker second. With the number of trips sharply down, the owner had instructed him to come out and cut costs. We discovered this when the office told us that they intended to reduce the number of safety kayakers on each trip. A reduction of that role would also have a real and dramatic effect on the locals who were employed by us. Working with over fifty Ugandans from a large collection of different villagers, tribes, and customs, called for constant awareness of how a seemingly irrelevant action could rebound in unimagined repercussions. The key was adapting our Western knowledge to that foreign environment.

We won the battle for the safety kayakers, but every week brought a new attempt to trim the budget. We lost the battle to keep our Ugandan equipment repairer who was skilled not only in fixing the gear but also in the crucial aspect of negotiating with the local economy for supplies. With him gone, we paid mazungu rates and were unable to keep up with the work needed to maintain our equipment. It was a demoralizing time.

I was lying on my bed one morning reading a book when Corey stuck his head in the door.

"Samo can let us in on a deal to smuggle coffee out of the Congo."

I looked at him with some confusion. "I don't have a clue what you're talking about. Who the fuck is Samo?"

"You know him. The really big Ugandan dude who came on the river a few times and wanted to learn to be a guide."

"You mean the one who couldn't swim."

"Yeah, that one. It turns out that he's an officer in an elite Ugandan special forces unit. I got talking to him the other night at Al's Bar. His job is to get rid of people that the government doesn't like. Remember that time we saw him in the bar and his hands were shaking and he was drinking one rum shot after another?"

"Yeah?" I had a vague recollection.

"Well, he had just come back from a mission."

"It seems a bit hard to believe," I said. "He seems like a nice guy."

Corey nodded. "I know. That's why he drinks so much."

I rolled up into a sitting position. "So what's this coffee smuggling shit you're going on about?"

Corey sat on the edge of the bed. "Apparently there are a bunch of Belgium coffee growers out in the middle of the Congo that can't get their crops to market."

"That would be because of the dirty great big war that's going on in there as we speak."

"Yes. Apparently if we put up the money to buy the coffee, Samo will supply the trucks and soldiers to go in and get it. Then they take it to Nairobi and sell it for a huge markup."

"How much of a markup are we talking about?"

"About four or five times what we buy it for. Samo will take costs off the top and then we split the profit with him three ways."

"I don't know," I said. "It sounds dodgy to me."

"Think about it, bro. We'd be smuggling coffee out of the Congo. How cool is that?"

"And dealing with some Special Forces lunatic who rubs people out for a living. What could possibly go wrong?" I pondered the proposal. "How much do you want?"

Corey grinned. "Four hundred bucks. We need to put up eight hundred to make it profitable after costs."

"And I suppose they have no cash themselves seeing as they're Ugandans."

"Naturally."

I inspected my money stash. "I can give you three hundred," I said.

"That'll work," he said eagerly. He counted the money while I calculated the most far-fetched profit we stood to earn. "There's a possibility to go in with them if we want," he added.

"You can't be serious."

"Think about it, bro. We'd get to see a war."

"I'm pretty sure that you don't see a war. You're in a war."

"They're leaving tomorrow as they only have the trucks for a few days, and it came up at really short notice. Samo told me about it last night."

"I think I'm going to pass on the war adventure of a lifetime. When will they be back?"

"Samo reckons about three days. Then they have to get the coffee to Nairobi and sell it. They can get a better price for it there."

"Are you going?" I asked.

"Only if you go."

"What's to stop them driving us in there and then shooting us in the head, dumping our bodies and doing the job anyway?"

Corey contemplated this scenario. "I'll let you know when they get back."

"You do that," I said.

I knew that I was getting the hang of the river when events began to slow down for me. In the beginning, a flip had flashed across my consciousness in a brief moment, but now it became a clearer picture. I had time to brace myself in the raft, to move to the higher side as the boat was taken and shoved sideways in the big hole, to drop my paddle and hold hard with both hands, waiting for the final moment when the raft would flip and I'd decide whether or not to release my grip. But I always had the fear in the pit of my stomach as I waited for my turn above one of the very big rapids. That never went away.

Because I never forgot that I was working on a deadly body of water. Local fishermen were regularly pitched from their primitive dugout canoes, and their bodies would sometimes be caught by the powerful eddies, trapping them there for days on end as they circled round and round with floating weed and other debris.

One corpse remained for two weeks in the large eddy at Big Brother rapid, its dark skin tone slowly whitening until it was the color of fresh milk. Finally we contacted the local police unit and asked if they could help us retrieve it, and we joked and laughed with them as we pulled our awful cargo to shore, anything to take our minds off what we were doing.

On occasion a large crowd of villagers on the bank would signal to us, and we knew that a fisherman was missing. Our kayakers hurried ahead, zipping through the island chains while troops of monkeys scrambled in the trees and enormous colonies of bats erupted into the sky disturbed from their perches by the unusual activity below. Sometimes we found the fisherman clinging to a piece of his broken canoe, and the villagers danced and clapped as he returned to them, the women's dresses flashing in the bright sunlight, the men jumping and waving their hats. But usually they were never seen again.

Over breakfast one morning, Scott informed us that another guide was coming out to work.

"We're barely getting enough work as it is," Eddie said. "Why the hell are they getting another guide?"

We murmured our agreement. "Apparently," Scott said, "the office wants to be able to put more boats on fewer trips. Something about their cost to profit ratio."

"This from the people who are all on fixed salaries," I said.

Scott stood up and spread his arms. "What can I tell you; don't shoot the messenger? He'll be getting here next week. Most of you should know him from Cairns. It's Noah."

I couldn't put a face to the name, but when he arrived I recognized him instantly. We shook hands, and he admitted that he'd been trying to put a face to my name as well. Noah was no nonsense and pretty much indifferent to the good opinion of other people. Like most guides, he was stocky, well-muscled and compact, and I knew him by reputation as an outstanding rafter. I wasn't on his first trip, but I awaited his opinion on the river with interest.

"How was it?" I asked him when they'd returned for the day.

He shrugged. "Not bad, pretty straightforward. Hit the holes and try not to drown. I don't see what the big deal is, to be honest. It's not that hard."

I kept my face immobile as he burst my bubble. The following day the other guides went on a trip, leaving Noah and I to our own devices. I offered to show him around Kampala and we set off in the pickup. We were a few kilometers down the road when a policeman stepped out and raised his hand. I gave him a brief look, and then I swerved to the side and shot past him.

"Holy shit," Noah said, stretching around to look behind him. "Why didn't you stop?"

In the mirror I could see the policeman standing defeated in the middle of the road. "No gun, no car, no radio," I said. "Any particular reason why you want to stop and have a long argument over an instant fine payment?"

Noah began to freak out. He called me insane and proceeded to give me a dressing-down. I held my tongue but resolved to have a quiet chat with Scott and inform him that Noah might not be cut out for Africa. Scott and Corey were also worried about Noah's adaptability. We consulted Milo, but he just shrugged his shoulders and said that Noah would get it or he wouldn't.

"Not everyone can hack it," he said. "Usually it's the ones who are big and tough and loud back home who fall to pieces here, but Noah isn't like that. Give him a couple of weeks and see if he comes good. If he doesn't, send him home."

A week later a few of us drove into the city, this time with Noah behind the wheel. He threw the car down the road, bouncing over deep potholes and swerving to avoid the numerous obstacles, all the while keeping up a steady strain of colorful abuse out the window. We hung on for dear life on the back of the pickup and looked at each other in obvious relief.

As Corey was the contact point for our coffee smuggling operation, I left him to deal with Samo. It had been several weeks since the Congo incursion, and with no sign of our money, I started to pressure him into getting our share.

The company owner came out for a quick visit from New Zealand. I had never met him before, and even though I had been there for a few months, he insisted on checking out my skills on the river. To make matters worse, that day was my first low water trip, which meant running the large waterfall at Overtime, but he seemed satisfied with my ability, so I guess I'd done well enough.

We suspected that the real motive for his trip was to see what Milo was up to with his new company. So far, all Milo had done was improve the amenities at Bujagali Falls, but he controlled the campsite, and we had to pay him money for entry. The owner was suspicious of Milo's true objectives.

He held a guides meeting where he and the accountant presented a new proposal for cost cutting. This met a good deal of resistance from us, with Corey taking the toughest stance, and as a result he found himself out of favor with management.

He wasn't fired; he simply stopped receiving trips, only getting work when the office had no other option. In order to make some money, Corey moved out to Bujagali, where he helped Milo to run the bar and do other odd jobs. He also began teaching kayak courses to tourists staying at the campsite.

With Corey out of town, it was up to me to get our money for the coffee. I had a couple of meetings with Samo at Al's bar when he wasn't out exterminating enemies of the State. Each time, he assured me that the money was coming and that we needed to be patient. I wanted to believe him, both because he was a nice guy with a big smile who really liked us, but also because he had hands the size of dinner plates and killed people for a living.

One day I called his mobile phone, and he told me to come around to his apartment. The address was for a rundown allotment in the inner city. Three blocks of neglected apartment buildings stood in a large U shape. A group of women were washing clothing in some buckets, and I asked them if they knew where Samo lived. They didn't know and didn't appreciate that I was there asking questions. I tried his mobile again, but it was either switched off or had no coverage.

A man was sitting on a flight of battered steps that led up to the apartments. I gave him a couple of cigarettes and asked him if he knew Samo. He pointed to another set of stairs leading down into some form of subterranean basement. I descended with care in the gloomy light and found myself in a passage leading off in two directions, apartment doors spaced at regular intervals on one side of the wall.

I heard voices behind the first door, so I knocked on it. A man opened the door and looked at me with amusement. The harsh sound of a cheap radio filled the passage. He said something in the local language to the people in the room behind him, and there was loud laughter. I asked him if he knew where Samo lived and his face lost some of its mirth. He came out into the corridor and pointed to the left.

"The number nineteen is the one you seek," he said, and then he stepped back into his apartment and closed the door.

There was no light in the passage, and I moved carefully, counting the doors as I progressed. By the time I located what I thought was number nineteen, I could only find the doors by feeling along the wall. I knocked on the rough wooden surface and then I was momentarily blinded by the sudden light from the open door.

"Adams!" said Samo, and he dragged me into the tiny apartment.

He seemed overjoyed to have a mazungu in his home. Around a circular table sat five other people, and room was made for me with some shuffling of chairs. Samo poured me a shot of rum and began to talk of inconsequential matters, and I wondered how to bring up the subject of money without getting killed in awful ways. The only item of value in the room appeared to be a beautiful Glock handgun that sat among bottles, cards, and pieces of fruit in the center of the table.

The room stank of stale sweat, cigarettes, and alcohol. One of the women present stared at me as she absentmindedly rubbed herself. Samo kept talking, and we had another drink. He began to shift in his chair, his gaze darting around the room, and I sensed that the initial novelty at my appearance was wearing thin.

I suddenly became very humorous and companionable, slapping people on the shoulder and pouring rum so that it overflowed from the cheap glasses, soaking into the soft fruit lying on the table. The big man smiled and nodded his head, drinking the rum with cool abandon and smiling at my antics, but giving no hint of any desire to speak to me in private. I became acutely aware that this was not a good place for me to be, and the mood in the room shifted as the others became aware as well.

I stood up from the table and told Samo I had to be going. He expressed displeasure at this news, but added that he would see me out as he got up and tucked the gun in his pants. I left the others huddled around the table, their eyes watching me, the same woman still rubbing herself as she ate the fruit soaked with rum.

I stayed close to Samo in the darkness until we arrived at the soft illumination at the stairwell. I asked him about the money. He smiled and said that it would be some time as they were having trouble selling the coffee, and as he said this he shifted the gun in his pants and smiled again. I decided that I didn't care any more about the money and left him there in the passageway. As I climbed out into the day, the light dazzled my senses, and I breathed out slowly as I walked away, a cold feeling in my lower back where I imagined a gun might be sighted.

18

Milo spun the wheel as the Landrover slid on the muddy roads, narrowly missing a couple of men pushing a fridge strapped to a bicycle.

"Something I've been meaning to tell you," he said to me. "If you can keep it to yourself."

"I'll put it in the vault."

"Good. I'm buying up all the major access points on the river."

"Why's that?" I said. I had trouble understanding why this would be a sound idea.

"Because I'm setting up a new rafting company." He seemed delighted that he could finally tell someone.

"Have you got a name?" I asked.

"Equator Rafting."

"Not bad. I like it. So that means you're buying up all the access points to literally control access to the river."

"Fiendish, isn't it?"

"Who's your partner?"

"A local Indian guy who owns a bank." He told me the name.

"Can you trust him?"

"Probably not, but I've set it up so he doesn't have to do anything, he makes a lot of money, and he can't do without me."

I saw two policemen standing in the middle of the road and waving at us. "Looks like they've got guns," I said, and Milo agreed that stopping was the superior option.

They looked friendly and desperate. "Mazungus!" they exclaimed.

"What can we do for you, boys?" Milo said.

"Ah mazungus," said one, "it is very bad. This man, he is a very bad man. He has beaten his wife and she might even die. But he has escaped and we must follow him, but we do not have the vehicles."

Milo and I exchanged a glance. "Get in!" we said, and the two policeman climbed into the open rear seats. I politely pushed aside the barrel of a machinegun that was sticking in the back of my head, and its owner apologized profusely. Milo gunned the engine and we careened up the road, reveling in our new status as official police pursuit vehicle.

"Is this a car chase?" I asked, catching Milo's eye, and we began chanting, "Car chase! Car chase! Car chase!" while bouncing up and down in our seats. The cops became very excited and cheered and bounced up and down as well until we all ran out of steam and one of them admitted that it was not, in fact, a car chase.

Milo and I were a little disappointed. "Well, is it a motorbike chase?" I said, and Milo and I resumed our excited chanting once again, our passengers joining us for a second time, until eventually they confirmed that it was also not a motorbike chase.

We passed a boda-boda bicycle, its owner pedaling his passenger up the hill at a speed not much greater than walking pace. "It's not a bicycle chase, is it?" Milo asked. We did not chant at this point as we were not at all excited at the thought of a lowly bicycle chase. The policemen did their best to assure us that this was not the case, until eventually they admitted that in fact we were in pursuit of someone escaping on pedal power.

There were many boda-boda bicycles on the road. As we approached each one from behind, one of the policemen got to a standing position and gave a rushed commentary that we had most certainly this time found the culprit, only for them to change their minds as we pulled alongside each passenger perched precariously on the rear seat.

This went on for a few kilometers until one of the policemen pointed at a distant bicycle, the swaying passenger anxiously scanning the road behind him.

"That is the one! Yes, it is him. He is the very bad man."

Milo stepped down on the accelerator and pulled neatly into the bike's path. The man on the pedals looked at us in alarm as the cops jumped out and pointed their weapons at his passenger. The criminal slumped in defeat.

"Ah, they have got me," he groaned.

The policemen thanked us for our assistance, and we drove away from the scene. "You know who I feel sorry for? said Milo. "The poor old boda-boda rider there. He peddled his guts out up and down these hills, only for his fare to be arrested before he can pay."

I pointed at the surrounding jungle. "It wasn't really the best escape plan though, was it? Jump on a boda-boda and get peddled down the road at walking pace. Why didn't he just run into the forest?"

"It's crazy, I know," Milo agreed. "They'd have never found him in there. And now he gets to go to Luzira prison—average life expectancy three months. That's what you get for trying to kill your wife."

The bar at Bujagali was empty that night, so Milo and I got stuck into his beer stocks under the light of a brilliant full moon. The askari guard sat slumped in a corner, his gun across his chest. Corey was spending time in Kampala with a flight attendant he had seduced.

"I've never fired an AK47," I said to Milo.

"I've never fired a gun," he said in turn.

"Do you reckon he'd let us use it?"

"We can only ask." Milo staggered over to the guard. "Hey sebo, can we use your gun to shoot the fish?"

The guard stirred and sat up. "Oh no, Mr. Milo. That is most very bad."

"I'll give you a beer," Milo said, and the guard broke down and agreed.

I removed the cork plug from the end of the barrel as we walked down to the edge of the river. "Do you think this is a good idea?" I said as I slipped the catch to single fire.

Milo snorted. "Is anything we do in Africa a good idea?"

I squared up and pulled the trigger. I saw a half-circle of stars and the recoil threw me to the side. Milo grabbed the gun and had a shot as well, and then we passed the gun back and forth, taking turns to shoot while hysterical with laughter. The guard became worried and begged us to stop, but he shut up after Milo told him to take another beer. We finished the clip and staggered back to the bar, where we proceeded to drink ourselves into a coma. I had just enough foresight to crawl into bed beneath my mosquito net.

The next morning I discovered Milo asleep in his chair at the bar. I made some coffee and the smell roused him from his slumber. I had a rafting trip, and leaving him to his hangover, I walked up the long hill to where the bus would arrive.

"You look like shit," Noah said as he stepped off the bus.

"Yeah, it was a big night," I muttered.

I did the trip and returned to the campsite in the late afternoon. Milo cracked me a beer and we settled into the deep armchairs overlooking the falls.

"Had a visit from the local police chief this morning," he said.

"Oh yeah?"

"Wanted to thank us for our help catching the criminal yesterday."

"That's nice of him."

Milo drank deeply. "Then he asked me if I had any idea who tried to kill the fishermen last night."

"Oh no," I said.

"Oh, yes. Apparently they were all out getting a midnight catch with the full moon when bullets started zipping over their heads. Seems they had to huddle in the bottom of their canoes for quite a while until the shooting stopped."

I contemplated this news. "Do they have any idea who they're looking for?"

"None at all, but I am keeping an eye out for suspicious people."

"That's good of you."

"They'll be making me an honoree copper soon."

The next day I had another trip, and when I returned, Milo proudly showed me a new stereo he had purchased for the bar.

"Where on earth did you find this?" I said. Locating decent electronic equipment in the country was near impossible.

"I had my feelers out. I've been looking for one for ages."

A few hours later an overland truck arrived, resulting in a night of dancing and cavorting in the bar to the groovy tunes emanating from Milo's new acquisition. But as drunk as he was, Milo still had enough sense to remove the stereo at the end of the night and lock it in his banda hut. Corey was still away, and Milo had to return to Kampala for a few days, so I agreed to mind the bar for him. This involved me lazing by the river, drinking beer and eating cooked food, while listening to music and watching the world go by. Each night I took care to secure the stereo in Milo's little hut.

The last morning before Milo's return found me enjoying a quiet coffee in the early hours before the arrival of day-trippers and hangers-on. The cook cluttered in the back, muttering to himself as he banged pots and pans. The manager of Milo's work crew entered the bar. He was dressed in his customary bright blue suit and was rubbing his hands together in a nervous manner.

"Morning, Raymond," I said.

"Oh Mr. Adams, we have a very big trouble," he said.

"Can this problem wait until I've finished my coffee?" I asked.

He shook his head. "I am most grieved to tell you that this problem is of so large a nature that your coffee must be interrupted."

"You have my full attention, Raymond," I said.

He drew in a deep breath. "Thieves have stolen the radio of Mr. Milo."

"Oh, fucking hell," I said, getting to my feet. I hurried up the hill towards the banda huts, Raymond trying to keep up with me. A small group of workers with downcast faces stood around Milo's hut. The thieves had cut the chicken wire on the window and reached in to open the door, and it occurred to me that the security measures were somewhat inadequate. I instructed Raymond to gather all the employees and bring them down to the bar, where I would question each of them in turn. He clapped his hands and issued the instructions, and the young men scattered to do his bidding.

I got another coffee and sat in the bar. Raymond and the askari guard brought the first lad to me.

"This is Moses," Raymond said, not unkindly.

"Good morning, Moses," I said.

"Good morning Mr. Adams," he mumbled. His glance darted back and forth between me and the askari guard standing to the side holding his machinegun with the cork stuck in the barrel.

"Where were you last night?" I asked him.

"In the village."

"Did you come down to the camp?"

He shook his head.

"Did you see anyone come down to the camp?"

He shook his head again.

"Do you know who came down to the camp to steal the stereo?"

I kept my eyes locked on him, and he meekly raised his head and shook it a final time. I looked up at Raymond. "Well, that's all I've got," I said.

"A most excellent line of questioning, Mr. Adams," he said.

"Are you sure? It seemed pretty rubbish to me."

"Oh no," he assured me. "I am certain Moses is telling the truth."

I eyed the downcast face. "Are we allowed to use torture?" I asked.

Raymond shook his head. "I am of the opinion that this is not permissible."

Moses now looked very nervous indeed. I told him to go and he hurried away. The rest of the interrogations followed a similar line. It was hopeless and I knew it, but I felt I had to be proactive in solving this problem. Milo was due out later, and I didn't want to tell him that I had been sitting around all day after finding his stereo missing.

I decided to report the theft to the local police unit. After instructing Raymond to keep everyone at the camp, I walked up to the main road and hailed a boda-boda bicycle. My rider struggled along the dirt road for a few miles until we arrived at a small group of mud huts.

"This is the policemen's house," he told me.

"Are you sure?" I said. He nodded enthusiastically. "All right, wait for me here." I walked inside, where a policeman in a tattered uniform looked at me in surprise. I asked to see the chief.

"Ah, Mr. Adams, you are the associate of Mr. Milo," said a jolly looking round man with a cap on his head. "I am the chief of this police station."

I shook his hand and began to tell him about the theft. The chief held up a hand and lead me to the next hut. There was a man sitting at a small desk.

"This is my top detective," the chief said. "You can make your report with him."

The detective indicated for me to sit on the other side of the desk. I sat down while he readied himself with pen and notepad.

"Mazungu, what is your name?"

I told him my name, and he wrote it carefully on the sheet of paper.

"And tell me, mazungu, in your own words, what has happened."

I began recounting the morning's events, but noticing his careful motion with the pen, I slowed my speech so he would be able to keep up. He motioned impatiently, so I went ahead for a few minutes until I noticed that his hand was still writing at the top of the page. I leaned forward to see what he had written.

'I, Mr adams, did put streo in hut banda. Because I go to bed, by myself, it is dark the night and maybe a little cold.'

"Is that all you've got?" I said.

The detective curled his arm protectively around his notepad. "Please be continuing," he said with a defensive tone.

"Oh, come on," I said. "We're going to be here all day at this rate. Just give it to me and I'll write it for you."

"No, no!" he protested. "I am the very good writer! You tell me the facts, mazungu, and I will write it."

"You've got to be joking."

"Mazungu, I be writing much better than you."

I looked around. "Is this some weird form of Ugandan candid camera?"

He held his pen poised in the air. "Please talk now, mazungu, and I will write the facts."

"You couldn't write a shopping list."

We went back and forth in a similar manner for a little while until the policeman eyed me for a moment, and then he leaned back in his chair, a sinister smile on his face. "Ah, mazungu," he said with great calmness. "You thought that you were a clever mazungu. But I am the top detective, and the truths cannot be hidden from this one. You do not deceive me."

"What the fuck are you on about?" I said.

He pointed at me across the desk. "You are the thief!"

A great fury rose inside me, and I launched myself across the desk, my hands latching on to his jacket as I picked him up off the chair and threw him against the wall. The chief and his deputies rushed into the room and pulled me off their companion as I heaped scorn on his abilities. The detective needed a moment to recover from his shock, but eventually he began to scream accusations of murder at me, continuing until the chief told him to shut up and get out of his sight. He hurried away without another word.

"I am sorry for that one," the chief said. "He has only just been made the detective, and perhaps he is lacking in some of the experience. Shall I get you another detective?"

I declined his offer. I figured I'd probably pushed my luck as far as it would hold. I thanked the chief for his help, and he waved me goodbye as my rider peddled me back down the road.

There was a mood of despondency at the campsite when I returned. The staff sat around the bar, their sad faces reflecting their precarious situation. Milo had left me with a mobile phone for emergencies, and I decided to use it to tell him what had happened.

"Dude, how's it going?" he said. "I'm on my way out now."

I could hear the sound of him driving in the background. "Not so good," I said. "It seems that someone stole the stereo."

There was a brief moment of awful silence. "I'll fucking kill the lot of them," he said and hung up the phone.

"Raymond looked at me with sad eyes. "What did he say?"

"You guys are fucked."

"Mr. Adams, I did not tell you this before, but we are worried for our jobs."

"No shit."

"I also did not tell you that we wish to hire a most famous witchdoctor to help us find the thief."

The events of the day continued their peculiar turn. "You're getting a witchdoctor?"

"With your permissions. We will only get this most famous medicine man with your permissions. He is very expensive, but we have collected the money from all the workers."

"How much does he cost?" I asked.

"Forty thousand shillings."

I whistled in admiration, the sum being more than the average monthly wage. I dreaded the thought of Milo's reaction when I told him I had ordered a witchdoctor, but their need was greater than my potential embarrassment.

"How long will it take to get him here?"

"We must organize a matatu to make the journey as he lives near the Kenya. It would be perhaps four hours in total."

I looked at my watch. "You better get moving then."

An hour or so later, Milo's Land Rover puttered into view. He got out and came over to where we were standing, his face unnervingly calm.

"Where'd they steal it from?"

"Your hut," I said.

Milo, Raymond, and I walked up the hill. "Have you interrogated them all?" he asked.

"Yeah, I did that. I also went down to the local police hut to report it."

He looked at me in surprise. "What did you do that for? They're just a bunch of buffoons."

"So I discovered."

We got to the hut and waited while Milo surveyed the damage. "Any ideas on who did it?"

"I don't know," I said. "The askari; the kid who cleans the huts in the morning; they'd be my best bet."

"Godfrey cleans the huts, and he has a key. He's also just smart enough to stage the theft by cutting the wire, but too dumb not to realize that we'd pick that up as well. Is he here?"

"He is still here," Raymond said.

"Good. I'll interview someone else first then."

"Don't be too hard on them, Milo," I said.

He turned towards me, and I realized just how angry he was. "Everyone told me not to hire the people from the local villages around this area. They warned me that they're notorious for being thieves. But I gave them a chance. I've given them too many chances. And this is how they repay me."

Raymond had gathered all the workers in front of a fire burning in a small pit. To the side was a shed used for storing tools. Milo selected a young man at random and told him to go and wait in the shed. The young man followed the directions while casting anxious glances over his shoulder.

Milo waited until he had closed the door, and then he selected a burning piece of wood from the fire, smacked it around a few times to extinguish the flames, and then strode over to the shed. He slammed the door shut behind him, and there commenced the most dreadful cacophony of bangs and shouts and screams of terror, until the shed door burst open and the terrified teenager fled up the hill and out of sight.

Half of the workers took off in every direction, their heads down and their arms pumping the air. The askari guard didn't know where to turn first, his gun held impotently in his hands. Raymond and I exchanged a worried glance. Milo emerged frothing at the mouth and threw the piece of wood back on the fire. What remained of the staff viewed him with supreme apprehension.

I stepped forward and spoke with my voice low. "Jesus Christ, Milo. You can't go beating the locals with burning bits of wood."

He assured me of his total dedication to the new art of flaming stick beating, and his voice rose as he began a torrent of abuse at his employees, the locals, and Africa in general. I remained silent until he ran out of steam.

"Did the kid tell you who did it?" I asked.

"Of course not. I asked if it was Charles and he said it was indeed Charles. Then I asked if it was Moses and he said that Moses was certainly the one."

"Well, if you can't get them to tell you who did it when you're beating them with bits of flaming wood, then I don't like your chances."

"I didn't really beat him with the wood. It was just for show to get this lot here shitting in their pants."

Further questioning proved fruitless, however. Either Milo's demonstration had all been for naught, or they truly didn't know the identity of the thief. At a certain point Milo gave in and announced he would sack everybody and start all over again with a new workforce. A murmur of discontent spread through the group and I decided the time was right to inform Milo of our cunning plan.

"There is one thing I haven't told you about," I said with some reluctance. Milo looked at me with suspicious interest. The remaining staff members hung on my words. I forced myself to say it. "There is the witchdoctor."

Milo was looking at me as if I were a total idiot. "Are you shitting me?"

"No, um...it was your employees' idea. They pooled their money to get the witchdoctor to find out who the thief is. They sent a matatu to get him." I looked at my watch. "He should be here in the next half hour or so."

"You're kidding me, aren't you? Tell me this is a fucking joke."

I sighed. "I wish it was. Come to think of it, I wish I could go back to bed and start this day again with no thief. But they're serious about it. They spent forty thousand shillings."

Milo was impressed and turned to Raymond. "How good is this witchdoctor?"

"Oh, Mr. Milo, he is the most very best and most respected witchdoctor in all of East Uganda. Why even the peoples from the Kenya use him in times of need."

"Well, that's good," Milo said in a calm tone. "If I'm going to get a witchdoctor then I want him to be the best witchdoctor on the market."

"So you're cool with the witchdoctor idea?" I said.

"Dude, what have we got to lose? Stranger shit has happened, so we might as well give it a shot. I still think you're a total moron though."

We saw a matatu arrive at the top of the hill, and Milo sent Raymond to keep the witchdoctor isolated from the staff. By this stage, most of the workers who'd run away had returned, and a large crowd was forming as word had got out about the famous witchdoctor arriving. We walked up the hill, and Raymond presented us to the witchdoctor.

He was a shriveled old man of indeterminate age. He had a shock of very white hair and a beard, and he wore a well-cared for brown three piece suit. In his hand was an old fashioned brown suitcase with a clasp tied around the middle. He shook our hands, showing a broad smile of perfect white teeth. I liked him at once, and even Milo was disarmed enough to fashion a dopey grin.

We led him over to the crime scene, the large crowd following in our wake. I showed him the broken netting on the door and he carefully inspected each detail. The little children in the crowd watched in solemn abandon; I'd never seen them so quiet. The witchdoctor set down his suitcase and undid the clasp. The crowd watched. He undid the fastenings with a click and opened the lid.

A chicken stuck out its head and gave a nervous cluck. The witchdoctor grabbed it by the neck and cut off its head with a single movement. I hadn't even seen the knife.

"What is this guy, a ninja?" Milo whispered.

We stood at the door, careful not to intrude into the space. A horde of faces pressed against the windows, and those in front relayed information to the waiting crowd behind. The witchdoctor began to dance around the room, jerking from one point to another, the chicken's neck in his hand spurting blood in a random pattern. Milo muttered about not being able to get the blood out of the mattress, but I told him he could name the hut as "The Witchdoctor", and he seemed happier.

The witchdoctor discarded the chicken when its blood was exhausted, and then he kneeled down in front of his suitcase once more. I stretched forward and saw a variety of little cloth bags. The old man took his time selecting the required items, his small hands darting forward to empty a bag when his decision was made. Bark, spices, berries, leaves, roots, and other unidentifiable items were thrown around the room in no discernible pattern.

The witchdoctor began to chant words in a weird language, and Milo and I looked around in surprise as the crowd of spectators began to murmur in unison. The witchdoctor retrieved the chicken and began a strange and erratic dance, his body jerking from one corner of the room to the other. He leaped on the bed with his arms spread in wonder, swept low in a circle on the floor, and then he moaned and shrieked words of power that reverberated with his audience, sending them into a hypnotic dance that mirrored his own. I watched a child of not more than five years jerk and dance and windmill his arms, his face slack, his eyes rolled back, and his feet a tiny cascade of drumming steps. The chicken's neck began to spurt blood once more.

And then with no warning the witchdoctor stopped and stood rigid and mute in the center of the room, and the entire audience fell silent as one. The stillness of the moment felt like a terrible burden after the preceding cacophony. The chicken fell to the ground with a small sound, and the witchdoctor leaped to the raw earth and pressed the side of his face into the floor, studying the carcass with intense observation, and then he pirouetted in a complete circle, his head glued to the one spot as he kept the chicken in view.

And then he got to his feet, brushed away the debris from his suit and asked if he might have a cup of tea. Milo sent one of his workers flying down to the bar to meet this request. The witchdoctor motioned for us to approach, and we moved towards him with Raymond in tow.

"It is a most very nice banda hut, and I am so sorry for the mess," he said.

We assured him of the unimportance of his concern. He motioned for us to come closer.

"The one you seek, he is not young, but not so old. Perhaps still to become a man. He is tall for his people, but very thin. He lives very close to the crime, perhaps at the closest village. And I see the color blue. I do not know if it is what he wears or something else, but blue I do see."

Milo and I looked at each other. "Godfrey," we agreed. It was the young man who cleaned the huts.

"Where does he live?" I asked Raymond.

"In the village at the crossroads."

"The closest village," Milo said.

The witchdoctor stood smiling with his hands hanging by his side. Raymond walked to the door and addressed the waiting crowd. "Where is Godfrey?" he announced, but Godfrey was nowhere to be seen.

The village was a short distance down the road and we marched there to confront the accused, the large crowd in tow. We met the police chief halfway there as he had come down to see how the investigation was progressing.

"Mr. Milo, so very good to see you," he said, and then he spotted me and a big smile came over his face. "Ah, the lunatic." He turned back to Milo. "I have heard that you have the services of a most powerful witchdoctor. Is this true?"

Milo assured him that he was correct while taking credit for this cunning turn of events. The chief was very impressed at our wisdom and pronounced us the finest mazungus that he had ever known. By now the crowd was very large indeed, and there was an almost carnival atmosphere as we descended on the unsuspecting village. Milo, Raymond, the police chief, the witchdoctor, and I were all in the front row, and children danced and skipped at the edges as the crowd lumbered along the narrow dirt road.

We came to Godfrey's hut, and the crowd halted in anticipation. Raymond reached forward and knocked on the door. It opened, and a middle aged woman peered out and then jumped back with shock. Raymond conversed quickly with her in the local tongue while the crowd stood in the background. The woman tried to put up some argument against our presence, but she had no chance of halting the inevitable, and Raymond signaled for Milo and me to begin the search.

"I will keep his mother outside," he told us. "Godfrey is not here."

The hut consisted of two rooms, and we stood in the first one, our heads bowed due to the lack of space. There was a bed against the wall, and Milo lifted the mattress only to jump back, his body pushing me into the police chief.

"Ah, Mr. Adams—not more assaults against the police?"

I apologized and asked Milo what the problem was.

"Dude, there's a bloody great cobra under the bed!"

I craned my neck forward, and the cobra hissed and spat in our direction. Milo and I rushed out of the hut while Raymond and the police chief ushered the snake outside with a stick. The crowd broke into fits of laughter when they discovered that the mazungus were afraid of a lowly cobra, and they continued to laugh as they beat the snake to death.

We re-entered the hut with some caution, and Milo pushed me forward to look under the bed. Godfrey's mother stood watching us in silence, her arms folded and her face an expressionless mask. Beneath the mattress we found a history of petty thievery, a small horde of almost worthless items pilfered from clients and guides. Amongst the booty we recognized Corey's missing waist-bag. The police chief grilled Godfrey's mother as we collected the loot, and she eventually broke down and revealed that her son had fled a short time before our arrival, the stereo in his possession.

"What now?" I asked Milo.

"I reckon we've pushed this as far as we can," he said. "We won't see Godfrey again, he'd be nuts to come back here, but we might find the stereo in a secondhand shop. I'll just have to keep an eye out for it."

"We could pursue the thief," the police chief suggested.

"Let me guess," Milo said. "On a boda-boda bicycle?"

"He would be caught very soon."

"I think we'll give it a miss. I've done enough chasing after Godfrey to last me a lifetime."

Raymond approached me while they were talking. "Mr. Adams, the witchdoctor is telling me of his other services that he has for sale."

"What other services?" I said.

"He can be putting a curse on the boy."

Milo stepped forward. "What kind of curse?"

"There is the one with the boils that fester on the legs until he can walk no more."

"Perhaps it would be better to talk about this over here," I said, steering the group away from Godfrey's mother. The witchdoctor went through a list of various ailments that he was capable of afflicting on the accused.

Milo wasn't satisfied. "It's nice and all, don't get me wrong," he said. "Nothing like a good attack of leprosy to put someone off nicking your stuff. But haven't you got anything stronger?"

"What kind of strong do you mean?" Raymond asked.

"What is the strongest possible curse that he can do?"

The witchdoctor stepped forward. "I can place the curse of living death, and in three days full death will occur to the accused."

"As opposed to partial death," I said.

"But it is very expensive," Raymond said.

The witchdoctor agreed. "The most expensive curse possible."

"How much?" Milo said.

"Sixty thousand shillings," the witchdoctor informed us.

Milo turned to me. "What's that? About forty dollars?"

"About that."

"That'll do," Milo said, turning back to the witchdoctor. "We'll have one curse of three day death please."

We walked back down to the campsite where the witchdoctor drank his cup of tea. I mentioned to him that I had a problem with my knee, and he assured me of his power to concoct a remedy, but in the end my courage failed me, and I muttered something about using his powers the next time he was out this way.

After he performed the curse he got back into the waiting matatu, and we waved him goodbye. Milo and I headed down to the bar for a much needed drink while the staff scurried back to work. We commented with some cynicism on their sudden work ethic.

"You don't really think that Godfrey is going to drop dead in three days, do you?" I said.

Milo laughed. "Of course not." He pointed to his employees. "But they do."

19

Corey found himself back in favor with the management and returned to work with us in Kampala. This was timely for him as he had been reduced to taking photos of the rafting trips to make a living. The hardest part had been trying to wrangle a fair deal out of the Indian guys who owned the main photo shop in Kampala. Rajal, the main man in the shop, developed a close relationship with the rafting company through these photos, and he arranged to sell our very popular t-shirts through his shop as well.

After a few days back in the house Corey came to me with some issues. "Since when do mosquito girls live in the house?" he said.

He had a point. Eddie had a semi-regular mosquito girl as his main squeeze, and we tolerated her presence in the house, even though we weren't comfortable with it. Thus far nothing had gone missing, but we kept a wary eye at all times.

But the real problem concerned Dave's behavior. His usual world-weary and cynical view had become darker, and he was taking more solace than usual in rum, drugs, and women. As we sat at breakfast, it was not unusual for us to be greeted to the sight of two girls emerging from his room, their fishnet stockings in disarray, high heels tottering on the tiled floor. These were hardcore working girls, and Dave seemed determined to sample and abuse as many as possible.

"Do you know that he doesn't use a rubber when he's with them?" Corey told me.

"Bloody hell," I muttered. "Tell me he hasn't slept with the one who signs her name 'HIV positive' on the chalk board at Al's."

"It's like he's on some kind of death wish. I don't know what we can do to help him, but I don't like having those sorts of girls in the house."

Dave was also becoming more abrasive with the rafting customers. His direct contact with the clients was minimal, but whenever they did chance across his path, I found myself holding my breath at his possible reaction. He was scathing of the tourists' ignorance of the harsh reality of their surroundings, and he was bitter at the increasing likelihood of approval for a dam on the section of river where we worked.

"I hate thinking of this river drowning," he admitted to me one day, and he began rambling about it turning into a long stagnant lake, the tops of skeletal trees poking sadly from the waters in whose branches red-tailed monkeys now sat and played. He knew that the possibility of electricity for the river villages was a pipe dream, and he despised them for not comprehending the impending destruction of their way of life.

These things disturbed him, yet when he tried to express his thoughts the words came out disjointed. The true meaning of what he needed to say was lost in his confronting manner and desperation to communicate. He came across as intense, hasty, unconnected, and aloof. People smiled and nodded and found an excuse to be somewhere else leaving him struggling alone in his isolated world, not knowing what was needed to change about himself and incapable of any act necessary for such a change.

The Kampala Races were held every September, but with goats instead of horses. Corey and I went along to see the fun with Jane, our English marketing girl. We tried to talk Dave into coming but he was supremely disinterested. Unlike the rest of the office staff, Jane was perfectly capable—and sometimes all too willing—of keeping up with our decadent social life. We sometimes had to rescue her from getting into too much trouble. Her other outlet for punishment was her determination to learn how to kayak, a hobby which resulted in some horrendous swims on the unforgiving White Nile.

The day was hot with a cloudless sky. The site of the races was a large field close to the city center, and I surveyed the small oval track with some doubt as to its capacity to cater for such an event. There were a large number of hospitality tents and the cream of Ugandan society mingled in their best race fashions. Corey inspected the race program as we waited for the first race to begin. Beside us stood an older English gentleman dressed in a remarkable safari suit, which from his manner and bearing did not seem intended as fancy dress.

The announcer's voice boomed and crackled over the crowd as he introduced each goat's sponsor for the first race. A group of little Ugandan boys led the goats, each boy and goat wearing corresponding numbered bibs. I noticed that the boys were carrying long thick sticks, and I wondered aloud as to their purpose. Jane wondered if she could borrow a stick to get through to the bar.

"I think it's for the kid to hit the goat," Corey said.

"Why would he want to hit the goat?" I asked.

"I suppose to get it to go faster. Haven't you seen jockeys using a whip on a horse?"

We stared over at the starting line. "Are you trying to tell us," Jane said, "that those kids are going to ride on the back of the goats?"

The English gentleman turned and addressed us. "It's quite simple really; each jockey is required to chase his goat around the track to the finish line. He uses the stick to keep the goat in line."

"Are you serious?" I asked him.

"Quite."

"Well there you go," Corey said. "Maybe I should be looking at the boys more than the goats when I place a bet."

"I always do," said the gentleman as he sipped from a glass of champagne.

By this stage the field for the first race was in place, and with a bang the starting gate crashed open. The group of goats leaped forward as each jockey began a mad thrashing with his stick. The crowd cheered and cried as the goats came around the track, but soon problems began to emerge. One goat came to a halt at a particularly delicious patch of grass and munched away, oblivious to the desperate blows raining on its back. The lead goat was doing well until it was brought down by a goat attempting to mount it from behind, its startled jockey just getting out of the way in time.

The spectators bayed and yelled, arms waving, bodies jumping, drinks spilling, as the leading goat came around the final bend, its jockey struggling to keep up. The crowd roared encouragement as the winner shot past the posts and a cloud of dust settled over us as the stragglers trotted home.

"So what do you think of our little event?" the gentleman said.

"It's like the last bastion of white colonialism," I joked.

He regarded me for a moment with disparaging eyes. "I have no idea what you're talking about," he said, and he turned away.

One day Dave announced his intention to get an AIDS test from Doc Clark. We went to Doc Clark whenever we had personal medical issues. An Irishman who had been living in Uganda for many years, he kept a clean and professional clinic in the heart of the city. I suffered from foot sores for my first few months in the country, and all of the guides had frequent malarial attacks. Thanks to my obsession with wearing long clothes at night and always sleeping under a mosquito net, I never came down with the mosquito-borne virus. At times I helped nurse my colleagues through the three days of malaria delirium, an experience which always helped to justify my obsessive concerns.

We drove him into the city and waited for him to finish the procedure. He came out and got in the pickup.

"Well?" Scott said.

"It's going to take a few weeks," he replied, his face staring straight ahead. He was quiet on the short trip home, perhaps the inevitability of his fate weighing on his mind.

"I'm not going to Al's Bar anymore," he said as we walked in the door. "I'm not going to any bars at all." He went to his room and we looked at each other with disbelief.

"I'll believe this when I see it," Noah said.

But Dave was true to his word. He cut back on his drinking and he began an exercise routine. He even attempted to be more sympathetic to the customers, engaging them in conversation and only reacting with condescension at the most extreme provocation.

The day of his tests results arrived. He left after breakfast, a nervous smile on his now healthy face, and we waited at home with a sense of foreboding. At last we heard the pickup come to a stop outside the window where we were sitting at the dining table. Nobody spoke as the car door slammed and his footsteps sounded across the yard. He strode into the dining room and tossed a large envelope on the table.

"Are you going to tell us?" Scott said.

Dave seemed distant and out of place as if he were in a bad dream. "Negative," he said with a flat tone.

"Negative?" Scott was incredulous.

"Yep, fucking negative."

I didn't say a word. Corey picked up the results. "So, that's good then," he said carefully. "You've slept with every hooker at Al's and Capitol Pub and you didn't get AIDS."

"Some kind of superman," Eddie mumbled.

Dave managed a laugh. "Yeah, yeah... I mean, who would have though it possible? It doesn't seem possible..."

"You dodged a bullet," I said.

"He dodged a missile more like it," Corey said, laughing.

Noah stood up from the table. "Well, shit, there you go. You haven't got AIDS, you're not dying. I think this is a momentous occasion, and I plan on joining the spirit of celebration."

"What do you have in mind?" Dave said.

"I'm going to follow your example. I'm going to burn all my pot. That's it—I'm not smoking the shit anymore."

We met his announcement with ridicule, but he instructed us to go to the upstairs veranda and watch. We grabbed a few beers and seated ourselves with a nice view of the garden. Noah marched back and forth from the house, emerging every now and then with some dope which he dumped on the back lawn. It grew into a pile as he scoured the house for places where he might have left a forgotten stash. Finally he positioned himself next to his hoard, struck a match, and tossed it onto the green mound. He grinned up at us as we cheered, and then he danced a little jig around the disturbingly large bonfire as narcotic clouds of smoke settled over the neighborhood.

Later in the afternoon I heard a motorcycle at the gate, and I looked out the window to see Noah negotiating the purchase of a packet of pre-rolled dope cigarettes with one of the local boda-boda boys. And a few days later we were coming home from a rafting trip when Dave instructed Isaac to stop outside Al's Bar, and he got off the bus and walked across the road without a word. I awoke in the late night to the sounds of him escorting a girl to his room.

Cheating death seemed to cause a great bewilderment in Dave. Just when he thought he had pushed the boundary too far, he discovered that the goal posts had moved once again. A white person living in Uganda was not bound by normal societal rules, and it was too easy to lose all sense of perspective in attempting to discover how far the boundaries could be pushed.

The deeper he went, the closer he got to the unseen edge. We were aware of his crisis yet powerless to help or intervene. Words of comfort were wasted on Dave; he sneered at us over a glass of rum and belittled any attempts to understand him. I wanted to shake him, to somehow reach him, but nothing I thought of saying seemed appropriate.

One morning we were getting ready to leave for a rafting trip, but Dave had not yet emerged from his room. His sleeping quarters were in line with the main entrance and protected by a heavy iron cage. The cage and the door to his room were both locked. The windows were also behind impregnable iron bars and we couldn't see anything through the curtains. With increasing desperation we scoured the house for keys while a few of us attempted to batter open the sturdy door. In the end we called a locksmith, who took some time to unlock the room.

Dave was lying on his back, his arms and legs outstretched, his body resting on a tarpaulin sheet. Two empty bottles of rum and a plundered box of Valium lay scattered on the floor, but a quick check showed that he was still breathing, albeit at a very slow rate. We carried him to the bus and sped to the hospital where Doc Clark was awaiting our arrival.

Two days later, Dave was released and came back to the house. We'd managed to locate an expat psychologist, and he spent a few hours with Dave in the privacy of his bedroom. His diagnosis was plain; Dave needed to go straight back to New Zealand for professional care and support. But his family refused to foot the bill, and despite three years with the rafting company in Uganda, the company wasn't willing to help pay his way either.

Even we weren't able to help him. Too little work and too much high living had left us all broke. A ticket home for Dave was beyond our means.

Dave became a shadow that drifted on the periphery of our world. He was unfit for work but unable to leave. He was trapped in the house, trapped in Africa, and increasingly trapped in his own mind. We had trouble meeting his disturbed gaze, and we began sleeping behind locked doors.

One morning I walked through the office and onto the upstairs veranda. Dave was sitting in a chair, curled up in the fetal position, rocking back and forth as he moaned and cried. The office staff was at their desks, just meters from this scene, working away as if nothing were amiss. I shut the sliding door and demanded that they do something, anything to help the situation. But for them there was nothing more they could do, and Dave was just an inconvenient problem that everyone hoped would somehow sort itself out.

Jane was closest to Dave, and perhaps even secretly in love with him. She was instrumental in getting them both tickets to her home town of London. On the day they flew out, Corey and I said goodbye to them in downtown Kampala. Jane gave each of us a hug as Dave sat in the passenger seat of the car, his eyes staring straight ahead and twitching involuntarily at the nightmares that plagued him even in broad daylight. He was not able to respond to our attempts to wish him a safe journey. Dave never returned to Africa. A few years later I heard the news that he had taken his own life.

Dave's replacement arrived within weeks. Hendri was a young South African, barely out of his teens. He had a friendly face, a vibrant personality, and a deep sense of adventure, and he quickly joined Corey and me in our excursions of discovery around the city and the wider country.

After the period of darkness in which we had passed, Hendri's arrival did wonders to lift us out of feelings of gloom and guilt. It didn't hurt that he was a little wet behind the ears when it came to the subject of women, and we got great mileage out of his attempts to woo the teenage daughter of Al, particularly as Hendri was ignorant of the rumors of her father's past gangster status.

With the end of the millennium approaching we felt the New Year celebrations deserved a special event, and we organized a special two-day rafting expedition to which we invited all of our favorite customers, some of whom flew in from overseas for the trip. The first day ran as normal. I had a big flip in the hole at Total Gunga which I had christened "The G Spot", the only name of mine for a rapid that ever stuck. Hendri kayaked with us as he filmed our exploits for the trip video.

We continued on past the usual finish point, negotiating another large rapid and then a series of jungle-covered islands. One of these islands was our campsite for the evening and we arrived to see the local villagers ferrying across our supplies under Scott's direction. A large tarpaulin provided shade and shelter, and there was a fire-pit as well as ample supplies of food and drink. Each client's bag was waiting in a small pile, and all we had to do was erect the tents and get dinner started. Scott and Grace then drove back to Kampala for some forgotten supplies.

The tents were up, and we were preparing the food when one of the customers approached me and Corey with a concerned expression.

"One of my friends is not well at all," she said. "I think she had some of that cake."

"What cake?" I asked, and she pointed at a couple of chocolate cakes sitting innocently on a table. "Whose are those?" I said as Eddie walked within earshot.

"They're mine," he said with a natural casualness.

I told Corey to go with the woman and check on her friend, and then I took Eddie by the arm and steered him away from the group. "Tell me that those aren't mull cakes," I said.

"They're mull cakes, so what? It's like a little New Year's Eve present."

I was acutely aware of the lethal nature of Eddie's infamous baking skills, having had a few unpleasant experiences with his creations in the past. "Did you tell everyone what they are before you put them out?"

Eddie seemed completely disinterested in the conversation. "I told some of them."

"How strong are these fucking cakes?" I demanded.

"The dark one is normal. The white one is pretty strong."

I didn't want to contemplate what one of his pretty strong cakes might be like. I hurried up the hill to the tents to see how Corey was faring.

"She's totally out of it," Corey told me.

The attractive young woman moaned in a sort of delirium. "I've had hash cookies before," she mumbled, her head falling from one side to the other. "I thought I was used to it..."

"Not these cakes," I said. "Did you have the dark chocolate or the white one?"

"The white one..."

I turned to Corey. "That's what Eddie calls the strong one."

"Holy shit."

"He just stuck them out there without telling everyone."

"Will she be okay?" her friend asked.

"You're going to have to get her to vomit it up. Get some salty warm water down her."

I went back down the hill and called all the customers together for an impromptu meeting. I was furious that Eddie had created this situation and that it was up to me to sort it out.

"Right, this is a little tricky," I told the group. "These two cakes are of the marijuana variety. They're also pretty damn strong. Much stronger than you'd be used to."

"How strong?" one of them asked.

I broke off a very small section, not much more than a crumb, and held it up to them for inspection. "This will be enough to get most of you pretty well off your face. If any of you have had some of these cakes then I need to know now."

A tall and well-built Spanish man in his early thirties gave me a funny look and then he dropped to his knees. His eyes glazed and he toppled over slowly to one side. His wife grabbed at him in panic.

I squatted down next to them as the other customers stood in dumb silence. "How much has he eaten?" I asked his wife.

"Two pieces. Is this too much?" she pleaded.

"Oh he's fucked," Eddie muttered as he walked away.

"Who else has eaten some of this cake?" I shouted above the general uproar overtaking the camp.

Corey prepared some salty water and forced all those afflicted to drink the nauseating mix. People ran to the side of the island to throw up, retching uncontrollably on their hands and knees. Others remonstrated with me, demanding to know how such a thing could happen. Eddie was nowhere to be seen and I tried desperately to calm the crowd. Throughout it all our group of Ugandan workers sat transfixed by the absurdity of the panicking white people.

We served dinner a few hours later. Most of the customers had recovered, although the Spanish man still looked rather green. He sat by the fire gazing unseeing into its depths as his wife mechanically patted his arm while throwing baleful looks of hate at an uncaring Eddie. Then Corey came to me with the news that Eddie's mosquito-girlfriend was bullying the Ugandan staff. We were already upset at her presence on the trip as Eddie had broken an unwritten rule of not bringing mosquito girls to work related activities.

I told her that she had two available options: either she could start behaving and get it out of her head that she had any sort of status on this trip, or she could be ferried across to the mainland where she could make her own way home to Kampala.

Eddie jumped up to intervene. "You can't talk to my girlfriend like that!" he protested.

"I can when her behavior is affecting the trip," I replied. "Get her to stop bothering the help or she's off the island."

"You're just a fucking racist," he said.

"Oh, I'm a racist, am I?"

"Yeah, you heard. A fucking racist."

"What do I have to do to prove that I'm not a racist? Start fucking the locals?"

Corey and Noah intervened and calmed the situation, but I had a bad taste in my mouth not just from the unfair accusation but how Eddie's actions were jeopardizing the trip we had spent so long to pull together.

I drank some beer and we watched some local drummers and dancers perform for us, and eventually we toasted the new millennium as the moon shone over the waters of the White Nile.

20

Kate went back to New Zealand with rumors flying as to why she left her job. With Jane gone, only Tim was left to run the office, and this forced the owner to fly out to visit us and deal with the situation. Rajal from the photo shop approached him with a proposal to help with marketing, and the owner liked his proposal so much he promptly installed him as the new general manager of operations.

The first we heard about this startling development was at a meeting the day before the owner flew back to New Zealand. It was as much a shock for us as it must have been for Rajal. He made a short speech where he presented his new marketing ideas and promised a sharp uptake in work for all the guides.

After the meeting a few of us went down to Al's Bar for a drink and to talk things over. We were in complete agreement of the supreme averageness of the new marketing strategy. Rajal's biggest idea was to bribe various hotel cleaning staff to place flyers in the hotel rooms around town. His other ideas were either a complete waste of time or things that we had already come up with and were already doing.

We didn't see any evidence of the anticipated surge in customer numbers. We weren't surprised, but our new manager had tied our hands. With all the free time we had, we spent most of it hanging around the various backpackers and hotels, trying to drum up customers. What little time we spent at work showed that our new manager didn't understand either the rafting or general tourism industries. I mentioned this to Milo, and he laughed at our naivety.

"Dude, I'll tell you why Rajal wanted the marketing job. He wants access to the t-shirt sales. He's got contacts all through Kenya where the t-shirts are made. This is what I reckon is happening: he's telling the owner that he's ordered let's say one hundred t-shirts, but he's actually ordered maybe five hundred. Then he sells all the extra t-shirts through his photo shop, where he makes a huge profit. Rinse and repeat. The fact that he was given the role of general manager just makes it even more hilarious."

"It's not hilarious for us. He doesn't have a clue what he's doing."

"Yeah, it'll be funny to see how long this lasts. But the longer it does, the better for me."

"When are you going to start your rafting trips?"

"I've ordered the rafts but they won't be here until the middle of the year. And there's still a lot of preparation that I'm doing. When this is launched it's going to blow you guys out of the water."

I was leading a trip one day, and we dropped into the Kampala Sheraton to pick up a large group of British Airways customers. Scott gave me a hand to round them up, but one customer was missing, so I went to the buffet table to get a coffee while we waited for him to arrive. One of the other customers asked what the holdup was, and I explained the situation.

"What's his name?" We looked at the booking sheet together. "Oh, he's with us, he's over here."

The missing client had been sitting there the whole time. I got out my forms for him to pay, but then I realized that he had been talking to the British Airways crew, who each received a discount on the trip. When they understood that I was going to make him pay the full amount, they announced that he was part of their group and entitled to the same reduced rate.

"I can't do that," I said. "He's booked through our photo office, and they want to see the corresponding amount of money from him for the trip."

"Just say that he didn't turn up," the leader of the airline crew said. "We can include him in our numbers and nobody will know the difference."

The last client was the difference in numbers between having two guides on the trip or three. They were forcing me into a corner, but the risk was losing the customer and dropping a guide. We were also wasting precious time as the trip had a tight schedule. Against my better judgment, I ceded to their demands, and then we headed off for the river.

Rajal was at the guide house that evening, and he asked how the customer had liked the trip. He was proud of the fact that he had managed to book someone himself. With the old management I would have just explained the situation as it stood, but Rajal didn't understand or appreciate the intricacies of our job. For him it was a clear cut matter of the customer pays the agreed amount and gets to go on the trip. I was tired from a long day on the river and didn't want to deal with having to explain the entire situation in length and receive a lecture from our incompetent manager. Plus, there was also the risk of him insisting that I pay the difference for the missing money. I told him that the customer in question hadn't showed.

A few days later our manager called a meeting at the house. We sat around the dining table as he proceeded to go through a long list of cost saving measures dreamed up by him and the accountant. Once again they were proposing to cut the number of safety kayakers on each trip.

Scott began explaining the necessity of having a number of safety kayakers on a high volume river like the Nile, but his heart didn't seem to be in it. Eddie was looking at the ceiling and probably wondering when this would finish so he could go down to Al's. Noah made some derisive snorts, and Corey protested at the plight of the Ugandan kayakers who had been employed and trained by us and depended on their daily river allowance. Hendri, being new to the team, wisely kept his mouth shut.

It was up to me. "Rajal, what do you think our safety kayakers spend most of their time rescuing?"

He looked bored. "People, obviously."

"Nope. They rescue paddles." I turned to Scott. "How much does it cost to purchase a paddle and fly it out here?"

"Over a hundred bucks." He was smiling.

"How many paddles do they stop us losing per trip?"

"At least three or four."

"How long do you reckon it will take us to run out of paddles with this new safety kayak roster?"

Noah answered before Scott could respond. "Not fucking long. And what do we pay the kayak boys each? Five bucks?"

Rajal broke into the conversation. "That's why I employ you guys. You're the best and have the most knowledge of this stuff. Tim and I just wanted to make sure we were on the right track, but obviously on this one we were a little off base with the customer safety analysis, so we'll scratch this cost saving. Thanks guys."

"You know, it's funny," Noah said, "but I thought you were going to implement all these amazing marketing ideas and see a big uplift in work. Now you're telling us that it's all just cost cutting."

It was obvious that Rajal wasn't used to having underlings challenge him in this way, but he tried to reassure us that he was in fact doing just that. At the end he spoke what he imagined were words of encouragement, an exhortation for us to dig deep and make some effort to go out and round up paying customers. He spoke of us "living the dream" and hinted that we should be thankful that we lived in such grandeur and privilege.

I took great exception to all of this, and with a calmness that I didn't feel, I pointed out that we were already spending a great deal of time traipsing around the steaming city, attempting to win clients. Every hotel doorman in Kampala knew us by name, and our drinking hole had switched from Al's to the two backpacker bars so we could listen to inane Swedes lamenting the plight of the average African while we attempted to cajole them out of their remaining dollars to spend on a rafting trip, and all this for no payment, even though our manager's very own photo shop still charged a commission on its bookings.

And we did all this while resisting any temptation to fudge each trip's accounting procedures, something which could be done in a number of different ways. The fact that we did not succumb to this activity, even in the face of our own pathetic wage, was proof of our loyalty to the company. Thus we resented the implication that we should be forced to work harder for nothing but the supposed high-life in which we presently luxuriated.

The other guides raised voices of approval at this impromptu speech, but I noticed that Rajal and Tim were smiling at each other in surprised satisfaction. The meeting broke up, and Tim intercepted me as I was heading outside with my colleagues. He told me that Rajal wanted to see me upstairs for a quick meeting, and I wondered if perhaps I had overstepped the boundaries of allowable behavior.

"Have a seat," Rajal said as he leaned against a desk. He was smiling without warmth, his eyes never lifting from my own as Tim handed him some papers. "There's a problem with some of your trip documentation, and we wanted to have a look at it with you."

I relaxed somewhat on hearing that this was just some paperwork that hadn't satisfied the bean counter. Tim mentioned a name and waited for a reaction on my part. I just looked at him.

"He went rafting with you the other day," he clarified.

"I have a hard time remembering their faces let alone their names," I said.

"I booked him from my photo shop," Rajal said. "And according to you he didn't turn up."

I held his gaze as I tried to understand what was happening.

"And then this customer who didn't show up for the trip, this customer who paid a deposit but then didn't want to go rafting after all, this very same customer arrived in my shop to purchase his rafting photos." He leaned forward. "So what I want to know is how someone manages to buy photos of himself on a rafting trip that he didn't go on."

"Just get Scott up here," I said. "He was there; he'll be able to back me up on this."

"We want to hear it from you."

I again protested that I required the presence of my head guide, but they insisted on hearing my explanation immediately. And so as the other guides shouted and played volleyball in the garden below us, I explained the situation as it had happened. As I spoke I noticed Rajal and Tim exchange some worried looks. We discussed various points back and forth, but it was now obvious that their assumption of nefarious activity on my part had been incorrect.

Rajal produced some more documentation and launched into his next attack. I had been responsible for babysitting some European journalists around Kampala and then on a rafting trip. I had no idea how this could have gone wrong, but then they showed me the incriminating evidence. There was an extra waiver of liability form for the group. This was from a few months previously, and I racked my brains trying to work out the discrepancy. Perhaps they had visions of me breaking down and confessing, but this was unrealistic seeing as I didn't know what I was supposed to have done.

In the end they spelled it out for me. They believed that I'd taken an extra person rafting, charged them for the trip, and then pocketed the money without recording their presence on the trip manifest.

I couldn't believe what I was hearing. "Do you two really think I would do all of that and forget to remove the waiver form? What sort of idiot do you think I am?"

Rajal spread his hands, his gesture communicating that he wasn't responsible for my level of idiocy. I protested my innocence, and they asked me to prove it. I was panicking at the thought of where they were taking this, and in my haste I was willing to grasp any chance that presented itself. I needed to prove my honesty, and so I did what at the time I considered an honest person would do in such a circumstance. I offered them my resignation.

Rajal sat looking at me, the documents forgotten in his hand. Tim held his breath, as one of his feet tapped erratically on the floor and the sounds of celebration from a winning play came from the garden.

"Okay then," Rajal said. "If that's what you have to do then I'll have to accept it. I'll leave Tim to take care of the details."

He walked out of the office as Tim struggled to avoid my eyes, and then I found myself getting to my feet and I realized that I had made a tremendous miscalculation.

I walked downstairs and out into the garden in a state of unreality. My colleagues stopped playing and formed around me in a small group, the concern on their faces reflecting the awfulness which mine portrayed. I gave them a weak smile, my hands resting in my pockets.

"I'm out," I said.

"What do you mean?" Corey said.

"You remember when you got banished to Bujagali?" I said, looking at him. "Well, now it's my turn, although I doubt there's much chance of me returning."

Scott looked uncomfortable. "What happened up there?"

I outlined the events for them. As soon as Scott understood the true situation, he marched into the house with a grim look on his face.

"What are you going to do?" Hendri asked me.

"I don't know. Without this job, I don't have a place to live. The big problem is that I don't have a ticket out either. And my cash reserves are about the same as everyone else here."

Noah was incredulous. "You don't have a ticket out? Are you saying that you came into Uganda on a one way ticket? That's the craziest thing I've ever heard. What the hell were you thinking?"

I shrugged. "It was a calculated risk. Losing my job for stealing wasn't part of the calculations."

We talked some more, and then Scott returned from inside the house. He shook his head as he approached, his face downcast. "They're obviously full of shit on this; I explained the discrepancies and backed your story. If they'd fired you, I reckon we could've got you reinstated. But the fact you resigned means they've got a free run here." He spread his hands. "Why the fuck did you resign?"

"I don't know. I wish I knew. They boxed me into a corner; they were demanding an explanation. I just panicked. It was like a panic contest and I lost. I felt that resigning would show them my good intentions or something."

Noah snorted. "Well that worked out well for you."

"What about staying here?" I asked Scott.

"They're giving you a week."

We thought about that in silence for some moments and then Corey caught my eye. "I reckon the only thing to do is to head down to Al's and have a really big session. And I for one am not going to ask one fucking backpacker if they want to come rafting."

I got up early the next morning and caught a matatu into the city. I had no real goal for the day, I simply wanted to remove myself from the house. I was the only mazungu squashed into the little van. I looked at the other passengers on their way to work and wondered what they did for a living, how much they made.

The younger women attempted to catch my eye, always the faint dream of landing a white man and living a life of luxury. The incongruence of the fact that I was travelling with them in a matatu never entered their heads. Not only that, but in some way they were better off than me. I had no job and, in a week, would be technically homeless. In less than a month my visa would expire, a visa that could only be renewed by my employer.

All my time in Africa I'd been disassociated from the knife-edge existence in which the general population lived. For many of them, only one bad decision or ill piece of fortune separated them from terminal disaster. I'd thought of myself as above their vulnerability, but in reality I too had been only one step away from the precipice.

As the van shunted me from side to side while the driver threw it along the potholes and crumbling edges of the impossibly crowded roads, I realized the true hopelessness of my situation. The thought of a quick death from a road accident suddenly held a macabre appeal; at least then I would be absolved from any need to make a decision.

I got out at the taxi-park and pushed my way through the hawkers and the beggars, the street urchins, the thieves, the women going to market, the men in ill-fitting suits filing into the city to work behind a Formica desk in a derelict office building still shattered with shell holes unrepaired from the last war.

I made my way to Jinja Road in the downtown area of the city, moving with the crowds, alone in my world of unreality. I felt as if I was floating above the people around me, and I wandered along the busy sidewalk until I found myself entering an internet café. I paid for an hour and sat in front of my designated machine. I checked my email for messages, but it was empty.

I surfed the internet without intent, merely using it to keep myself occupied while my mind whirled in a quiet and confused panic. It was almost five years to the day since I'd left Perth for Sydney, and in all that time I'd never asked for help from anybody at home. No matter how bad things had seemed, I'd always found a way on my own. It was something I took pride in, something that represented my efforts. More than that, it enabled me to proceed on my own terms.

If I never asked for help then I was always free to make my own choices and free to make my own mistakes. Nobody could ever point a finger and accuse me of not paying my way. But the moment I asked for help I'd leave myself vulnerable to someone taking the decision away from me. The only real thing I had left was the power to make my own decisions and pay whatever price they demanded.

I sat at that computer for a very long time. And then I wrote an email to my father asking for help to pay for a ticket out of Uganda. I pressed send before I had the chance to second guess my decision.

"Where do you want to go?" Milo said.
"I don't know. Somewhere that's not Africa."
"So how did you ask your father for the right amount if you don't know where you're going?"
"I asked him if he would put up the funds that I need to get to my next job. Where that next job is, I have no idea. But if I'm going to be looking for a job, I need to know that I can get there."

Milo cracked another two beers and handed me one. We were sitting on his back porch in the house he shared with Alison and her baby son. "Have you considered staying in Uganda?"

"I didn't think that was an option."

"I'm going to be up and running by the middle of the year. I'm going to need guides."

"Yeah, but that's six months away. What am I going to do in the meantime?"

"I'll need help with the set-up. To tell the truth I need help now. You can stay out at Bujagali, run the operation there, and be my backup for when I need it. Just no witchdoctors this time."

The offer was appealing, but for some reason my instinctive reaction to being fired was to seek an immediate exit from the country.

"The big issue is my work visa," I said.

"When does that expire?"

"Just under a month."

"Were you getting the standard three month extension?"

"Yeah. And this is the problem. Even if my dad does come through with the money for me to get to my next job, the northern summer season doesn't start for another three or four months. So what do I do? Get a job in Switzerland and fly there to find it's the middle of winter and I have no way to support myself while I wait for the season to start?"

Milo thought for a moment. "I could probably help you with the visa through my company, but it'll be tricky. And it would mean that I'd need a commitment from you to stay."

"How long?"

"At least a year. I won't be able to pitch it to my business partner any other way. And you'll be living at Bujagali."

"Living at Buj for a whole year," I said. "That's a special kind of fun."

"Think of all the backpacker and overland truck chicks. I'll bring you a steady supply of rubbers."

I smiled. "They're my favorite bit of safety equipment."

That night a few of us went to a club. It was not one of our usual destinations, and we were the only whites there. The clientele were young upper-middle class Ugandans, but on seeing our group, the women approached us en masse and began displaying behavior that put the mosquito girls to shame. My companions let them down good naturedly, but I brushed aside their unwelcome and obvious advances with disdain.

Some of them took offense at my attitude. The women's leers turned to sneers and they began to cast aspersions on my manhood, accusing me of being impotent or preferring the company of boys. Their male companions joined in, ingratiating themselves in an attempt to get lucky by mocking my refusal to sleep with their own women. I ignored their attempts to humiliate me until eventually they became bored.

The club held no attraction, and I told the other guides that I intended to leave. They wanted to finish their drinks, so I went outside to wait. There was a long line of people waiting to get in, and I stood off to the side and leaned against a low wall. One of the bouncers ambled over in my direction, his pump-action shotgun slung over his shoulder. He looked me up and down.

"Mazungu," he sneered. "You cannot wait here. You wait over there." He pointed to a piece of identical wall a few meters away. The crowd watched. It appeared that he wanted to have some fun at my expense, show the audience how he could boss around a mazungu.

I remained silent, my face expressionless. He repeated his demand, but with no reaction on my part he began to get worked up. This wasn't going the way he had envisioned. He demanded that I move. Didn't I know who he was? He was the boss here, and he decided where I could stand. He went on and on, the words tumbling from his mouth in a meaningless tirade. Still I made no effort to move or speak. I just watched him, my arms hanging loosely by my sides.

The crowd began to murmur, and he realized that he had to do something to finish what he had started. He unslung the shotgun from his shoulder and repeated his demand for me to move from my piece of wall.

I glanced down at the gun and then back at my antagonist. "What the fuck do you think you're going to do with that?" I said.

The combination of me speaking for the first time and the unexpected response to his ace in the hole seemed to unravel his thought processes. He didn't know how to proceed, but then the crowd began to jeer, and he forced himself towards me until our faces were quite close together. He was about my height, a little stocky, but he looked slow.

"You move now, mazungu," he said.

"I thought you were going to shoot me."

"You move, you move now."

"Go fuck yourself."

Someone in the crowd called out for me to move, and others began to join the chorus. I ignored them all. There existed only the bouncer and myself. We were alone in our little world that he had created to score some cheap and easy points at my expense. I liked my piece of wall. It felt comfortable. And I wanted him to start something. All my time in Africa, all the crap I had put up with, all of my frustrations, it was all ready to be released right then.

I saw his eyes change as he realized my intentions. He swallowed and his glance darted back to the crowd at our side. He could see what he would have to do to get me off my little low wall. I breathed with a slow and steady rhythm. He stepped back and began to call me a crazy stupid mazungu. Only someone as stupid as me would not understand what he could do if he wanted. It was only because of his generosity that he decided to let me stay at my wall.

The crowd jeered and hooted at me, but their hearts were not in it. They just wanted to go inside. I folded my arms and leaned back against the wall, ignoring the insults and staring into space. A few minutes passed, and then the other guides emerged into the night air. They saw me and walked over, and I stood up from the section of wall and walked away with them. The bouncer called out some jeering remarks as we left.

Corey looked around not understanding. "What was that about?"

"It's time to get out of Africa," I said.

I went back to the internet café the following morning. My inbox showed a new message, and with my heart in my mouth I clicked on it. It was from my father, and I read it with a growing sense of disbelief. The tone was curt, not the one of warmth or understanding that I'd been hoping to find. It seemed that my timing couldn't have been worse. My father and his partner had just had a baby daughter who had been born with a heart defect requiring radical new laser surgery. She was in fact the first baby to undertake the procedure in Western Australia. The operation had occurred a few days previously and had been successful, but from his tone I understood what sort of stress he was under.

The email outlined this information and then ended with my father's conditional offer. He was only prepared to provide me with the funds for a ticket back to Perth. In that moment I couldn't begin to articulate just why this news was so disappointing. All I knew was that I felt terribly let down and betrayed. The thought of being forced to return to Perth after all this time and under these circumstances was unacceptable to me.

I got up from the computer in a daze and made my way down to the busy street below. I looked around at the heaving mass of pedestrians and vehicles, bewildered by my senses and unable to fathom just what I was going to do. I didn't even have enough strength to put one foot in front of the other as I was incapable of choosing a direction in which to walk.

It was as if my ability to process information and make decisions had shut down. What did it even matter which way I walked? I had nowhere to go. I just stood there as the crowd surged around me, my body creating a small obstacle in their path like a rock in a river around which water flowed. And then I spotted the familiar staff shirt of one of the guides. It was Corey. He raised his hand and gave me a smile.

We got a mediocre coffee in the lobby of the Kampala Sheraton hotel, the calm luxury of our surroundings a welcome counterpoint to the chaos of the city streets. In a flat voice I outlined the details of my father's reply, and then I sat there shaking my head and staring down at the carpet.

"At least you now have an option," Corey said.

"It's not a fucking option," I said without meeting his gaze.

"Why not?"

I sighed and sat back in my chair. "I don't know, it just isn't. I can't go back to Perth, what am I going to do there? Go back to tending bar, after all that I've been through?"

"It can't be that bad," Corey ventured. "So you work in a bar for a bit until you get back on your feet, so what?"

"It's not just that. Look, this is my second overseas trip. The first was a total fucking disaster ..."

"Most first trips are; you should've seen how bad my first attempt went at guiding overseas."

"Yeah, I get that. It happens to everyone. But now my second trip is going to end as a disaster too, and even worse than the first one. I mean, at least I got myself back home from Canada. And that was to Cairns where I could just pick things up where I left off. Now I have to go home with my tail between my legs, my fare paid for by my father, and I'll probably have to stay at his house as I won't have any other immediate options. I can't live with that."

"You'd feel like a failure," he said.

"Exactly. When I left home five years ago and I got to Sydney and it all went to shit, I didn't go home a failure then. I made it stick and I kept going and getting on with things. If I go back now, like this, I don't know...it's as if I'll have gone back on everything I've achieved. If I'm going to go back, I'll do it on my own terms, not because I'm forced to."

"So are you going to stay here then and work for Milo?"

I looked at him. "I can't. That moment at the nightclub...it made me realize that I've been here too long."

"Yeah, what the hell happened outside there last night?"

"It doesn't matter—Africa shit, that's what happened. The point is if I stay here, I think I'm at risk of ending up like Dave. I don't mean that I'm going to go down like he did. I think each of us have our own special ways of self-destructing. And I think mine will be that I'm going to keep putting myself in situations where eventually I'll just get killed or at least seriously fucked up."

"Yeah, I've thought about that myself. You get confronted here by the darker side of yourself."

"It's because we're above the normal rules," I said. "You keep pushing, like you're trying to find where the boundary is. But sometimes the boundary is so far that when you find it, you can't go back anymore. That's what happened to Dave."

We sat in silence for some moments and sipped our coffee. "So you can't stay here," Corey said, "and you can't go back to Perth. And you haven't got a job to go to or enough money to get there even if you had one. So what are you going to do?"

I pondered my situation for the rest of the day as the two of us graduated from coffee to lunch, and then to a long series of beers at the little bar overlooking the taxi park. That night we met up with some British Airways flight crew that we had taken rafting on my last trip.

After an eventful night, I woke up with bleary eyes in an unfamiliar bed in the Sheraton with one of the stewardesses. She was a lovely English rose, long limbed and elegant and a wonderful distraction from my immediate reality. We wiled away the morning in bed, ordering breakfast and the papers, and then we made our way down to the hotel pool, where I collapsed on a lounge chair under the tropical sun.

Corey and his own conquest joined us not long after, and we had a swim to try and clear our heads, but when our hangovers refused to leave, we did the only sensible thing and ordered a round of drinks. My body felt immediate relief as the first vestiges of alcohol entered my system. Corey gave out a sigh of great satisfaction and sank down onto a lounge.

The sun beat down on my tanned skin, the feeling of warmth a soothing tonic to go with my satisfied daze of sex and alcohol. The pool filled up with hotel guests, and I stroked the bare thigh of the woman beside me, imagining pleasurable fantasies where she spirited me back to some country manor in England.

But there was no escaping my own head, no escaping the fact that I needed to do something, anything to take control of the situation. I had analyzed my plight a hundred times, turning the facts and possibilities around and around in my head, searching for some way to wriggle out of this mess. And then as I baked under the hot sun, a cool gin and tonic in my hand, the sounds of people frolicking in the pool, the warm touch of a beautiful woman by my side, suddenly I had a moment of complete calm settle over me.

I knew what I needed to do.

I turned and looked at our little group. "Does anyone know if there is a public internet point in the hotel?"

"There's one in the lobby," Corey's date said. "I have an access card if you want to use it."

"That'd be great," I said as I stood up.

"What are you going to do?" Corey asked me.

"I'm going to send a reply to my dad that I won't be able to accept his offer."

Corey sat up. "Do you have some other plan?" he said.

"Nope. That's my plan; rejecting the offer. It'll force me to get moving, or at least it will set things in motion. At the very least, I'm making my decision, I'm taking control. I'll get out of here on my own steam."

"You're sure of that?"

I laughed without humor. "Nope. But it's the one thing that I can do, and I have to do something. I'll get out of this hellhole and go and do another overseas trip, and that by God will be a fucking success."

"What are you guys talking about?" Corey's girl said.

Corey glanced towards me and I told him to go for it. "Adam's been fired from his job for supposedly stealing, which he didn't do, and he doesn't have a ticket out of the country or any money to buy one, and his visa's going to expire in a few weeks, and so now he's going to tell his dad that he doesn't want his help to fly out of here on the first available plane."

"You forgot the part about not having a place to live either," I said.

"Oh yeah, there's that too."

The two girls took a few moments to digest this information. "You guys are crazy," my date said.

"It's a distinct possibility," I said, and then I walked back into the hotel.

21

The following day everything started to come together in an unexpected rush of momentum. The gloom and depression had lifted and I felt clearheaded for the first time since losing my job. It wasn't my way to try and push through the feelings of blackness; I had to let them settle before I could make rational decisions once again. Rejecting my father's offer had something to do with it, but mostly I just needed the time to get my head straight. There was no trip that day, and after breakfast I went up to my room to sort out my things. A little later, my colleagues knocked at the door and came into the room.

"What's up?" I said.

"We all spoke to Rajal and told him that he has to give you time to save up for a ticket out," Corey said. "So you're still working at least for the moment."

"And you can stay here," Noah added. "They've even agreed to extend your visa."

I was dumbfounded. "How on earth did you get them to agree to do that?"

The guides all looked at Scott, who gave me a satisfied grin. "I did a snoop. It turns out that Tim found the discrepancies and took them to Rajal, but instead of coming to you to get your side of it, he sent an email straight to the owner saying that he had discovered you were a thief."

"Why would he do that? Why wouldn't he come to me first?"

"Maybe he wanted to prove that he's actually doing something as the manager, which we all know he's not. If he found a so-called thief, then he gets the owner off his back for a bit. So he's told the owner that you're a thief and he's doing a bang-up job, and then it turns out that you're not one after all. It all looks pretty fucking messy. So I told him that it would be a good idea to let you stay on and keep working until you have enough for a ticket out. And he saw the wisdom of this idea."

"You're back on, bro," Corey said as he slapped me on the shoulder. "So you can stop packing your stuff."

"How long do you reckon I've got?" I asked Scott.

"I think you'll be good for a few months."

I did a quick calculation in my head. "I don't know if it'll be long enough to save up for the fare. What are we doing at the moment, one trip a week each?"

"We're going to slip you some of our trips," Corey said. "Plus, I have some kayak courses coming up at Bujagali. You can take those as well. They'll give you some decent coin, and you can stay out there away from the office shenanigans while you're doing them."

I hardly knew what to say to their generosity. I thanked them, and then we went downstairs and sat out in the garden away from the office.

"So I have a place to stay and a way to get the cash together to get out," I said. "Now I need a destination."

"What are your ideas?" Hendri said.

"I could try Canada. There's a rafting operation up in BC that was very keen to have me a few years ago. The only problem with that is the ticket will be pretty expensive."

"Maybe the rafting company could pitch in to cover the difference," Corey said.

"What about you, Noah?" I said. "You came here straight from the European season, right?"

"Yeah, I was working in Norway. It'd be pretty easy to organize to go there. What is it now, February? The season up there starts around late May so the timing's right. Fucking cold rivers though. I froze my nuts off up there."

"But there's Norwegian chicks," Scott grinned.

We all made murmurs of appreciation at this thought but Noah scoffed and shook his head. "You reckon the rivers are cold? The chicks up there shit ice blocks. Even I couldn't get anywhere with them."

Scott guffawed. "What do you mean, 'even you'? Like you're God's gift to women."

Noah raised an eyebrow. "Didn't you know?"

"Where else?" I said, trying to keep the conversation on track.

"How about the Zambezi?" Hendri suggested. "I've got a bunch of good contacts down there."

"No offense, Hendri, you being South African and all, but right now it's 'fuck Africa.'"

"No, I get that."

"Some mates of mine worked the season in Italy last year and they said it was pretty good," Noah said. "Apparently the money was brilliant. I've got the contact for the head guide."

I felt immediately intrigued at the idea of working in Italy. It was weird how something could be completely outside your radar, and then in just a moment it could consume your imagination.

"Whereabouts in Italy?"

"Somewhere up in the Alps. Apparently they don't speak a word of English up there."

"Italy could be cool," I said.

Corey agreed. "And it's close, about as close as you're going to get. You'd just need to get a flight to London and then a cheapie low cost fare from there."

Scott spread his hands. "And don't forget...Italian chicks! They've got to be warmer than those up in the fjords."

We all agreed that Italian mountain girls held some distinct promise. I decided to try both the Canadian and Italian options so as to give myself the best chance of hooking up a job. But the thought of having to learn a new language in Italy stuck with me. I instinctively liked this idea. I wanted to be able to push myself intellectually as well as physically, and attempting to learn a new language seemed like a good fit. Noah went upstairs and came back with details for the Italian company.

"Here's the email of the contact in Italy, a guy called Davide. Ask him if he has two jobs."

"You serious?" Corey said.

"I've had a gutful of Africa too," Noah replied. "I've been here six months and I'm already going nuts. Plus there's no work; we're just sitting around and spending all our money down at Al's Bar. And first you get the shaft and end up sitting on your butt out at Bujagali for months until you're flavor of the month again, and now they've gone and done it to Adam too. Fuck that shit, I'm not waiting around for them to find out that they don't like something about me."

I held the scrap of paper in my hand. "Two positions then," I said to Noah, and he nodded, and I felt glad that he might be going with me.

I sent the emails that day, and then I went around to see Milo and bring him up to date. He was far more interested in the internal political maneuverings than the fact that I wouldn't be working for him in the future. I had sent a long and desperate email to the owner proclaiming my innocence but hadn't received so much as a response.

"Yeah, he won't take you back no matter what evidence pops up," Milo said. "This is all about him taking back control from me."

"From you?"

"Sure. The whole time I was head guide we stocked the roster with guides who are loyal to me, not to him. This is his chance to start splitting apart that group, which he wants to do before I start my rafting operation. Otherwise, what's going to happen? Well, I take all his guides in one hit, leaving him right in the shit. Come to think of it, it's a bit of a bummer for me, but I can still get guides."

"So I've been caught in the middle of the owner's battle with you as well as Rajal's efforts to try and prove that he's actually doing something when he's not."

"Yeah, it looks that way. You never really had a chance on this one. If you had kept your head down and not mouthed off all the time then you could have stayed out of it, but you were a pain in the butt to Rajal, and he must have actively searched around for a way to get rid of you. Maybe resigning like you did wasn't such a bad idea after all. If they had fired you, I doubt that Scott would have been able to blackmail Rajal into putting you back on. But this is all just speculation. When are you heading out to Bujagali to do Corey's kayak courses?"

"At the end of the week. I want to hang out here first and see if I get any immediate responses to my emails."

The Canadian company was swift to respond to my inquiry with a firm offer, but the cost of the flight was more than double that of a ticket to Europe. I emailed back explaining my predicament and asking if they could help with the fare. I felt uncomfortable doing this as it made my application look considerably shaky, but I had no real choice. Sure enough, their response was not encouraging, and I got the feeling that I had blown my chances with that job. Noah's Italian contact replied to me, explaining that he was no longer working for the company in question. However, he gave me the owner's email, and I sent through an inquiry that received a response a few hours later. The Italian company was prepared not only to give us both jobs, but to reimburse a substantial proportion of the airfare on our arrival.

I showed Noah the email, and we went through the instructions the Italian had given us. He needed detailed histories of our rafting careers and our current first aid qualifications to pass on to the Italian Rafting Federation. When I dug up my Canadian Wilderness First Aid certificate, I realized I had a problem.

"It expires in May," I said to Noah. "And I can't afford to do a first aid course here. I can't even afford the bribe."

Noah inspected my certificate. "We need to fax these through, right? So you can alter the date with a pen."

I stared at him. "Alter the date with a pen? They can't be that stupid."

"It's not about them being stupid. Fax machines smudge these things all the time. It'll just look like a dirty mark or something."

"I can't believe I'm going to do this," I mumbled as I held a pen above my certificate.

"Don't write on the original," Noah said. "Make a copy on the fax machine first and see how that comes through. Then alter the copied version and fax that. It'll look more authentic."

"Damn that's devious," I said as I followed his instructions. We inspected the copy together. "I could alter the year from 2000 to 2001," I said.

"Try it."

I carefully made the adjustment and we looked at it for a while. "Looks fine to me," Noah said. "They're not going to inspect it too closely anyway, particularly not the company that wants us. People see what they want to see."

I was not as sure of this as my surprisingly dodgy colleague, but I had no choice and sent the fax with grave misgivings.

We headed into the city, our goal the Italian embassy located in an old colonial building on a leafy avenue. A pair of dogs slunk away from the gate as we approached, and I threw a stone in their direction to keep them moving. Noah inspected the opening hours.

"Shit, look at this. They're only open twice a week for a couple of hours a day. We'll have to come back tomorrow."

"I have to head out to Bujagali tomorrow. This is rubbish." I pushed on the buzzer a few times, and eventually a voice answered.

"Si?"

"Hi, we need information about getting visas to work in Italy?" I said, speaking slowly and carefully.

"You need to come back during business hours," said the voice, the metallic sound shrieking in the quiet confines of the street.

"Yes, I see that," I said. "But we want to know what to bring so we don't have to come back again."

The voice said an unintelligible word, and then there was only silence. "I don't think you got very far there," Noah said. But then we heard the sound of approaching footsteps and the gate was opened by a Ugandan guard. He looked us over and handed me a piece of paper with instructions for our visa application. I thanked him as he slammed shut the heavy gate, and then we headed back to the house to get our applications in order.

We presented ourselves to the embassy at the opening of business the following day, where we spent a few hours filling in a myriad of forms and providing sufficient identification. The staff was delightfully Italian, and we departed with assurances of a smooth and simple process.

I headed out to the river in a matatu and arrived in the late afternoon. The bar was crowded with Westerners and Ugandans and the park itself thronged with day visitors. Milo's improvements had made a big impact, and it was obvious that his plan was going well.

"I'm taking more on the gate each day than the rafting operations earn in a week," he told me as we sat and ate a simple but wholesome meal prepared by his cook in the new kitchen. It was a welcome change from having to scrabble about in the Jinja markets for meagre cooking supplies. Milo introduced me to the young English couple who were going to spend the week with me learning how to kayak, and after a pleasant evening I retired to one of the banda huts nestled in the coffee trees overlooking the falls.

The next day I discovered that my students were total novices, which gave me pause seeing as the river was of the more threatening variety. But I was desperate for the funds, so I spent the next three days standing waist-deep in a small eddy, attempting to teach them how to perform an eskimo-roll in a kayak.

At night I sat in the bar and studied a book on Italian grammar that I had purchased in Kampala. After another day explaining the basics of reading rivers and getting their paddling technique sorted out, we spent the final day of instruction negotiating the strong currents at the base of the falls across to the middle islands. I was in a state of constant anxiety as we ferry-glided back and forth, acutely aware of the monster rapids located just downstream and the terrifying consequences if one of them took an inopportune swim. Thankfully the day passed without incident, and we toasted their success with beers in the bar, where they paid me with a satisfyingly large roll of US dollars.

They left the following morning as the rafting vehicles arrived for a rafting trip. I said hello to Corey and Scott, and we spoke about how the kayak course had gone. Brum's girlfriend had also come out with a couple of her friends, their plan to spend the day hanging out at the falls. Sometime later I was relaxing at the bar when she came running up to me.

"Adam! You must come quickly!" she said. "There is a tourist in trouble in the river!"

I followed Grace down to the bank where a small crowd had gathered. The fearsome rapids thundered less than a hundred meters away. The bank was on the side of what seemed to be an enormous pool, but was in fact an eddy. The water turned in a large circle off the side of the main current, only to be drawn back into the base of the rapids. The swimmer had been deceived by the apparent placidness of the water, unaware of the huge underlying currents. She was barely fifty meters away from the huge plume of white-water cascading and thundering in the afternoon light. She had one arm raised and was waving it back and forth in desperation.

I stepped into the water and began to swim out towards her. I was well aware that without a lifejacket I was putting myself in grave danger. I did not like this one bit, but someone had to do something, and the unfortunate fact was that I had been cast in the role of savior.

I wanted to swim as close to her as possible without being drawn into the main current. It was also very important to keep a small distance from her. Even though she was small and lithe, panic would make her strong, and I had no intention of being drowned by the person I was trying to save.

I stopped within a few feet of her. She eyed me warily, panic mixed with crazed hope that I could help her. She was quite beautiful and was not wearing a top.

"I want you to swim towards me," I said. My tone was forceful yet calm.

"But…I am in trouble. I cannot." She was French.

Little by little I coaxed her in my direction, always careful to keep a small distance between us. I could feel the current dragging us towards the rapids, and it was a tricky business to tread water and swim backwards while facing the woman. I soothed words of encouragement whenever she appeared to be on the edge of losing herself to panic. And then, after some long minutes of this, I felt a change in the water and knew that the two of us were safe. I reached over and pulled her the rest of the short distance to the bank where Grace was waiting with a towel.

The crowd murmured its approval, and I stepped from the water with a keen sense of embarrassment, both for the woman and for myself. Her small firm breasts bobbed in the afternoon sun, and I looked away until she had covered herself. She thanked me in a hurried tone, and I mumbled some response, and then I walked back up to the bar and resumed my drink, not wanting to become involved for some strange reason.

I returned to Kampala only to find that the Italians had made no progress with our applications. The embassy staff spread their hands in a gesture of helplessness as I attempted to explain the necessity of obtaining the work visas by early May. I instinctively knew that I couldn't trust the system to come through for me, and the consequences if they didn't were too awful to contemplate. My only option was to present myself every day they were open for business. Noah accompanied me for a good many of these visits, and we got to know the layout of the embassy buildings and became friendly with the guards on the gate.

"All those movies where the spies or terrorists do unbelievably complicated shit to scope out places are rubbish," Noah observed as we sat in the visa application room one day. "All they'd have to do is pretend to want a fucking work visa. I don't even know why we're bothering to go through all the bullshit at the front door every time either."

"Do you plan on tunneling in or something?" I said.

He pointed to a side corridor. "Staff entrance over there. It's a separate side door. So instead of standing at the front door and doing the explanation on the intercom and the video inspection and then the bloody wait in the holding room, we can just walk around the side, open the door, walk down the corridor, and take a seat right here."

"Remember, it's not Africa in here; this is Italy."

"Oh it's fucking Africa all right."

On top of jumping through visa hoops, I wasn't saving enough money, and I started exploring other options to get out of Uganda. I was on friendly terms with Captain Paul, a British Airways pilot who I had taken rafting on a few occasions. I emailed him and asked if he had any ideas on alternative escape routes. He had some contacts in the air freight business and set about seeing if he could get me a jump-seat on a cargo plane. Another option was to convince one of my air hostess conquests to get me a cheapie flight on British Airways, but I knew they only got a couple of discounts a year, and this really wasn't my style.

The average price of a one-way ticket to London hovered around the thousand dollar mark, which I couldn't afford no matter which way I turned it. I was doing a couple of trips a week, but that left a lot of free time for me to fill. Just because I had managed to stay on the roster didn't mean that management wanted me around, and my bedroom was right next to the very office where they were even now most probably plotting my doom. Stepping out of the house, however, meant spending money, whether on food or drink or other entertainment options. Mostly I alternated my days on the river with days spent sitting at the embassy. The rest of the time I hitched a lift out to Bujagali and spent time sitting at the bar, reading my grammar book, and watching the Nile flow swiftly to the Mediterranean Sea.

To my surprise, my forged first aid documents passed muster, and we both got jobs for the Italian summer. The only remaining hurdle was to figure out how to get there. The cargo plane option hadn't come through, and the same went for other more ludicrous ideas such as hopping a lift on an overland tourist truck through the Sudan and into Egypt.

I was sitting around the house when Tim came downstairs and told me I had a phone call. I followed him up to the office and picked up the phone.

"Dude, it's Milo. Listen, Alison has just found out that there's a travel agency in the city that's having a fire sale special on tickets to London."

My stomach dropped at this news. "What's the address?" I said as I frantically motioned Tim to give me a pen and paper. I wrote down the details and tried to picture the location.

"It's down that street where the British and American embassies are located," Milo said.

"Bomb alley?"

"That's the one. Now if I were you, I'd haul butt and get down there now. It was only luck that Alison heard about this."

"I'm going." I slammed down the phone and turned to the accountant. "I need the car," I said.

Tim gave me a look. "Well, that might be possible."

"I wasn't asking for permission, I was asking for the keys."

"You really are a piece of work," he said as he sat in his chair, his arms folded.

I laughed. "Do you lot want me out of here or not?" I saw his face register this information, and he reached back and tossed me the keys. I turned and raced down the stairs and out the front door. The dogs scrambled to their feet at the sight of me moving so fast.

Hoping that nobody was planning on choosing today to detonate some large explosives, I sidestepped over a couple of leper victims and made my way inside the travel agency. A few Ugandans slouched on uncomfortable chairs waiting to be served. I took a ticket and studied the travel agents. They were all Ugandan and had the standard expression of contempt and boredom mixed with a good dose of hubris at having a job. If I was going to grab one of the deals, I would need someone who was on my side.

The electronic counter ticked over until it reached my number. I headed over to the available booth and sat in front of a young woman. I said hello, and she gave me a big smile. I gave her a big smile in return. We chatted briefly, and I was astounded to discover that she seemed to possess that most rare of qualities in Uganda; initiative.

"I heard you have some specials on one-way tickets for London," I said.

Her fingers danced over her keyboard with a clickety-clack. "We do indeed. It is a South African Airways special for next week only. Is South African Airways acceptable to you?"

I was prepared to fly with Air North Korea if it would get me out of her country, but I merely nodded my head and said that I was perfectly happy with that particular company.

"The ticket is for six hundred and fifty dollars American only."

We looked at each other in silence across her desk. I tried to remain calm. "You have to get me one of those tickets," I spluttered. "It's a financial emergency."

"There are ten seats available on the special at this stage."

"Have you had many inquiries for them?"

She tilted her head. "You are one of the first, so you might be very lucky indeed." Her fingers danced again. "The full price for those flights is just over a thousand dollars."

"Mary," I said after glancing at her nametag, "I really, really, really, really need one of those tickets."

She smiled again, a warm smile, a smile that spoke of watching the sun set over a beautiful African savannah. "I like you very much, Mister Adams. I will do my best to get you one of these tickets. Can you come back in two days?"

"I'll be here."

"And please bring your money and passport."

I went back to the guide house and found Noah. "I'm going for an all-out attack on the embassy to get my visa," I said.

He didn't appear convinced. "We've been haunting that place for months."

"Well, I have the sniff of a cheap airfare and I'm not going to be brushed off this time."

"They're open for another hour," he said, looking at his watch. We jumped into the car as Tim came downstairs for the keys, his hand held out in futility as we reversed with screaming tires out of the compound. By the time we had negotiated the lunch hour traffic, there was very little time remaining. We got through the front gate only to be greeted with the sight of a long line of Ugandans outside the door.

"Fuck that," Noah said as he headed for the staff entrance. I hesitated a moment and then hurried after him, following him through the door and down a narrow corridor to the now familiar waiting room. One of the head diplomats turned around as we entered.

"How did you come in here?" he said in surprise. Noah pointed back the way we had come. "But you cannot be doing this!" he exclaimed. "This is a security breach. You must return outside and join the others who are waiting."

"Look," I said, stepping forward. "We've been coming here every day you're open for months now, trying to get our work visas. We've done all the paperwork and followed all the instructions, and you guys keep putting us off every single time. And now we're set to leave next week, and we need those visas right now, today. If we waited outside with that lot, we wouldn't make the cutoff time."

The bureaucrat regarded us in silence. One of the girls in the office looked up and then quickly glanced away. Finally he held out his hand. "Give me your passports," he said with real anger in his voice. We did as requested, and he stormed out of the room.

"Probably going to write in them that we're banned from entering Italy for the next fifty years," Noah grumbled.

We sat down, both of us prepared for a long and futile wait. The diplomat returned not ten minutes later and thrust our passports at us without a word. I took mine and thumbed through it until I saw a very impressive visa imprint.

"Is okay?" the diplomat demanded.

"Thank you very much," I said meekly. The man stormed off. "We got them," I said in disbelief.

Noah showed me his passport. "The visa is only valid until mid-August," he hissed. "The season's longer than that."

"I'm taking it," I said. "What do you want to do, tell him you don't want it? We can work it out once we're there."

He wasn't happy, but he followed me out the front door.

I went back to the travel agency, money and passport in my pocket. My favorite travel agent gave me her characteristic smile and waved me over. If I managed to get this ticket then I would have a couple of hundred dollars left over to fund the trip from London to Italy. I didn't want to contemplate the possibility of having to pay full price.

"Did you bring your documentations, Mister Adams?"

"I did. How did you go with getting me a ticket?"

"You are a most fortunate man. It is my pleasure to tell you that you have a one-way ticket to London departing in six days."

"I could kiss you right here," I said with genuine warmth.

"Oh Mister Adams! Please be not doing such a thing. I would be in the most terrible trouble." We both laughed, and as I walked outside I felt a deep sense of relief. The sun seemed to have a different aspect; it felt warmer, more comforting, and brighter.

I found Corey, and we went to get a beer at our favorite bar overlooking the Taxi Park. We sat and watched as the cacophony of noise drifted up to our isolated perch high atop the struggles of the seething masses below. Corey had his bag with him as he was on his way out to do a week-long stay at Bujagali. He dug into his belongings and brought out his expensive river dry-top, a special jacket with rubber seals on the neck and hands so that water couldn't get inside.

"You'll be needing this where you're going. I imagine it's pretty cold in the Alps."

"Damn, I hadn't even thought about the fact that I'll be on a cold river again. I don't even have a wetsuit."

He laughed. "I know. That's why I'm giving you this."

"Thanks, man. It's been a crazy time."

"I'll be seeing you on a river somewhere."

I went to the Kampala casino with Milo and Alison on my final night in Africa. Milo had gotten hold of some mind-altering substances, so by the time we walked through the lobby, my eyes were revolving inside my skull. I found a poker table and managed to lose what little money I had budgeted for the night in a very small space of time, as did Milo. We moved to another table and sat down next to the South African who had sold Milo his Landrover. We engaged him in conversation while pilfering from his stack of chips. He was quite unfazed at our obvious thievery.

At one point, after having lost yet more of his money, I leaned across and looked him in the eye. He regarded me with cautious interest.

"I'm on drugs," I managed to say, and then I swept my hand through his pile and dragged half his remaining chips to my side of the table.

"I didn't doubt it for a moment," he replied.

Milo appeared at my shoulder. "We gotta go, dude. It's late."

"What's the time?" I slurred.

"Five in the morning," said the South African as he recovered his chips.

"What time's your flight?" Milo asked me.

I attempted to remember. "I think tomorrow afternoon. Maybe it would be good to sleep first."

We pried Alison away from the bar that was holding her up, and then we made our way down the steep stairs with great caution. Milo slid behind the wheel of Alison's little car and began jabbing the key at the side of the steering console. Finally he managed to fit the key in the ignition, and with a triumphant grin he gunned the engine and drove straight out of the car park and through the plate-glass window of a jewelry store across the road. The glass came crashing down, and alarm bells began to shriek.

Milo looked around. "Holy shit. There's jewels and shit everywhere."

"Just drive the car," Alison slurred from the back seat. Her arms flailed in the air as she attempted to add weight to her pronouncements. "I don't want any jewels, so just drive the fucking car."

"But the jewels are everywhere..." Milo began.

"Drive-the-fucking-car!" Alison wailed, emphasizing each word.

I couldn't speak, my mind unable to process what was happening. Milo came to life, reversed out of the mess of broken glass and glittering baubles and we careened away into the first light of dawn.

I woke in an unfamiliar bed in an unidentifiable room. There was a girl sleeping next to me and I recognized her as one of the local expats. I tried to remember how events had transpired to place me in this position, but nothing came to mind. I sat up and searched around for my clothes. The form on the bed stirred and looked up at me in annoyance.

"Whas the time?" she slurred.

I looked at my watch and a sudden feeling of dread passed through me from head to foot. I had less than three hours to make my flight. "Have you got a phone?" I said to her.

"I donno...maybe, somewhere round here."

I grabbed her by the shoulders and tried to clear her head with my stare. "I need your phone or I'm in the deepest shit possible."

She shook herself and thumped around on the sheets with her hand until she held up her phone with triumph. I snatched it off her and dialed Milo's number. It went to his message bank and I cursed in frustration. I tried again to no avail. I couldn't believe what was happening.

"Try once more," said the girl. "Third time lucky." She looked as if she was about to pass out.

Milo answered. "Yeah?" said a muffled and haggard voice.

"It's me, Adam. You gotta help me or I'm going to miss my plane!"

"Dude? What time is it?"

"It's half past one," I said.

"Damn, I've missed most of the day. What time's your flight?"

"Four o'clock. And I don't even know where I am right now."

"Oh, you're fucked."

"Look, I'll get a special hire to the guide house and pack my bags. You meet me there. Go there right now, just get in your car and go, and then you can take me out to the airport. I can't afford a taxi fare out there."

"Yeah, I can do that. I got something I want you to take to London for me anyway. I fucking need a shower though."

"No shower!" I said. "Just get in the car and go." I hung up the phone and looked at the girl. She had fallen asleep, so I grabbed my stuff and ran outside. The bright sun hit me with the force of an iron bar across the face. I held up one hand and looked around for a special hire. There were none to be seen so I started down the road at a half trot, each stride sending a jolt of pain through my throbbing skull. I came to an intersection with a main road and I waved my hand frantically until a derelict vehicle pulled to a halt beside me.

"Gabba road, sebo," I said as I fell into the back.

"Oh that is very far indeed, good mazungu. I must be having very much money to go all the way..."

"Drive the car!" I screamed at him, and he leaped into the air, his hands wringing in panic as he attempted to get the car started. He drove with all the urgency of a condemned man being led out to the firing range, and I pounded the seat in frustration at his every false move. Finally I directed him down the road to the house and thrust some money at him as I ran into the compound, through the door, and up the stairs. I started grabbing everything I had and stuffed it frantically into my bags.

Scott wandered into my room. "What's going on?" he said. "Aren't you flying out today?"

"I slept in," I said as I dived from one corner of the room to the other, yanking out drawers and looking under pieces of furniture to see if I had missed anything. "Milo's on his way to get me to the airport."

"You should have a shower."

"I haven't got time for a shower. Why is everyone so focused on showering? We should be focused on the fact that if I don't get to the airport on time then I'm going postal and shooting anyone that looks at me funny."

"Well, you look like shit, and if you turn up to immigration in the UK looking like that, they might not even let you in. They'll probably put you on a plane straight back here; file you under yet another derelict Aussie trying to get into the country with no return ticket, no job, and no visa."

I stopped in mid-stride, the full horror of what he had just said registering on my fuzzy brain. Then I retrieved my toiletries bag from my backpack and dived into the bathroom. I was almost done when Scott called through the door that Milo had arrived.

"Five minutes!" I yelled. "Tell him I'll be five minutes."

I finished up, dumped the last few items in my bags, and scurried downstairs. The house staff had collected to see me off. Haddie began a drawn out speech detailing my many outstanding mazungu qualities but after a few minutes I cut her off with a profuse apology, thanked all the staff, said goodbye to my colleagues, and pushed Milo into the Land Rover. We careened through the gate and I looked back as the large blue obstacle swung slowly shut on me for the final time.

Milo swigged from a bottle of Nile Special beer as he drove.

"Is that wise?"

"It's the only thing that's enabling me to deal with my existence at the moment."

I thought about that. "You got another one?" I said, and he pointed to a small cooler behind him. I cracked the top and drank deeply, the alcohol entering my system in a soothing rush.

We were out of the city limits when I spied a police block on the road. Milo took a good look and then began to slow down. He had spotted that they had guns, which meant they probably had a radio too. As one of the policeman walked towards us, Milo thrust his bottle of beer at me. I looked around for a place to stash it, but I was too slow, and the cop caught sight of me sitting there, cradling the two large beer bottles.

His face lit up into a huge smile. ""Ah, mazungus! You are drinking! This is very bad! We must arrest you."
"No, no, no, no, no," said Milo. "You don't want to do that."
"Oh yes. You are drunk and very bad people. You must be punished!"
"We're not drunk!" said Milo. The cop pointed at the bottles of beer. "Well, maybe a little bit, but where we come from that's ok."
I looked at Milo with some confusion. The cop looked equally dubious. "This I cannot believe. You are making fun of me."
"It's true!" Milo protested.
"Where do you come from?" he asked with great suspicion.
Milo and I answered together with enthusiasm, "Australia!"
He sneered. "This is not possible. I cannot believe in the Australia you can drink and drive your car."
"Well," Milo began, "It's like this. In Australia, if you drink a lot and get drunk, then you have to drive more slowly, because it's harder to drive, so we drive slower, and then we have less accidents, so drinking and driving in Australia is encouraged, and we have very, very, very safe roads. It's really a very safe country."
The cop looked at me. "Very safe," I confirmed.
His attention returned to Milo who smiled weakly up at him. I held my breath. Milo's argument was quite possibly the most ridiculously stupid explanation I had ever heard, but there was no way I was going to say anything contrary. The policeman looked at Milo. He thought for a very long time, the silence drifting across us like the smoke from roadside fires. And then he jerked his thumb over his shoulder.
"Okay, you can go."
We drove away in shocked silence. "Didn't even have to pay a bribe," Milo said.

We parked directly in front of the terminal, and I jumped out with my bags. Milo handed me a package made up of layers of bubble wrap and duct tape. It was shaped like a short cylinder.

"What's this?"

"It's the EPIRB I told you about. The thing I need you to take to London for me."

"You didn't tell me it was an EPIRB."

"I didn't tell you it was anything. The address is taped here on the outside where I need you to drop it off. They're going to service it for me, and then I have someone else who's going to bring it back in a couple of months."

"It's not drugs, is it?"

"Nope. We used all them last night."

We walked into the building, and Milo waited for me to check in and deposit my bags.

"And that?" the lady at the counter said, pointing at the EPIRB package.

"Carry-on luggage," I said, and she nodded and gave me my passport and boarding pass. I showed them to Milo, and he gave me a thumbs up, and then we made our way over to the security screening area. I put my laptop bag on the conveyor belt, and then I placed Milo's package on there as well. At that moment a thought came to me.

"You know," I said to Milo, "if there's one thing an EPIRB looks like, it's a bomb. It probably looks more like a bomb than a bomb does."

He looked at me and let out a sigh as we both realized that we would have to unwrap the package to prove it wasn't a terrorist item designed to explode a plane into a million pieces in the sky.

"It took me ages to get that all wrapped up nice and safe," he grumbled.

The package went through the X-ray machine, and the large woman inspecting the monitor let out a cry of horror.

"Eih! What is that one?" she said in alarm, pointing at the emerging package.

"We know, we know," I said. "It's an EPIRB, but I'll un-wrap it so you can see for yourself." I started to attempt to pry open Milo's devilishly intricate wrapping project.

"It's a what?" she said.

"An EPIRB," Milo said helpfully.

"What is that?"

"Well, it's a satellite emergency beacon. If you're in trouble and you want to be rescued, you activate the EPIRB and it sends a message up to a satellite in the sky, and then the satellite sends the message to the rescue people, telling them where you are, and they come and rescue you."

The woman had been attempting to follow this argument, but the faces she pulled, from initial confusion to dubious uncertainty to total disbelief that something like an EPIRB was not actually the bomb that it so closely resembled convinced Milo of the hopelessness of his position.

"Never mind," he said. "We'll just get it out and show you."

But then she shook herself as if emerging from a dream. "It's okay. You can go," she said, and she waved her hand in a loose dismissal.

Milo and I started at each other. "Well, cool. That's all right then," Milo said.

"No it isn't fucking all right," I protested.

"What's the problem?" he asked me.

"I'll tell you what the problem is—I'm about to get on a plane that lets things that look like fucking bombs get through without security even inspecting them. If she lets this through, what else is getting on that plane?"

Milo turned to the woman. "He does have a point," he said to her.

"It's okay. Is not a bomb."

"Oh really?" I said, stepping forward. "If it's not a bomb, what is it then?"

She thought for a moment. "Is an E-Whah."

"It's a what?"

"A E-Whah," she repeated angrily.

I turned to Milo. "She doesn't even know what this is. I'm unwrapping it."

"No, mazungu," she said. "You are holding up the line. This is E-Whah. I am security person and I have decided."

"What does it do then?"

She stared at me with confident defiance, and then she placed her hands on her hips. "It goes up and then comes down, and then we rescue the people."

235

I started yelling at her while attempting to tear open the package, but some other security personnel wandered over, and they too began to berate me for wanting to prove that the EPIRB was not a bomb. Finally they began threatening that I would not be allowed on the plane, and Milo dragged me away from them, intact package in hand.

"Dude, just get on the plane. If you blow up, you blow up."

"This country is insane," I muttered.

"Well, you did it. You got out of Africa. It's been great having you around," he said.

I realized that this was our goodbye, and I suddenly experienced a surprising sense of loss. "Thanks for everything, Milo."

"I'm just sorry that the whole Uganda trip didn't work out better for you."

"Are you kidding? This trip has been amazing. It's the best thing I've ever done."

He smiled. "Well, I'm glad then. Let us know how you get on in Italy."

"I will. And you keep sane out there."

We slapped each other on the back, and then he walked away, back to his funny old Land Rover parked illegally in a strange country.

I thought about all the times I had left good friends behind, never knowing when or if I would see them again. The job and the lifestyle meant that we developed close and complex friendships, but the trade-off was one of perpetual departure. I shouldered my bag and walked to the boarding area, the EPIRB tucked safely under my arm.

I saw a young English expat who I knew from around Kampala. He was traveling on the same flight, and after boarding he changed seats and sat next to me. We spoke for a bit, and then I asked him if he knew if Australians required a visa to get into Britain.

"I don't think so," he said. "But I do know that every day young Aussies get turned around at the airport and sent home on the next flight because they can't meet entry requirements. Apparently a lot of them turn up on working holiday visas without the minimum funds."

"I just need to stay for a week or so until I can organize a trip to Italy."

He yawned. "Tell them that then. Hopefully you won't have any issues."

The conversation was not comforting as now I had something new to agonize over on the flight to London.

The plane was close to full, with a fair number of Ugandans, some flying for the first time to judge by the state of their apprehension. The engines revved, and I felt a moment of nostalgia as the wheels left the ground, and then I breathed a sigh of relief and smiled as we lifted up and into the sky.

I watched the vast green land falling away beneath the plane, and then finally I felt a sense of sublime satisfaction that I had gotten out on my own terms. The lights flickered and a chime sounded around the cabin and people began to relax and settle into the flight. A stewardess pushed a trolley in a rattling cadence down the narrow aisle, catching my elbow before I could react.

Corey would be at the bar at Bujagali Falls now, a drink in his hand as he sat on his privileged perch beside the thundering river, an army of geckoes scurrying in the beams high above his head as they hunted for oversize moths and dusk insects, while the cook banged together a simple meal and village fishermen gathered at their long dugout canoes as they prepared for a night trawling the waters for a catch to take to Jinja market. In the grand scheme, little had changed, but for me, everything had changed.

In time I would look back on this period and know that I had been one of the lucky few. Were you there when, did you know such and such, what did it look like before they did this and that? Ah, you missed the golden time, the best time to have been there, it's nothing like it was when I was a river guide rafting the White Nile in Jinja town. But every generation says the same thing, and every time is special and unique for the people who were there. Change is always happening, and the only thing you can do is be out in front of it, hoping that your faith will be rewarded.

22

Milan airport was loud and confusing, and I tried to make sense of the machinegun Italian being spoken around me. After staying with relatives for a week in London, I had hopped a plane to Italy, courtesy of Captain Paul, who had come through with a complimentary flight.

I noticed a guy about my own age waiting for his bags. He wore brightly colored adventure-style clothing, and there was a whitewater helmet strapped to the outside of his shoulder bag. I walked over and asked if he was a river guide. Not only were my instincts correct, but we were both due to work for the same outfit. What an amusing coincidence. My new colleague, named Ralf, took this to be a profound sign from the universe that we were on the right path.

We retrieved our bags and made our way through a somewhat inattentive immigration control point. Ralf was carrying a guitar as well as his bags. As we walked through the airport corridors we caught the sound of music and singing.

"That's Kiwi music, bro," Ralf said, and he strode off to investigate.

I followed in his wake, and we discovered a large group of Maoris sitting among a pile of luggage off to the side of the corridor. Most of them were playing instruments and singing. Ralf spoke with one of them for a minute, and then he turned to me with an update.

"They're a famous Kiwi music group. They're here to do a tour. I'm going to jam with them for a bit."

He pulled out his guitar and sat down and began playing. The girls sang beautiful harmonies while the deep male voices created a warm baritone sound underneath. I chatted up one of the girls and told her what we were doing in Italy.

"We're all just on one big adventure," she breathed, and I smiled and held my tongue as this was all getting just a bit hippy and lovey-dovey for my tastes.

"Do you play, bro?" one of the Maori lads asked me, and I held out my hand and accepted the offered guitar.

A large crowd had gathered, which soon attracted airport security. They asked us to stop as the crowd was blocking the corridor. I handed the guitar back to its owner, who beamed at me as we shook hands. Ralf was quite content to chatter away, but I had one eye on the time—we still had a large distance to cover to reach the mountain valley where we would be working, and I wasn't prepared to pay for a night in a Milanese hotel. I managed to extricate him from his newfound chums, and then we set off to look for the bus that went to the Milan Central train station.

"What a great way to start our Italian trip!" Ralf gushed.

"Yeah, it was very cool," I mumbled as I dodged groups of travelers pushing mountains of suitcases in a haphazard manner. I squeezed past a few of these mobile leviathans only to discover that Ralf was no longer at my side. He was about twenty meters behind me, standing in the corridor with a concerned look on his face. I jostled my way back around the same people I had only just cleared.

"What are you doing?" I said, irritated.

"Bro, we didn't get their contact details. We have to go back and find them."

"No way. I'm catching the bus to the train station. Then I'm going to catch a train to Verona, and then I'm going to find a train for Trento, and so on. I want to get there today, and it's already 2pm. So are you coming with me or not?"

Ralf hesitated for a moment, and then he picked up his belongings and continued with me down the corridor.

The Milan Central train station was very imposing in a neo-gothic sort of way. We got off the bus, keeping a wary eye out for pickpockets, and made our way into the cavernous interior, where I located a pay phone. I called the rafting base, and a lady named Carla answered the phone. She spoke excellent English, and after some hasty conferral, we discovered that it was not possible for us to reach the valley by public transport today. She told me to call back in ten minutes so as to give her time to formulate a plan. I sent Ralf to get some more change for the phone while I guarded our luggage, and then I rang Carla back at the specified time.

"Catch the next train to Verona," she said. "One of our guides will meet you at the station. His name is Tobia, and you can stay the night with him and come up to Val di Sole tomorrow."

"Val di Sole?" I said.

"It's Italian for Valley of the Sun."

I thanked her, and then I brought Ralf up to speed as we scanned the gigantic departures board for the next train to Verona. With a train firmly in mind, we got in line at the ticket office and began to rehearse how to negotiate the purchase of tickets in Italian. Ralf had a similar phrase-book to mine, and we flicked through them and tried to memorize the key words.

Our turn came and I stepped forward. "Um…due big-a-letti per Verona, prego…" I felt quite pleased with myself.

The woman behind the counter regarded me with a look of confusion and contempt. "Cosa dice lei?" she said.

I had no idea what she was saying, so I attempted to repeat my request. Ralf stepped forward with his phrase-book and tried to help me.

"How do you pronounce this word that means ticket?" I pleaded with him, holding up a hand in an attempt to placate the now rather irritated woman at the counter.

"Big-a-letti," Ralf said.

"I tried that, but she just looked at me as if I was a total imbecile."

"Give me a shot," he said as he pushed past. "Per Verona," he said as he held up two fingers. The woman gave us both a long look, but eventually she presented us with the required tickets.

"I biglietti devono essere timbrati," she said.

"What did she say?" I asked Ralf.

"I have no idea."

"Just nod and pretend we understand what she's on about."

"Should we ask her which platform we need to go to?"

"Brilliant. How do you say 'platform'?"

We both dived into our respective books, but I came up with it first. "Binario?" I asked the lady.

"Diciasette," she replied. We didn't understand, so I mimed writing the number on a piece of paper, which she eventually did with some bad grace, thrusting the number at us while beckoning to the next person in line to come forward.

"Seventeen," I said triumphantly as the newcomers pushed us aside, and we hustled through the crowds to where a long train sat waiting on the platform. A guard was standing beside the train, and we repeated the name "Verona" until he understood what we were on about and nodded his head. We scrambled aboard. The train was packed, and the only spot we could find was in a small gap at the end of a carriage where we managed to wedge our bags.

"Late afternoon rush hour," I said to Ralf.

As the train sped towards Verona, I gazed outside at the passing fields and towns. I saw isolated farmhouses with tall walls topped by bright orange rounded roof tiles that hung dangerously over the edges, and brutal apartment blocks that backed onto the railway line, the tiny balconies crowded with plastic chairs and tables. In the background sat the foothills of the Alps, with the occasional mountain peak emerging from the pollution haze through which the red disk of the sun peeped in muted defeat. Ralf and I spoke for a while about what sort of rivers we might find in the mountains, and the carriage rocked from side to side as we raced over the Lombardy plain.

We stood outside the Verona train station in the early evening light as we waited for our contact to arrive. Ralf chattered beside me, but I wasn't really listening to him. A feeling of dislocation had settled on me, as if in reaction to finding myself in yet another strange city, another unfamiliar locale. I was tired and hungry, and my back ached from dragging around the weight of my bags.

A tiny Fiat came to a flying halt at the pavement, and the young driver beckoned to us.

"Adam and Ralf? You are Adam and Ralf?"

"I reckon this is our ride," I said to my companion.

Somehow we managed to stuff our bags into the compact space while still leaving room for us. I got in the front, but this proved to be somewhat of a miscalculation. Our guide hurtled through the narrow cobbled streets with a maniacal nonchalance, one hand on the wheel and the other on my seat as he spoke excitedly, craning his head around to look at Ralf. There were crowds of rushing mopeds and scooters, and for a moment it seemed like Africa again, but with cobbles. We drove for around twenty minutes, and then Tobia slammed the car to a halt beside a picturesque apartment building.

"This is my house," Tobia told us. "Bring your bags."

We hauled our gear up the stairs and into the apartment. It was a lovely mixture of rustic and modern, raw red brick walls and earthen wooden beams contrasting with plain white walls and new appliances.

"Nice place," I said.

Tobia smiled. "I am here for a little while, but it is not my own house. I am, how do you say, sitting on it?"

"What is that sensational smell?" Ralf said.

"I have prepared a traditional Veronese meal for you; a pasta with ragú. There is also red wine. Sit and eat, please."

We sat at the table and piled into the food while Tobia answered our questions. He was twenty one but looked younger, and he had been rafting since he was fifteen years old on the same river where we would be working. We asked him many questions about the river and the location.

"What is the company like to work for?" I asked.

"The big boss, he is a very strange man, crazy sometimes. He can be good, he can be bad. But lots of work, the money is very good."

Tobia rolled a joint and passed it round, and we smoked and drank and talked into the night, and I was thankful for his hospitality that had so lifted the spirits of this weary traveler.

Tobia drove us to the station, where he helped us purchase tickets for Trento. Our train was not due to leave for a few hours, so we stowed our luggage and our new friend gave us a lift into the city center. He would be coming up to the valley at the end of the week, but for now he had other things to do. We said goodbye and then set off to explore the city.

The people hurrying past us were all dressed in an elegant manner, and I glanced down at my own scruffy clothes.

"We're not really dressed with Italy in mind, are we?" I said.

"I've never seen so many good looking people," Ralf said as he looked at the crowds through which we walked.

"I don't know; it's not that they're so good looking. More the fact that they all seem to have just stepped off a catwalk."

We came to an imposing medieval archway, a clock stamped incongruously in its center. It was part of the original town walls, and I imagined archers firing volleys in our direction while their fellow defenders readied cauldrons of boiling pitch. Cars and scooters shot beneath the arch, their horns sounding in a continual cadence, while the crowds poured along the sidewalks and around the groups standing beside one of the many cafés that fronted the road.

On the other side of the arch was a large piazza dominated by an ancient Roman amphitheater. We stood and stared at it in silence for some time.

Ralf broke the spell. "I think we need to get a coffee, bro."

We made our way to one of the many cafés fronting the amphitheater, long rows of tables stretching out towards the ancient monument, the hundreds of seats empty in the early morning light.

"It's probably not tourist season yet," I said as we sat and ordered from a smartly dressed waiter. We sipped our cappuccinos as we admired the beautifully dressed women parading before us on their way to work.

Ralf stretched out in his chair and smiled a satisfied grin. "What are the poor people doing right now?"

"Not having to pay this outrageous bill," I said as I inspected the ticket. "These must be the most expensive coffees of all time."

"Worth it," said Ralf. "How many times in your life do you get to do this?" He swept his hand at the scene before us, and I had to admit his point.

We spent a few hours touring the inner-city streets until our schedule forced us to return to the train station. We left Verona, the train heading back towards Milan, but after a short while it turned towards the mountains, and soon we entered a wide valley with steep cliffs pressing in from the sides. I spied a lonely monastery high on a mountain peak, and I wondered how the monks were able to reach it. We swept past small hilltop forts and castles, the foreground dominated by fields of vineyards and everything clothed a deep shade of green.

Ralf chattered on about the multitude of beautiful women whom he had left behind in New Zealand. I knew he was exaggerating, but I didn't mind. I even found it instructive in a way, remembering my own previous troubles with insecurity.

And as he spoke I thought back to the time when I had left Perth on my motorbike to journey across Australia and my then precarious state of mind. I would not have even imagined the physical and emotion journeys that would result from that decision, and then I wondered if that was the point. If you restrict yourself to the safe and simple path, then you close yourself off to all the wondrous possibilities the world could have offered. It is enough to journey, to set out, to have the leap of faith to start in unknown directions, and then take the opportunities as they present themselves.

And finally there is the courage to take the step, to move towards a presented opportunity and embrace it as your own. And then perhaps one day you will find yourself sitting on a train in a strange land, and you will marvel at how much your life has changed. And then you will be left with the excitement of what is to come and how much more you still have to experience and learn. I had a new country to explore. A river to conquer. A language to master. And a visa with three months on the stamp.

CPSIA information can be obtained at www.ICGtesting.com
Printed in the USA
LVOW10s1252220516

489441LV00038B/720/P